Funding for the LIFE Project in Turkey provided by the United States Government

ELMALI KRÜMEL

THE CUISINE OF *life*

RECIPES AND STORIES OF
THE NEW FOOD ENTREPRENEURS OF TURKEY

LIFE

CONTENTS

- 8   **RECIPES BY COURSE**
- 11   **ABOUT THE PROJECT**
- 12   **THE LIFE PROJECT CONSORTIUM**
- 14   **LIFE PROJECT ADVISORY COUNCIL**
- 15   **ACKNOWLEDGEMENTS**
- 17   **FOREWORD**
- 19   **A WORD ON FOOD SUSTAINABILITY FROM THE EDITORS**
- 21   **INGREDIENTS AND SOURCING**

- 31   **WRITING A RECIPE, RECORDING A JOURNEY,** Dr. Johanna Mendelson Forman
- 32   **Ayşe Es** and her recipes:
- 34   Peynirli Sıkma (Cheese-Filled Wraps)
- 36   Saçta Kıyma Böreği (Lamb-Filled Skillet Borek)
- 38   **Esin Yıldız** and her recipes:
- 40   Hünkar Beğendi (Sultan's Delight)
- 42   Portakal Suyu ile Zeytinyağlı Kereviz (Celery Root with Olive Oil and Orange Juice)

- 45   **STORIES AROUND DISHES,** Filiz Hösükoğlu
- 46   **Filiz Hösükoğlu** and her recipes:
- 48   Pirpirim Aşı (Purslane Dish)
- 50   Astarlı Sütlaç (Rice Pudding)

- 53   **MSA for LIFE,** Cem Erol
- 54   **Fatima Fouad** and her recipes:
- 56   Shurbet Khudar w Dajaj (Vegetable Soup with Chicken)
- 58   Zurbian (Rice with Lamb)
- 62   Zahawiq (Green Chile Sauce)
- 64   Harissa/Harisa (Peanut Dessert)
- 66   Muz Fattah (Banana Bread)
- 68   **Fatima Hammo** and her recipe:
- 70   Kibbeh bil Sanieh (Kibbeh in a Tray)

73	**FOR LONG-TERM REFUGEES, SUSTAINABLE LIVELIHOODS REPRESENT MORE THAN SURVIVAL,** Kathleen Newland
74	**Fatma Hülya Tek** and her recipes:
76	Tavuklu Pazı Sarma (Swiss Chard Stuffed with Chicken)
78	Gonca Gül Tatlısı (Rosebud Cookies)
80	**Gülhan Salcan** and her recipes:
82	Harput Köftesi (Bulgur Koftes in Tomato and Pepper Paste Sauce)
84	Hedik/Diş Buğdayı (Wheat Boiled with Chickpeas)
87	**TURKEY'S FOOD ENTREPRENEURS,** Yigal Schleifer
88	**Hanaddy Kheawe** and her recipe:
90	Makloubeh (Upside-down Rice with Eggplant and Lamb)
92	**Hayat Ali Naji Al-Laith** and her recipes:
94	Shafoot/shafut (Bread in Yogurt Sauce)
96	Fahsa (Beef Stew)
98	Shorbet Lahme (Wheat and Lamb Soup)
100	Bint Al-Sahn (The Daughter of the Plate)
104	Asida (Corn Porridge)
107	**FOOD, THE ULTIMATE SOCIAL MEDIATOR,** Mert Fırat
108	**Iman Batikh and Mohamad Yahya Kawakibi** and their recipes:
110	Mahshi Betincan Ma Fitir (Mushrooms Cooked with Stuffed Eggplants)
112	Dalae Mahshi Bil-Ruzz (Stuffed Rack Of Lamb)
114	Mamuniyeh (Semolina Helva)
117	**UNLIKELY ENTREPRENEURS,** Dalia Mortada
118	**Inam Alshayeb** and her recipes:
120	Baba Ganoush (Smoky Eggplant Salad/Dip)
124	Fattoush (Bread Salad)
126	Muhammara (Walnut and Pepper Dip)
128	Shakriyeh (Lamb Stew with Yogurt)
130	**Latifa Smaili** and her recipes:
132	Mhajeb/Mahjouba (Vegetable and Cheese Turnovers)
134	Kuskus (Couscous with Lamb)
137	**MIGRATION AND THE KITCHEN,** Zeynep Kakınç
138	**Maha Al-Tinawi** and her recipes:
140	Ouzi (Lamb and Rice Pilaf Wrapped in Phyllo Pastry)
142	Laban Bi Khiar (Cucumber with Yogurt)
144	Mujaddara (Lentil Pilaf)
146	Tabbouleh (Fine Grain Bulgur Salad)
149	**THE MIGRATION OF FOOD IN ANATOLIA,** Nevin Halıcı
150	**Maysaa Algherawi** and her recipes:
152	Shish Barak (Dumplings Cooked in Yogurt Sauce)
156	Fakhdet Lahmeh (Leg of Lamb)
158	Salatet Jarjeer (Arugula Salad)

161	**FOOD, THE GREAT EQUALIZER**, Joan Nathan
162	**Mohamad Shady Khayata** and his recipes:
164	Kibbeh Mabrumeh (Rolled Kibbeh)
166	Esh El Bolbol (Nightingale's Nest)
168	Kunafe Nabulsieh (Kunafe from Nablus)
170	**Muyassar Hamdan** and her recipe:
172	Mansaf (Lamb Cooked in Yogurt)
177	**SHARING IS LOVING**, Artun Ünsal
178	**Naglaa Ashour** and her recipes:
180	Om Ali (Bread Pudding)
182	Basbousa (Semolina Cake)
185	**IDENTITY, CULTURE, AND CUISINE**, Musa Dağdeviren
186	**Nizar Akram Elkharrat** and his recipes:
188	Batersh (Smoky Eggplant Puree)
190	Basmashkat (Rolled Steak with Rice Filling)
192	Tatar Barak (Dumplings in Yogurt-Tahini Sauce)
194	Siliq Bil Zeyt (Chard with Oil)
196	Siliq Mutabal (Chard Stalks in Yogurt Sauce)
199	**A TASTE FOR CHANGE?**, Paul Newnham
200	**Nisan Doğan** and her recipe:
202	Cevizli Kayısı Kavurması (Dried Apricots with Walnuts)
204	**Özgül İnali** and her recipes:
206	Hangel (Mantı Without Filling)
208	Patlıcan Güveç (Eggplant and Lamb Stew in an Earthenware Pot)
211	**FOOD TO CREATE NEW BEGINNINGS**, David Hertz
212	**Sawsan Bawadekji** and her recipes:
214	Safarjaliyeh (Quince and Lamb Stew)
216	Ris El Freekeh (Freekeh with Rice and Lamb)
220	**Sawsan Lutfi** and her recipe:
222	Batata Bel-Firin ma Dajaj (Potato Baked with Chicken)
225	**NATURAL TALENTS FOR A LIVING**, Anissa Helou
226	**Shathaa Alramadhani** and her recipe:
228	Kibbeh El Riz (Rice Kibbeh)
230	**Yelda Kumbasar** and her recipes:
232	Aşure (Noah's Pudding)
234	Kuru Baklava (Dry Baklava)
237	**FOOD POWER**, Mitchell Davis
238	**INDEX**

RECIPES BY COURSE

MEZES, SALADS, AND CONDIMENTS

120	Baba Ganoush (Smoky Eggplant Salad/Dip)
124	Fattoush (Bread Salad)
142	Laban Bi Khiar (Cucumber with Yogurt)
126	Muhammara (Walnut and Pepper Dip)
158	Salatet Jarjeer (Arugula Salad)
94	Shafoot/Shafut (Bread in Yogurt Sauce)
194	Siliq Bil Zeyt (Chard with Oil)
196	Siliq Mutabal (Chard Mutabal)
146	Tabbouleh (Fine Grain Bulgur Salad)
62	Zahawiq (Green Chile Sauce)

SIDES AND SOUPS

104	Asida (Corn Porridge)
144	Mujaddara (Lentil Pilaf)
34	Peynirli Sıkma (Cheese-Filled Wraps)
48	Pirpirim Aşı (Purslane Dish)
42	Portakal Suyu ile Zeytinyağlı Kereviz (Celery Root with Olive Oil and Orange Juice)
36	Saçta Kıyma Böreği (Lamb-Filled Skillet Borek)
56	Shurbet Khudar w Dajaj (Vegetable Soup with Chicken)
76	Tavuklu Pazı Sarma (Swiss Chard Stuffed with Chicken)

MAINS

190	Basmashkat (Rolled Steak with Rice Filling)
222	Batata Bel-Firin ma Dajaj (Potato Baked with Chicken)
188	Batersh (Smoky Eggplant Puree)
112	Dalae Mahshi Bil-Ruzz (Stuffed Rack Of Lamb)
166	Esh El Bolbol (Nightingale's Nest)
96	Fahsa (Beef Stew)
156	Fakhdet Lahmeh (Leg of Lamb)
206	Hangel (Mantı without Filling)
82	Harput Köftesi (Bulgur Koftes in Tomato and Pepper Paste Sauce)
40	Hünkar Beğendi (Sultan's Delight)
164	Kibbeh Mabrumeh (Rolled Kibbeh)
228	Kibbeh El Riz (Rice Kibbeh)
70	Kibbeh bil Sanieh (Kibbeh in a Tray)
134	Kuskus (Couscous with Lamb)
90	Makloubeh (Upside-down Rice with Eggplant and Lamb)

110	Mahshi Betincan Ma Fitir (Mushrooms Cooked with Stuffed Eggplants)
172	Mansaf (Lamb Cooked in Yogurt)
132	Mhajeb/Mahjouba (Vegetable and Cheese Turnovers)
140	Ouzi (Lamb and Rice Pilaf Wrapped in Phyllo Pastry)
208	Patlıcan Güveç (Eggplant and Lamb Stew in an Earthenware Pot)
216	Ris El Freekeh (Freekeh with Rice and Lamb)
214	Safarjaliyeh (Quince and Lamb Stew)
128	Shakriyeh (Lamb Stew with Yogurt)
152	Shish Barak (Dumplings Cooked in Yogurt Sauce)
98	Shorbet Lahme (Wheat and Lamb Soup)
192	Tatar Barak (Dumplings in Yogurt-Tahini Sauce)
58	Zurbian (Rice with Lamb)

DESSERTS

50	Astarlı Sütlaç (Rice Pudding)
232	Aşure (Noah's Pudding)
182	Basbousa (Semolina Cake)
100	Bint Al-Sahn (The Daughter of the Plate)
202	Cevizli Kayısı Kavurması (Dried Apricots with Walnuts)
78	Gonca Gül Tatlısı (Rosebud Cookies)
64	Harissa/Harisa (Peanut Dessert)
84	Hedik/Diş Buğdayı (Wheat Boiled with Chickpeas)
168	Kunafe Nabulsieh (Kunafe from Nablus)
234	Kuru Baklava (Dry Baklava)
114	Mamuniyeh (Semolina Helva)
66	Muz Fattah (Banana Bread)
180	Om Ali (Bread Pudding)

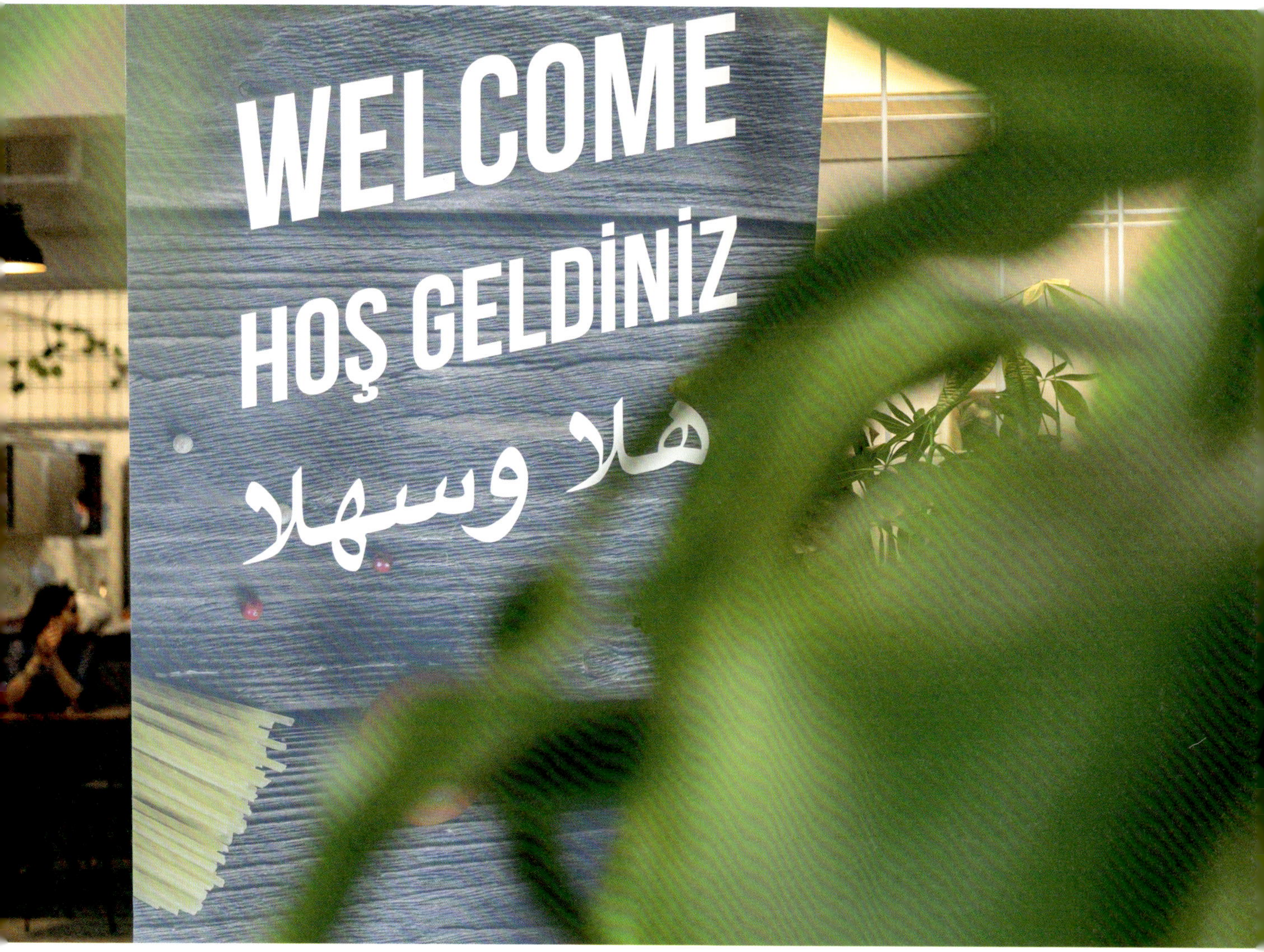
WELCOME
HOŞ GELDİNİZ
هلا وسهلا

ABOUT THE PROJECT

The Livelihoods Innovation through Food Entrepreneurship (LIFE) Project supports and encourages entrepreneurship, job creation and cross-cultural engagement in the food sector in Turkey. The LIFE Project launched the first food incubators in Turkey, where members from the refugee and host communities start and scale businesses, contributing directly to their livelihoods and economic development in their communities.

Two Food Enterprise Centers (FECs), in Istanbul and Mersin, serve as hubs for training and business development support. Modern facilities offer commercial grade kitchens, coworking and meeting space, and are venues for networking, community events, and workforce development. Anchored in the FECs, the LIFE Project incubates fledgling businesses, equipping entrepreneur members with the knowledge, skills, and networks necessary to build successful food businesses. Activities include training, business coaching, support services, and pitch competitions. Through the practice of gastrodiplomacy, the program provides pathways for cultural preservation while building community among diverse populations through the medium of food.

The project is implemented by an international Consortium of partners consisting of the Center for International Private Enterprise (CIPE), Idema (International Development Management), the Stimson Center, Union Kitchen, and the William Davidson Institute at the University of Michigan. An international Advisory Council provides additional expertise from luminaries in the food industry and related fields.

The recipes and stories featured in this cookbook come from LIFE Project members who participated in the incubation program in Istanbul.

THE LIFE PROJECT CONSORTIUM

The Center for Private International Enterprise (CIPE) is an affiliate of the U.S. Chamber of Commerce and works with business leaders, policymakers, and civic organizations around the world to build the institutions vital to democratic society. CIPE's key program areas include enterprise ecosystems, business advocacy, democratic governance, and anti-corruption & ethics. CIPE has a track record of working successfully with local partners to support entrepreneurship in Syria, Turkey, across the MENA region, and globally. As the LIFE Project Consortium lead, CIPE has a dedicated team to manage the project and its partnerships across the globe: Stephen Rosenlund and Marie A. Principe (Washington, D.C.) and Osman Çakıroğlu (Istanbul).

International Development Management (IDEMA) works with local and international experts, in addition to its team of experienced consultants, to create solutions to a wide range of socio-economic and development challenges. IDEMA is committed to providing meaningful impact through developing and implementing projects, realizing innovative solutions towards development obstacles, and serving as a hub for development practitioners to form global partnerships. IDEMA serves as the lead implementing partner of the LIFE Project in Turkey, from designing and managing the FECs in Istanbul and Mersin, to delivering entrepreneurship support, workshops, and events. IDEMA co-founders Dr. Ali Ercan Özgur, PhD, Güler Altınsoy and Bilge Turcan, lead the implementation of the LIFE Project in Turkey.

From climate change to its impact on migration and access to food, the **Stimson Center** is a nonpartisan policy research center at the forefront of the conversation about food's connection to public diplomacy and economic development. Stimson's food security program analyzes governance, innovative technology, and public-private partnerships to offer creative solutions to the transnational threats that food insecurity presents.
Dr. Johanna Mendelson Forman, Distinguished Fellow and director of the Center's Food Security program, is the Center's lead for the LIFE Project.

Union Kitchen is among the leading food and beverage business accelerators in the U.S. With a production facility, distribution company, and several retail stores in Washington, D.C., Union Kitchen builds successful food businesses in the D.C. market that can scale regionally and nationally. Union Kitchen provides the LIFE Project with tried and true expertise on facility design and management, entrepreneur incubation, and follow-on support services. Union Kitchen also fosters relationships with investors, distributors, and retail chains for their members. CEO and Founder Cullen Gilchrist and Executive Vice President Andrew Varnum lead Union Kitchen's role in the LIFE Project.

The William Davidson Institute (WDI) at the University of Michigan, is an independent, non-profit research and educational organization guided by the founding principle that thriving businesses drive economic development and improve social welfare in low- and middle-income countries. Within the education sector, WDI offers management training and entrepreneurship development programs, and partners with profit-seeking firms and nonprofits to develop and apply proven business practices. In designing the curriculum for the LIFE Project, WDI has shared knowledge and best practices in entrepreneurship with LIFE Project members and worked with trainers to optimize pedagogy. Vice President Amy Gillett and Senior Project Manager Kristin Babbie Kelterborn lead WDI's role in the Consortium.

LIFE PROJECT ADVISORY COUNCIL

Didem Altop, Co-Founder and Managing Partner, 2C Consulting and Project House
Christina Bache, Visiting Fellow, the London School of Economics and Political Science (LSE)
Vanda Berninger, Co-Chair, One Journey Festival
Lauren Bernstein, President and CEO, The Culinary Diplomacy Project
Jabber Al-Bihani, Founder and CEO, Komeeda
Brenda Brown, Co-Founder and CEO, Frontier Kitchen
Waterman Brown, Director, Business Operations, Hope and Main
Mitchell Davis, Chief Strategy Officer, James Beard Foundation
Ebru Baybara Demir, Chef and Founder, First Mesopotamia Cooking School
Mert Fırat, Actor and Goodwill Ambassador, United Nations Development Program
Patricia Funegra, Founder and CEO, La Cocina VA
Nicola Gryczka, CEO, Gastromotiva
Semi Hakim, Co-Founder, Kök Project
Sezai Hazir, President, Habitat Turkey
Anissa Helou, Author and Cookbook Writer
David Hertz, Chef and Founder, Gastromotiva
Hans Hogrefe, Managing Director, Equal Rights Consulting
Filiz Hösükoğlu, Food Writer and Consultant
Nasser Jaber, Co-Founder, Komeeda
Paula Johnson, Curator, National Museum of American History, Smithsonian Institution
Shirley Kaston, Co-Founder, Kök Project
Michael A. Levett, Senior Fellow in Social Innovation, Babson College
Gideon Maltz, Executive Director, Tent Foundation
Capricia Penavic Marshall, Ambassador-in-Residence, The Atlantic Council
Nate Mook, Executive Director, World Central Kitchen
Joan Nathan, Author and Cookbook Writer
Kathleen Newland, Senior Fellow and Co-Founder, Migration Policy Institute
Paul Newnham, SDG Advocacy Hub Coordinator, World Food Programme
Kathleen O'Keefe, Co-Founder, Up Top Acres
Ryan Ross, Chief Innovation Officer, Halcyon
Yigal Schleifer, Co-Founder and Editor, Culinary Backstreets
Natalie Shmulik, Food Consultant, The Hatchery
Shen Tong, Founder, FoodFuture Company
Noobstaa Philip Vang, Founder and CEO, Foodhini

Members of the Advisory Council work with the LIFE Project in a personal capacity; their activity should not necessarily be taken as an endorsement by their employer, organization, or any other company.

ACKNOWLEDGEMENTS

This cookbook was made possible by the valuable contributions of a number of individuals in Turkey and elsewhere. First and foremost, heartfelt gratitude goes to the members of the LIFE Project for sharing their recipes and personal stories for publication.

Sincere thanks to the vast team at the Mutfak Sanatları Akademisi (MSA Culinary Arts Academy of Istanbul) for testing and standardizing the recipes, and coordinating the professional photography of the dishes, especially the founder, Mehmet Kemal Aksel. Managing Director Sitare Baras had the vision to understand the importance of this project; her leadership and willingness to engage her entire team in the LIFE Project made this collaboration work. Ayşe Uğural, Marketing and Communications Manager, provided guidance on the publication process, lending her knowledge of cookbook production to our team. Head Chef Cem Erol and Assistant Chef İsmail Emre Çakır worked with their students to translate, test, and fine-tune these recipes alongside our members. The beautiful photographs were taken by Danielle Villasana, Filiz Hösükoğlu, Sami Sert, and Seren Dal, with assistance from Can Mete.

Three individuals served as this volume's co-editors. Filiz Hösükoğlu, a leading expert in Turkish gastronomy, served as principal co-editor and curator of the recipes, translating the dishes produced in the LIFE Project FEC kitchen into written documents. Alaa Alarori, CIPE's Project Coordinator in Istanbul, supported Hösükoğlu by coordinating with the staff at the FEC, the members, and serving as a liaison with the MSA. His work on all aspects ensured seamless communication between the contributors and the rest of the team. He also systematized the archive of photographs you see in this book. Johanna Mendelson Forman, the Consortium's gastrodiplomacy lead, captured the spirit of this project and the stories of its members; she curated the essays with a vision to highlight the importance of food as a tool for social cohesion in Turkey and globally. Together with Hösükoğlu, she engaged the MSA Culinary Arts Academy as a key collaborator.

Kara Elder, our copy and recipe editor, transformed the words of so many individuals into an enjoyable and useful volume.

This cookbook could not have been possible without the ongoing support of CIPE, specifically Senior Program Officer Stephen Rosenlund who had the initial vision and provided oversight, and Program Officer Marie A. Principe, for her management that made this vision a reality. Osman Çakıroğlu, CIPE's Project Director in Istanbul, played an important role in coordinating the publication of this cookbook with our book designer Yeşim Demir Pröhl, and printer. Finally, our Consortium partner and field implementer, IDEMA, provided the staffing and translation necessary to engage our members and collect the recipes. Special thanks to Rama Alkalas, Asu Aksoy, Motasem Abuzaid, Sahar Alsharie, Elif Nazlı Aksoy, and Esra Arslan.

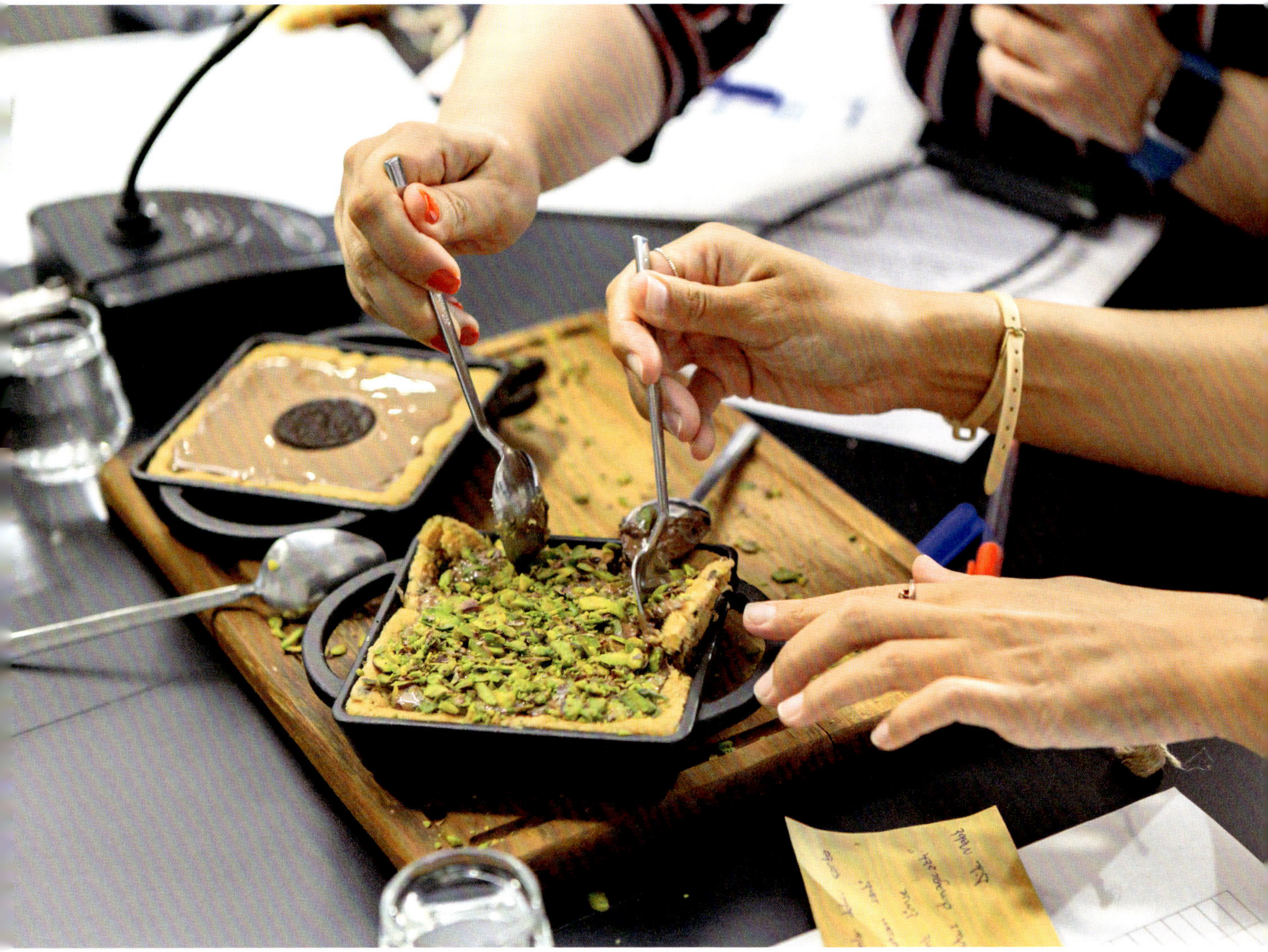

FOREWORD

Abdulwahab Alkebsi

Managing Director, Programs. Center for International Private Enterprise

This book is a unique collection of wisdom, stories, and culinary treasures shared with us by some of the leading minds in the food industry internationally and rising stars on the food scene in Turkey. The recipes are contributed by members of a larger community of entrepreneurs who are part of the LIFE Project.

We are in the midst of the largest refugee crisis since World War II, fueled by oppression, conflict, violence, and persecution, with nearly 71 million forcibly displaced people worldwide. Turkey is at the epicenter of this global crisis, hosting more refugees than any other country, with over 3.6 million registered Syrian refugees along with over 365,000 from other nationalities. With that comes strained resources and understandable social tensions between refugees and host communities. Women are disproportionately affected in a variety of ways as families are disrupted and they assume new household and financial responsibilities.

Within this context, there is an urgency to shifting priorities from a humanitarian response focused on aid delivery to a developmental response that supports sustainable livelihoods. Entrepreneurship and job creation is of the utmost importance in fostering self-sufficiency. Entrepreneurs create new ways of organizing, new methods of production, new products, new services, and new markets. In other words, they expand the pie, rather than cut it into smaller pieces. This drives economic growth and innovation and expands opportunity within host societies.

The food sector is one of the largest employment generators in countries around the world. Across the food value chain, this sector provides tremendous opportunities for entrepreneurship. Meanwhile, food provides a medium for cross-cultural engagement and understanding unlike any other. As an immigrant myself (Yemeni by birth and culture, American by choice and lifestyle), I know firsthand the importance of food in preserving culture while building community in one's new surroundings.

This book combines short essays about the special role of food in building community with recipes you can prepare at home. Through the contributions made by the women and men of the LIFE Project, we learn how their lives have been transformed by their participation in this project. We are proud to tell the stories behind the food.

Often our first exposure to a new culture is through our palates. What better way for you to get to know the new food entrepreneurs of Turkey than through their signature dishes. As you cook their recipes, enjoy the journey from the salads of Syria, through the flavorful rice dishes of Yemen, to the sweets of Turkey, and many stops in between. Whether it's afiyet olsun in Turkish, sahtain in Arabic, or the universal bon appétit – eat well and enjoy your meal, with good health and happiness!

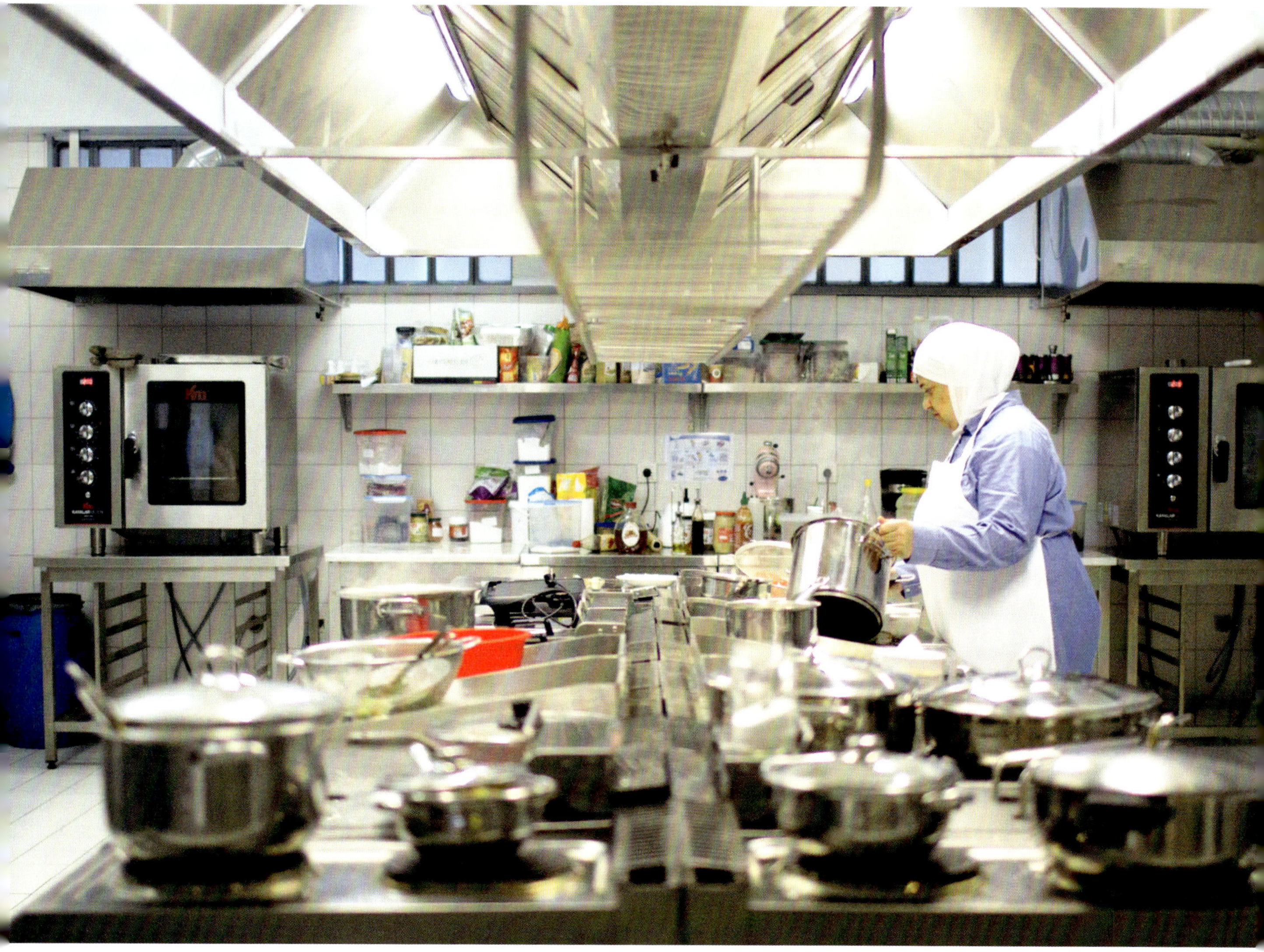

A WORD ON FOOD SUSTAINABILITY FROM THE EDITORS

Johanna Mendelson Forman

Sustainability of our planet's resources is an important concern for many of the members who participate in the LIFE Project. Food waste happens everywhere but it is often the most vulnerable who suffer. In a world where people are forced to migrate, or where resources are scarce, using every part of a vegetable or an animal is second nature.

Many who authored these recipes are refugees from Syria, Yemen, and other war-torn countries. Many Turkish contributors came from regions where food scarcity was often a problem. What all contributors have in common is an awareness about using every ingredient they select. Many of the recipe authors insisted that there would be no waste when dictating the methods of preparation. For example, Inam Al-Shayeb (see page 118) noted that she used vegetable leftovers like the juice and seeds of fresh tomatoes for other dishes. Nizar Akram Elkharrat (page 186) includes one recipe using Swiss chard leaves and another for the stems. And these pages include many interesting ways of using stale bread, including soaking it with an herbed yogurt sauce, as seen in Hayat Ali Naji Al-Laith's recipe for shafut (page 94), or adding it to Fatima Fouad's recipe for muz fattah (page 66), a comforting mix of toasted flatbread and banana slices drizzled with honey and cream.

Food waste is a global problem. Reducing the amount of food that is wasted is a goal that not only will help reduce hunger, but will also reduce the emission of greenhouse gases, one of the main contributors to climate change. The United Nations Sustainable Development Goal number two is all about reducing food waste to end global hunger by 2030, and chefs and cooks have become a driving force in this movement. We are pleased that the LIFE Project reinforces these goals in the training that has been central to the empowerment of food entrepreneurs who will use these new skills to build sustainable livelihoods in Turkey.

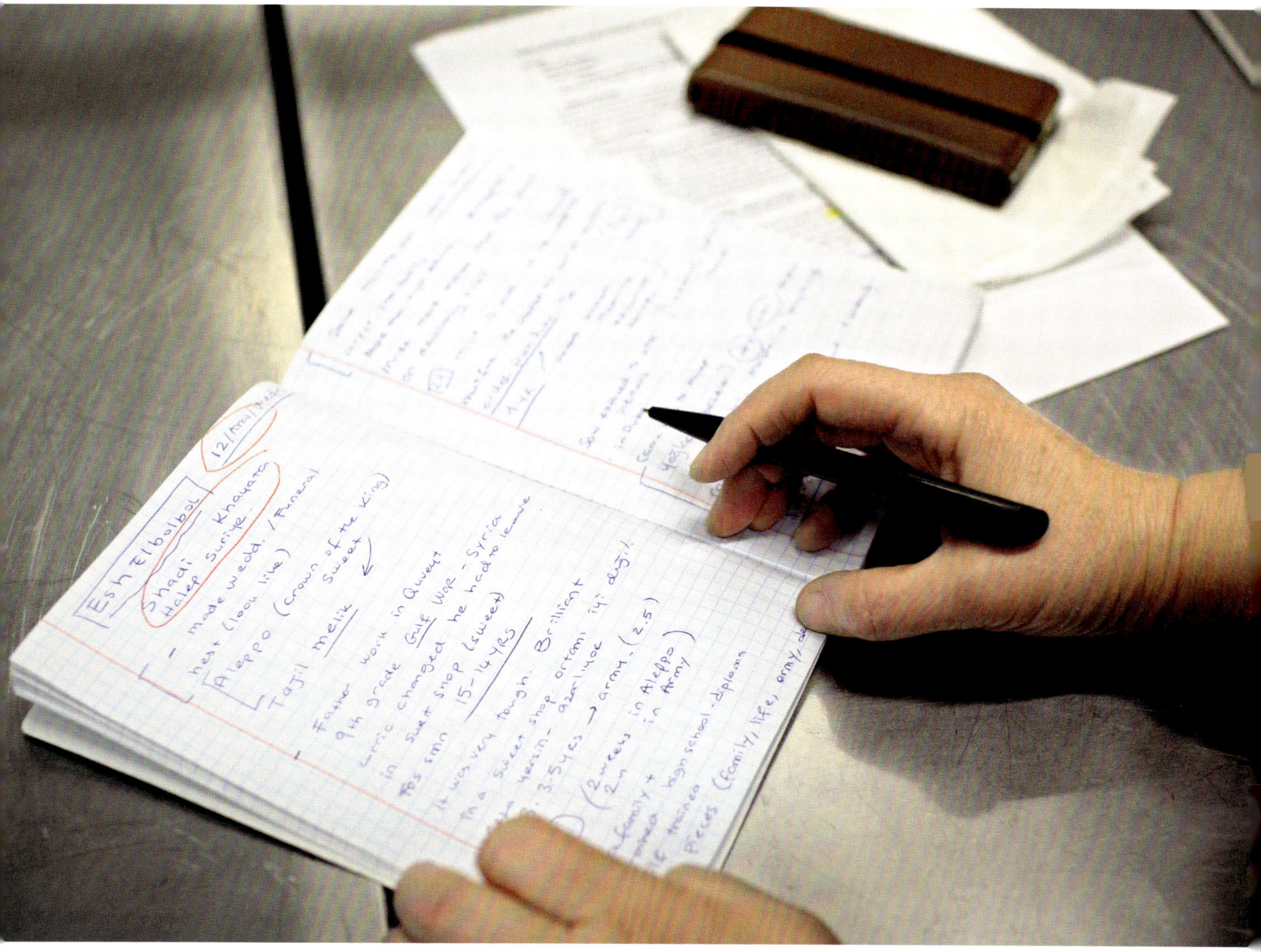

INGREDIENTS AND SOURCING

Kara Elder, Filiz Hösükoğlu

When translating recipes from one language to another -- especially ones that have only been passed down orally, from generation to generation -- there are bound to be variations when it comes to ingredients. Consider the potato: in most Turkish stores, there is one thin-skinned variety available, in different sizes. For the recipes in this book, waxy varieties -- such as Yukon Gold, Red Bliss, and new potatoes -- will work well.

Often, of course, the variety is of little consequence -- yes, the type of onion or grain of rice will affect the cooking time and taste of a finished dish, but using a yellow instead of a white onion, or a slightly larger instead of a slightly smaller one, won't ruin the food by any means. The recipes here are designed and tested for the cook to succeed, but they are not so rigid as to dictate every last detail. It's up to you, the cook, to take these stories and flavors, follow your intuition, and be inspired in your own kitchen, always feeling free to adjust the salt here, a spice there, until you've made something to enjoy with your own friends and family, remembering and honoring those who shared their stories in this book.

Unless otherwise specified, the recipes in this book were tested using fine-grain salt, whole milk, and whole-fat, plain yogurt. Eggs are large; butter is unsalted. Rice is white, medium-grain. Flour is all-purpose. Nuts are raw -- if you are to toast or use peeled nuts, the recipe will say so. In general, virgin olive oil is used for cooking (you may use extra-virgin instead), and light olive oil (Riviera olive oil in Turkey) for deep-frying.

Recipes were tested at MSA, primarily using the metric system. Conversions to American volume measurements and Fahrenheit have, in most cases, been rounded to the closest common usage (for example, 180°C is exactly 356°F -- in the recipe, though, it will appear as 350°F).

The following describes a few common pantry ingredients. In most cases, they will be available in Turkish, Middle Eastern, and/or Indian markets; some well-stocked grocery stores or specialty markets may also carry these items. When applicable, we have listed suitable substitutes and recipes for homemade versions.

Bulgur is made from cracked, par-boiled wheat and comes in different levels of coarseness, often labeled by numbers: #1 (fine), #2 (medium), #3 (coarse), #4 (extra course).

Corn flour is not the same as cornmeal, cornstarch, polenta, or masa harina. In the U.S., look for Bob's Red Mill brand, or others such as My Spice Sage online. If you can't find it, grind cornmeal in a high-powered blender or dedicated spice grinder for several minutes, until finely ground, then strain through a mesh sieve (you may regrind the larger particles if you like, or add them back to your bag of cornmeal).

Fenugreek seeds have a faintly sweet, maple-like scent; they are available whole or ground. When soaked in water, ground fenugreek becomes almost gelatinous and, when whipped, thickens into a cloud-like foam. (The leaves, which are not called for in this book, have a similar sweet smell, with notes of grass and alfalfa.)

Freekeh (firik) is durum wheat harvested while still green, then roasted over fire and cracked. It cooks quickly and has a subtle smoky flavor.

Kaymak is a dairy product similar to clotted cream, made from buffalo, cow, sheep, or goat milk. It is commonly rolled and cut into sections, looking like thick blankets of pure cream. In American markets, you may see it sold in small plastic tubs.

Nigella seeds, also called black onion seed, black caraway, black cumin, black sesame, fennel flower and kalonji (in Hindi), are tiny, tear-shaped seeds with angular sides. They have a distinct taste and aroma that is faintly bitter and often compared to oregano and anise, but their flavor is truly one of a kind.

Red pepper paste comes in spicy and sweet (also labeled mild) varieties. It is used, much like tomato paste, to add depth to various dishes and sauces, as well as to make muhammara (walnut and pepper dip, see page 126). You can make your own from roasted red peppers (either sweet or spicy, depending on the recipe): puree in a blender and then cook slowly in a nonstick skillet, until a paste forms.

Safflower petals are used primarily for their ability to add a yellow hue to dishes (and as a less expensive substitute for saffron). You'll most often see them dried, near other herbs and spices.

Clarified butter is prized for its high smoke point and ability to be stored at room temperature without spoiling. Variations in milk type, spices added, and process are found throughout the Middle East, Africa, and the Indian subcontinent -- you may know it as samna (in Egypt), semn (Yemen and Syria), ghee (India), or niter kibbeh (Ethiopia).

In the U.S., you can buy it in stores (where it will most likely be called ghee), but a basic version is easy to make: Melt 4 sticks of butter in a small saucepan over low heat, uncovered, without stirring. After about 10 minutes the butter will start to bubble and spit; foam will form at the top, then subside. Keep cooking until the butter is golden yellow and you can clearly see the milk solids settle at the bottom of the saucepan. Remove from heat and strain into a glass container for storage; it will keep for about three months at room temperature or up to a year in the refrigerator.

Semolina, called irmik in Turkish, is ground durum wheat. You may find it sold in coarse or fine varieties, or sometimes simply labeled "semolina flour."

Tahini is a paste made from ground sesame seeds. Each country has its own version, so try different brands to find your favorite. You can even make your own: in a food processor or blender, grind 1 cup of sesame seeds (any variety works; toasted if you like) until a paste forms. Drizzle in 1 to 2 tablespoons of a neutral-tasting oil, blending until incorporated. Add more oil, 1 tablespoon at a time, until the mixture is as thin and smooth as you'd like. (This will make about ¾ cup of tahini.) Tahini does not require refrigeration, but the oil may separate from the solids -- stir well to combine before using.

Vanilla powder, made from dried and powdered vanilla beans, is typically used rather than extract. You can substitute vanilla extract one-for-one in these recipes.

Wheat starch acts as a thickener; corn starch may be substituted.

If you can't find items in stores, most ingredients are available via the following purveyors:

burlapandbarrel.com -- For spices (ships to the U.S. and Canada)
foodsofnations.com -- For spices and other Middle Eastern and international grocery items (ships to the U.S. and Canada)
myspicesage.com -- For spices, grains, and flours (ships to the U.S.)
pereg-gourmet.com -- For spices, grains, and other Mediterranean and Middle Eastern grocery items (ships to the U.S.)
sadaf.com -- For spices, grains, flours, rose water, and other Mediterranean and Middle Eastern grocery items (ships to the U.S.)
tulumba.com -- For red pepper paste and other Turkish grocery items (ships worldwide)

MOMENTS OF LIFE

24

MOMENTS OF LIFE

25

MOMENTS OF LIFE

MOMENTS OF LIFE

27

MOMENTS OF LIFE

MOMENTS OF LIFE

29

WRITING A RECIPE, RECORDING A JOURNEY

WRITING A RECIPE, RECORDING A JOURNEY

Dr. Johanna Mendelson Forman

Writing down a recipe is more than putting words to paper. Often it is the embodiment of an oral tradition mixed with a story that binds traditions of place and time together. The recipes gathered in this project may reflect the first time that many of these women and men have ever had their family's traditional foods appear on paper. The process of transferring knowledge from an oral tradition to a written one is a way of memorializing the past, but the process is fraught with challenges.

Modern cookbooks about the foods of other lands often try to do the impossible. They create a means for others who are not part of the same culture or tradition to share in the wonders of a regional cuisine. The challenges for the transcriber and for the cook are manifold, but the end result can provide both the creator and the donor of the recipe a way to share a taste of their homeland, an entry into a world that may no longer exist.

It is said that for immigrants the first thing a new generation loses is language, but the foodways often linger. In the United States even people many generations removed from parts of Central Europe can still perfectly replicate the dumplings that their great-grandmothers brought with them on the journey across the Atlantic. Our palates become our atlas of places that we may no longer remember or visit, but still consider part of our heritage. There are no DNA tests for confirming these food roots, yet they are very much a part of who we are.

Watching professional chefs in Istanbul test a recipe for a Yemeni refugee's rice dish confirmed this notion of how difficult it is to recreate what the recipe author meant when she talked about cooking the onions until well browned: Were they to be caramelized? Or just sautéed? And when it came time for seasonings, how much cinnamon, turmeric, and salt would recreate the taste of this zurbian, a lamb and rice dish that is common in both western Yemen and parts of southeastern Turkey? Professional chefs could not agree, but the proof would be in how the dish tasted when it was finished.

Over the course of the LIFE Project I have come to understand and respect the distance that so many home cooks have traversed not only from the lands that they fled, but also from the kitchens where no one used a recipe to an entrepreneurship program where training required that they create written ones from their food memories. This is a new step in the creation of a food entrepreneur, but also an important step forward as women and men start new lives in the kitchen by using the past to create new beginnings.

Dr. Johanna Mendelson Forman is a Distinguished Fellow at the Stimson Center, leading the Food Security Program. Her experience as a policy maker on conflict and stabilization efforts drove her interest in connecting the role of food in conflict, resulting in the creation of Conflict Cuisine®: An Introduction to War and Peace Around the Dinner Table, an interdisciplinary course she teaches at the School of International Service at American University in Washington, DC, where she is an Adjunct Professor. Mendelson Forman is the gastrodiplomacy lead for the LIFE Project Consortium.

AYŞE ES

Ayşe was raised in Mersin, a port city in southern Turkey. When Ayşe was a little girl, her mother frequently used a wood-burning ocak (old-style furnace) to cook, although they had access to a portable gas stove as well. One of her mother's specialties was yufka, a thin, round, flatbread cooked on a saj (iron griddle) set over the open flames. Making yufka required a whole day and many helpers, with some rolling the dough while others tended the saj; by the end, there would be enough yufka to last several months. As they were working, they'd make simple sıkma and saj börek, two types of stuffed flatbreads cooked on the saj.

Today Ayşe and much of her family -- including her mother -- live in Istanbul. (She came to study Food Engineering at Istanbul Technical University and decided to stay.) Ayşe and her mother would often get together to prepare sıkma and börek, always joking that they should start a business selling the wraps in Istanbul. But within this joke was a kernel of truth and hope: Ayşe had always wanted to work for herself, so she quit her corporate job to pursue her passion, joining the LIFE Project shortly after to develop her business plan. She plans to open a cafe serving sıkma and börek, to bring a little taste of her hometown specialties to Istanbul.

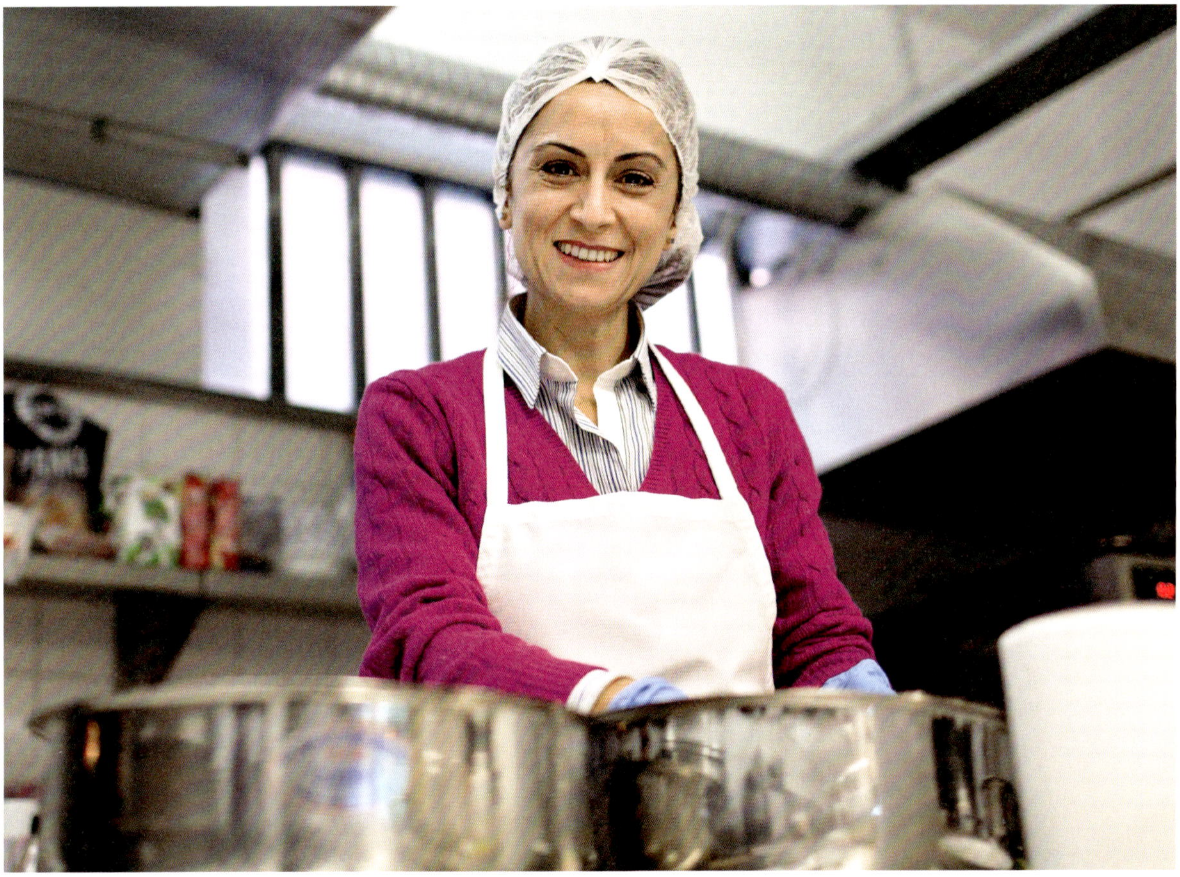

PEYNİRLİ SIKMA

(CHEESE-FILLED WRAPS)

15 to 16 servings

Every season

Sıkma is a special flatbread of the Turkish nomads in Anatolia (called yörük in Turkish), widely prepared in Adana and Mersin. Very thin pieces of dough are cooked over a saj, then wrapped and pressed with a filling, almost like a burrito. Visitors from other cities particularly liked these dishes, so they became a treat prepared for guests.

Ayşe prepares these in a nonstick skillet. They are a delight with tea, orange juice, or ayran (a yogurt drink).

INGREDIENTS:

For the dough:

- 2 cups (300 grams) whole-wheat flour
- 1 cup (150 grams) all-purpose flour
- 1 teaspoon salt
- 1 tablespoon (15 milliliters) oil, preferably sunflower
- About 1 cup (250 milliliters) water (amount varies depending on your flour)

For the filling:

- 200 grams curd cheese (such as ricotta or quark)
- 200 grams feta cheese
- 200 grams aged kasseri cheese (may substitute Swiss cheese)
- 4 to 5 scallions, finely chopped (may substitute 1 small onion)
- ½ cup finely chopped parsley (20 grams)
- 2 green or red peppers, such as Anaheim, finely chopped (70 grams)
- 3 to 4 tablespoons melted butter, for brushing (may substitute olive oil)

METHOD:

Whisk the flours and salt in a large bowl, then use a wooden spoon to stir in the oil and water. Mix and finish kneading with your hands, to make a soft, not-too-sticky dough. Divide into 15 to 16 portions, set on a lightly floured work surface, cover with a towel or plastic wrap, and let rest for 20 minutes.

Grate and crumble all the cheeses into a large bowl and stir in the onion, parsley, and pepper.

Roll out 1 portion of the dough into a circle about 18 cm (7 inches) in diameter. Heat a large nonstick pan over low heat, then cook the round until it's golden on both sides, about 15 to 20 minutes per side. Be careful not to overcook, or the wrap will become brittle.

Once it's done, place on a piece of cloth, brush with butter, and fill with 1 to 2 tablespoons of the cheese mixture (to taste). Wrap and roll tightly. Repeat with the remaining dough and filling.

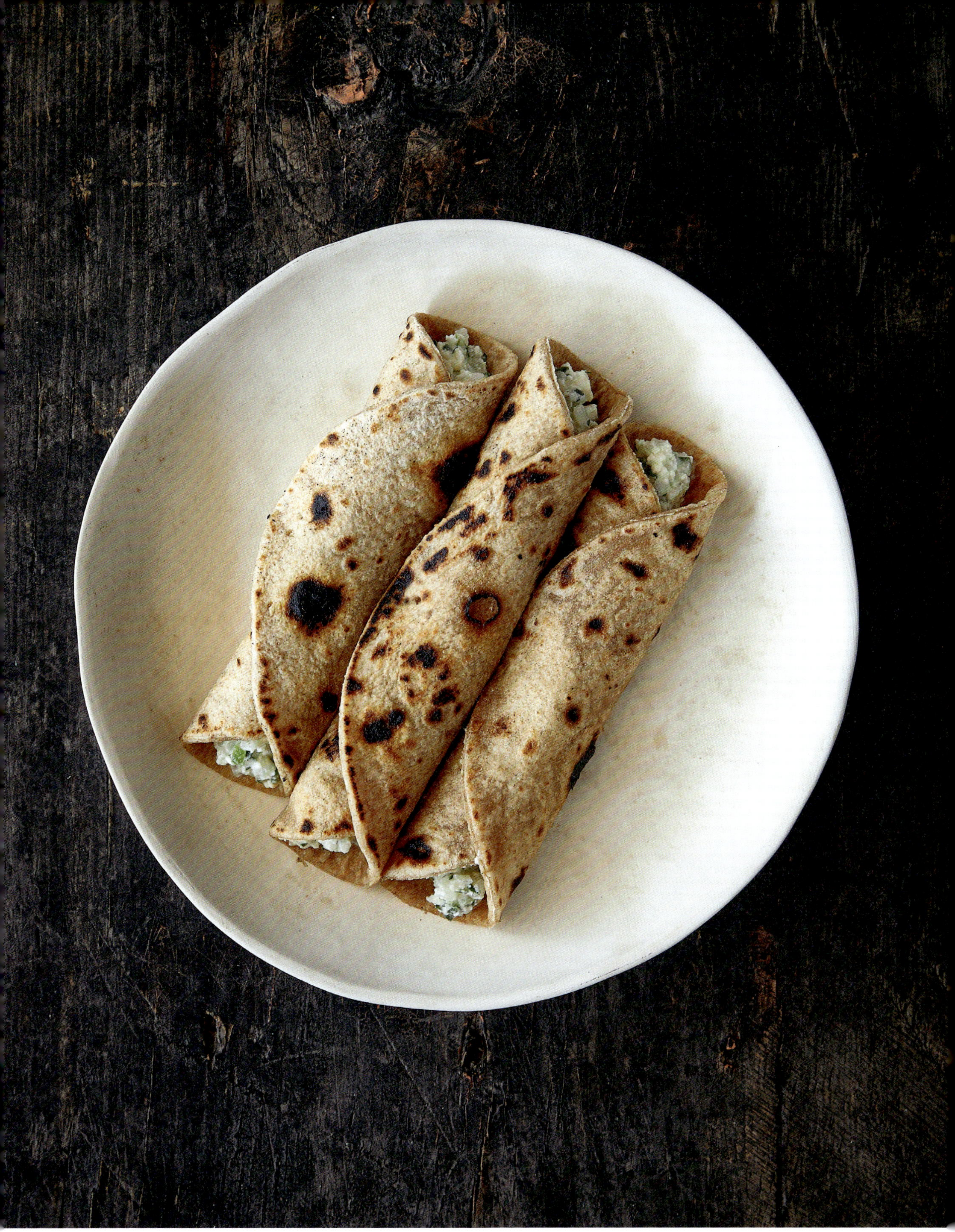

SAÇTA KIYMA BÖREĞİ

(LAMB-FILLED SKILLET BOREK)

15 to 16 servings

Every season

This type of börek features a thin dough similar to sıkma, but the cooking method differs: once rolled out, the filling is evenly distributed over top, then the dough is folded to create a large half-moon shape before being cooked on a skillet.

Serve them as a snack with tea, or make it a meal with a salad. You can adapt the filling to what you've got on hand -- try cheese, parsley, grated zucchini sautéed with onion, or boiled potatoes seasoned with onion and herbs.

INGREDIENTS:

For the dough:

- 2 cups (300 grams) whole-wheat flour
- 1 cup (150 grams) white flour
- 1 teaspoon salt
- 1 tablespoon (15 milliliters) oil, preferably sunflower
- 1 cup (250 milliliters) water (amount varies depending on your flour)

For the filling:

- 250 grams ground lamb or beef
- 2 tablespoons (30 milliliters) olive oil
- 1 teaspoon (10 grams) tomato paste
- 1 teaspoon (10 grams) pepper paste (see page 22)
- 1 medium onion (200 grams), finely chopped
- ½ cup parsley leaves and stems (20 grams), finely chopped
- ½ teaspoon freshly ground black pepper
- ½ teaspoon crushed red pepper flakes
- ½ teaspoon salt (if your tomato and pepper pastes are salty, decrease this amount)

METHOD:

Whisk the flours and salt in a large bowl, then use a wooden spoon to stir in the oil and water. Mix and finish kneading with your hands, to make a soft, not-too-sticky dough. Divide into 15 to 16 portions, set on a lightly floured work surface, cover with a towel or plastic wrap and let rest for 20 minutes.

Mix the filling ingredients in a large bowl.

Roll out one portion of the dough into a circle 15 to 16 cm (6 to 6 ¼ inches) in diameter. Spread 2 tablespoons of filling over one half of the circle, then fold the other half over to enclose. Pinch with your fingers to seal and trim with a pastry cutter. Repeat with the remaining dough and filling, keeping the trimmings to make another ball of dough.

Warm a large nonstick skillet over low heat and cook 2 pieces at a time, about 20 minutes per side. Serve warm.

AYŞE ES

ESİN YILDIZ

Esin worked for 27 years in information technology. Although her career was intense and busy, she enjoyed cooking as a hobby. As the years went by, she grew more and more interested in starting a business of her own -- and after retiring in 2016, she decided to return to school to learn all she could about not only cooking, but the technical skills needed to run a food business. She completed apprenticeships in cooking and pastry, as well as trainings in cakes and food hygiene, all in preparation to start her own catering company. The Women Entrepreneurs Association of Turkey (KAGIDER) introduced Esin to the LIFE Project, where she was able to connect with other entrepreneurs and deepen her understanding of the food business climate. She now runs a catering company called 1DK Events and specializes in preparing food for private dinners, birthday parties, and other celebrations. Esin was born in İzmit, Turkey.

Find Esin on Facebook and Instagram: @1dk.events.

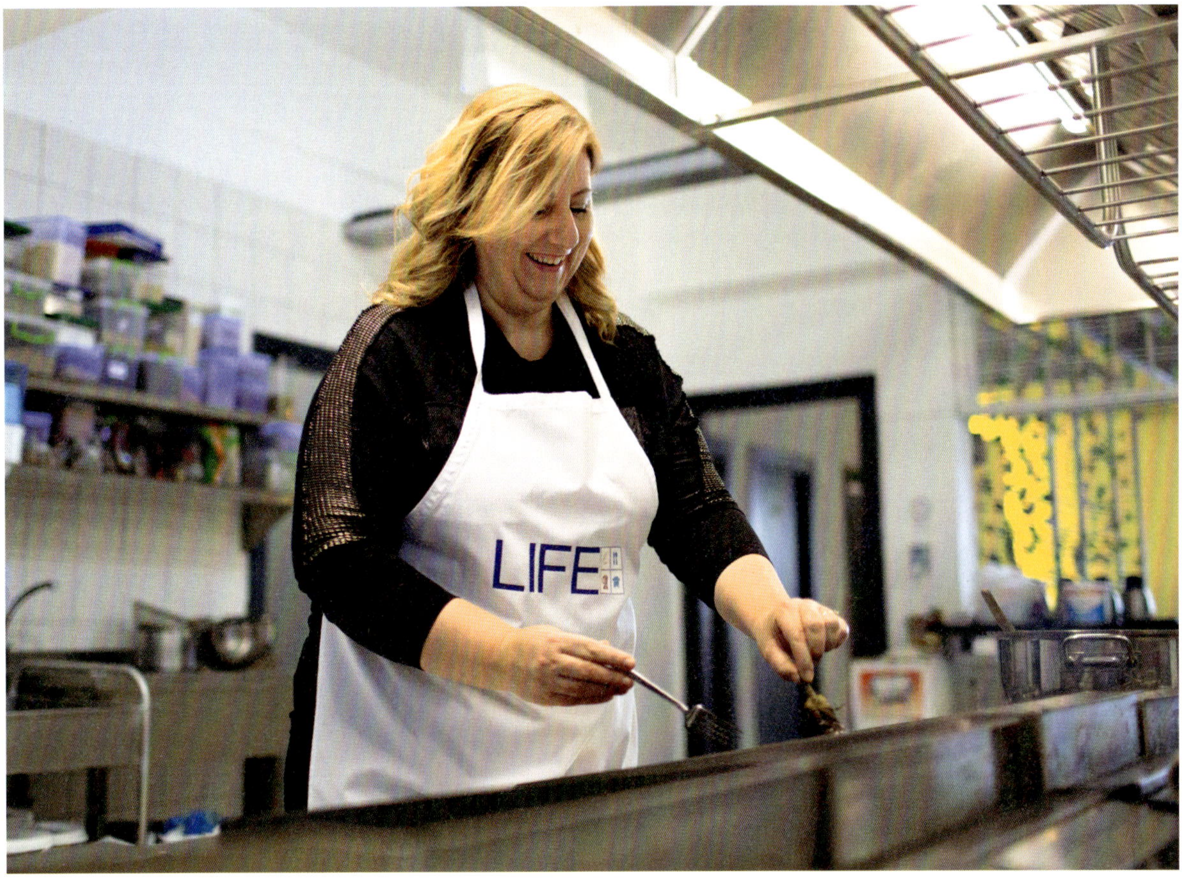
LIFE

HÜNKAR BEĞENDİ
(SULTAN'S DELIGHT)

8 servings

Summer, when eggplants are best

One origin story of this dish, as Esin explains, goes back to 1867. The sultan Abdulaziz visited France and invited the emperor, Napoleon III, and his wife, Eugenie, to visit him in Istanbul. Unable to get away from his work, Napoleon III sent Eugenie in his place. She brought her chef along, who, one day, prepared béchamel sauce, to much interest from the palace kitchen chef, who happened to be making roasted eggplants at that very moment. The palace chef combined the two, making a new dish which he served with lamb -- much to the delight of the sultan.

INGREDIENTS:

Topping:

¼ cup butter (or 100 milliliters/6 ¾ tablespoons olive oil)
2 medium onions, diced (500 grams total)
1 kilogram boneless lamb chop, cut into 2- or 3 cm (¾ - or 1-inch) cubes
2 cloves garlic, crushed
1 green bell pepper (85 grams), diced
2 medium tomatoes (330 grams total), peeled, seeded, and diced
1 teaspoon tomato paste
½ tablespoon salt
½ teaspoon freshly ground black pepper
3 cups (750 milliliters) water

For the eggplant base:

1 ½ kilograms globe eggplants
½ cup (100 grams) butter
2 tablespoons (25 grams) flour
2 ½ cups (625 milliliters) warm milk
½ teaspoon salt
1 cup (100 grams) grated kaşar (kasseri) cheese (may substitute mild cheddar or mozzarella)
½ teaspoon grated nutmeg

Note: *For a gluten-free option, make the base with ½ cup mashed eggplant, 2 tablespoons milk, 2 tablespoons grated hard cheese (Grana Padano or Parmesan), and a pinch of grated nutmeg.*

METHOD:

Preheat the oven to 200ºC (400ºF).

First make the topping: Melt the butter in a large, heavy-bottomed pot set over medium-high heat. Add the onion and cook for about 10 minutes, until the onions are slightly golden on the edges. Stir in the cubed lamb and cook on low until the liquids that released have evaporated. Add the garlic, bell pepper, and tomatoes, stirring to combine. Add the tomato paste, salt, pepper, and water, give it a stir, then simmer for about 1 hour, or until the meat is tender and almost all of the liquid has evaporated.

While the meat is cooking, make the base: Prick the eggplants with a fork; place them on a foil-lined baking sheet and bake in the oven for 40 minutes, turning occasionally, until charred on all sides and collapsed. Wrap with the foil and let sit for 15 to 20 minutes. (To add a smoky flavor, char the eggplants over the flame of a gas stove, turning occasionally until collapsed.)

Carefully remove the charred skin, placing the flesh in a large bowl, then finely chop the eggplant flesh and mash with a fork or a wooden spoon.

Melt the butter in a large skillet set over medium heat, then add the flour and cook until it's almost golden and smells toasty. Add the mashed eggplant, warm milk, and salt; cook, stirring frequently, over low heat until the mixture is very creamy, about 15 minutes. Turn off the heat; add the grated cheese and nutmeg. Put the eggplant puree on a serving dish and scatter the meat mixture over it.

Hünkar Beğendi can also be garnished with finely chopped parsley.

WRITING A RECIPE, RECORDING A JOURNEY

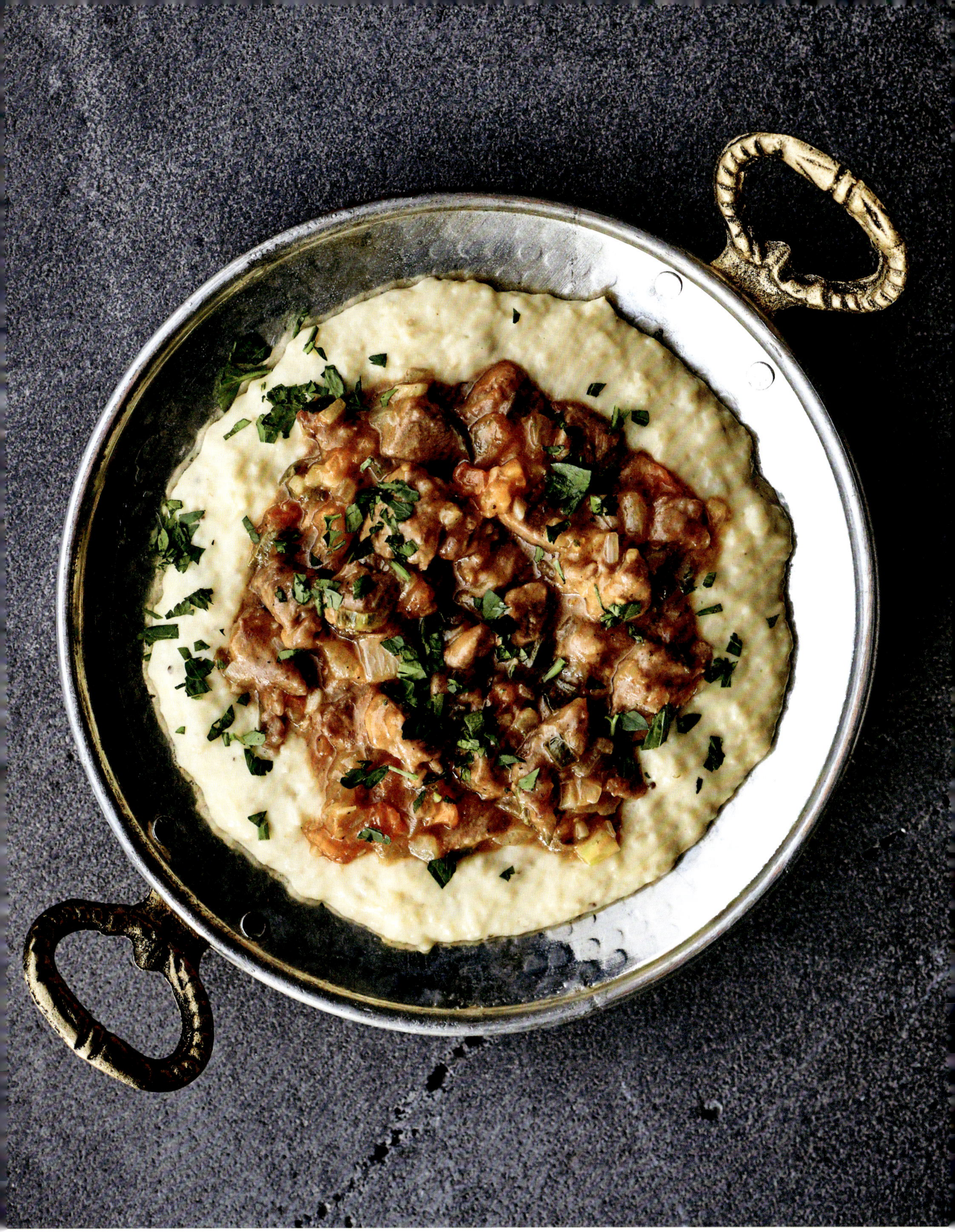

PORTAKAL SUYU İLE ZEYTİNYAĞLI KEREVİZ
(CELERY ROOT WITH OLIVE OIL AND ORANGE JUICE)

8 servings

Winter

Esin used to be a picky eater and particularly hated celery root. After many years of picking it out of things her mother would cook, she stopped by a friend's home, who practically demanded that she try the dish she had prepared -- with celery root. To her surprise, Esin loved the dish and now makes it often.

INGREDIENTS:

1 lemon
3 medium celery roots (660 grams)
1 large potato (350 grams)
1 onion (220 grams) finely chopped
½ cup (125 milliliters) water
¼ cup (60 milliliters) olive oil
1 carrot (160 grams), julienned
2 cups (500 milliliters) orange juice
1 teaspoon salt
1 teaspoon sugar

METHOD:

Squeeze the juice of the lemon into a large bowl of water, then, as you peel and cut the celery roots into 2.5-cm (1-inch) chunks, drop the chunks into the water to prevent discoloring. Peel the potato and cut into 2-cm (¾-inch) chunks, adding them to the water as you go.

Put the onion and ½ cup water into a large saucepan set over medium-high heat. Bring to a gentle boil and cook until the onion is soft, about 20 minutes.

Add the olive oil, give a good stir, then add the carrots and cook for 3 minutes. Add the potato slices, celery root slices, orange juice, salt, and sugar. Cook, covered, over medium heat, until the vegetables are tender, about 25 to 30 minutes. Chill before serving.

Note: *Celery leaves can be added while cooking, as well as for garnish.*

ESİN YILDIZ

STORIES AROUND DISHES

STORIES AROUND DISHES

Filiz Hösükoğlu

My story working in food began early as the daughter of a woman who was both a creative and uncompromising cook when it came to ingredients and techniques she used in her kitchen. While I objected to being her apprentice when I was young, I was not aware of how valuable these hands-on lessons would be later on in my career.

Although engineering is my formal training, my passion for food has always been with me. My journey began when I served as a translator for renowned American cookbook author Paula Wolfert. This led me to other opportunities centered around Turkish food culture -- I worked as a consultant for the European Union Turkish Business Centres (ABIGEM), created to promote food companies in Turkey and develop a market share in Europe. I've also held positions with companies like Culinary Backstreets and Oldways, as well as participated in the first migration project of Turkey, which aimed to solve the problems of constant movement from rural to urban areas.

Food is more than a passion: it is a powerful tool to build understanding and create new relationships. And working as the editor and curator of this cookbook fulfilled a dream to use food in cultural diplomacy. While testing recipes, some of the contributors spoke of heart-touching memories of their homelands; we exchanged stories around tables, dishes, and people. Translating these food memories from narratives to something written and permanent was very meaningful.

Filiz Hösükoğlu is a project manager and culinary culture consultant who serves on the LIFE Project Advisory Council. She has consulted for cookbook writers, food journalists, documentary producers, and researchers on cultural heritage and traditional Turkish cuisine since 1993. Ms. Hösükoğlu has also presented on traditional culinary culture heritage at national and international conferences, written articles for national and international food and cultural heritage magazines, offered cooking lessons, and organized cultural heritage and food tours and programs. In 2015, she worked with a team to develop the successful application by Gaziantep Metropolitan Municipality to be included in UNESCO Creative Cities Network in Gastronomy. She holds a degree in mechanical engineering.

For me this is not only a cookbook. This is the story of an entrepreneurship program that is creating jobs through cultural engagement and developing capacities in the process of sharing recipes and learning new skills. This cookbook is also the story of a team of people who have come together to brainstorm on the best ways to integrate newcomers into the community.

My hope is that the readers of this cookbook will be inspired by the stories and narratives of those who worked together to make it.

If one of these stories helps to create a personal mission that inspires others to use the power of food in community building, then we will have fulfilled our goal of using food to connect people across borders.

FİLİZ HÖSÜKOĞLU

Filiz's work has led to many exciting and fulfilling opportunities, including working closely with the LIFE Project to help empower others in their new lines of culinary work.
She believes that cooking is an art that offers limitless creativity -- but it's also a tool to bring people together with a common language of joy, sharing, and tasting, all inspiring for the next generation. These are a few of her favorite recipes.

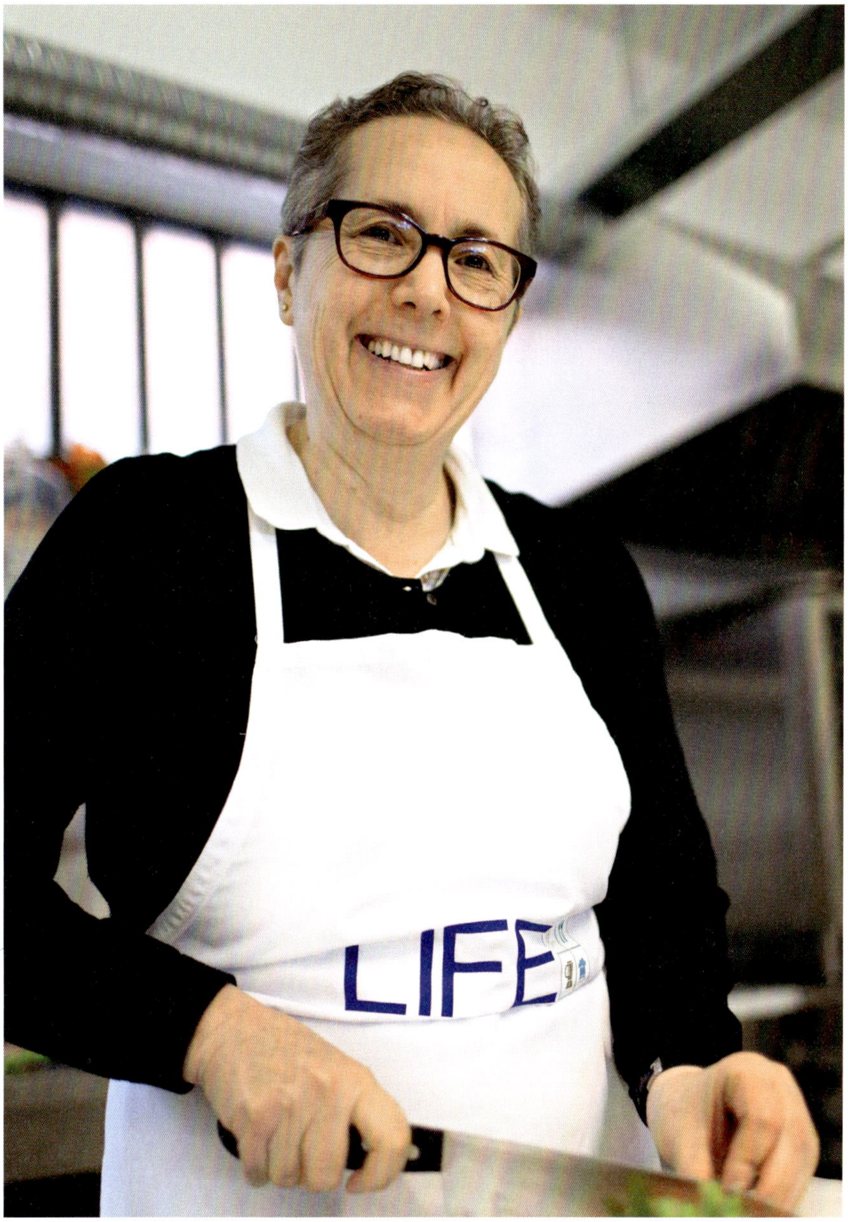
LIFE

PİRPİRİM AŞI

(PURSLANE DISH)

Serves 10 people

Summer

Due to its short shelf-life, purslane used to be dried during the summer and kept in fabric bags to be cooked during the winter. Now that it's more frequently available, this dish can be made with fresh purslane throughout the year. Purslane also happens to be very good for you, as it's high in omega-3 fatty acids.

If purslane is not available, use spinach or Swiss chard. You can also use canned or dried tomatoes in place of fresh.

Serve with pita bread, homemade pickles, and spring onions.

INGREDIENTS:

For the soup:

3 tablespoons (15 milliliters) olive oil
1 onion (220 grams), finely chopped
1 sweet red pepper, cut in 1-cm cubes
1 tablespoon (15 grams) tomato paste
1 tablespoon (25 grams) pepper paste (see page 22)
2 tomatoes (500 grams total), peeled and cubed
½ cup black or green lentils, boiled
½ cup black-eyed peas, boiled
½ cup chickpeas, boiled
½ teaspoon (1 gram) freshly ground black pepper
6 cups (1 ½ liters) hot water, plus more as needed
1 tablespoon (15 grams) salt
1 tablespoon (20 grams) pomegranate molasses (may substitute 2 tablespoons lemon juice mixed with ½ teaspoon sugar)
4 cups purslane, chopped
⅓ cup (70 grams) coarse bulgur (see page 21)
3 to 4 cloves (15 to 20 grams) garlic (to taste), crushed with a pinch of salt

To garnish:

5 tablespoons (70 grams) olive oil, butter or a combination of both
1 tablespoon (3 grams) dried mint
1 tablespoon (2 grams) crushed red pepper flakes

METHOD:

Warm the oil in a large skillet set over medium heat, then add the onion and cook for 5 minutes.

Add the cubed pepper and cook for 5 more minutes, then add the tomato and pepper pastes and cook another 5 minutes. Add the tomatoes, cover, and cook for 7 to 9 minutes. Add the lentils, black-eyed peas, chickpeas, black pepper, and 6 cups of hot water. Cover and cook for 10 minutes.

Stir in the salt, pomegranate molasses, purslane, and bulgur, then simmer, covered, for 15 minutes. If the mixture gets very thick, add up to 1 cup of hot water, so that it has a creamy texture. Add the crushed garlic, give a good stir, and turn off the heat.

For the garnish, warm the oil and/or butter in a small skillet over medium heat, then add the pepper flakes and the dried mint and cook for several minutes, until it's sizzling and fragrant. Drizzle this mixture over the soup.

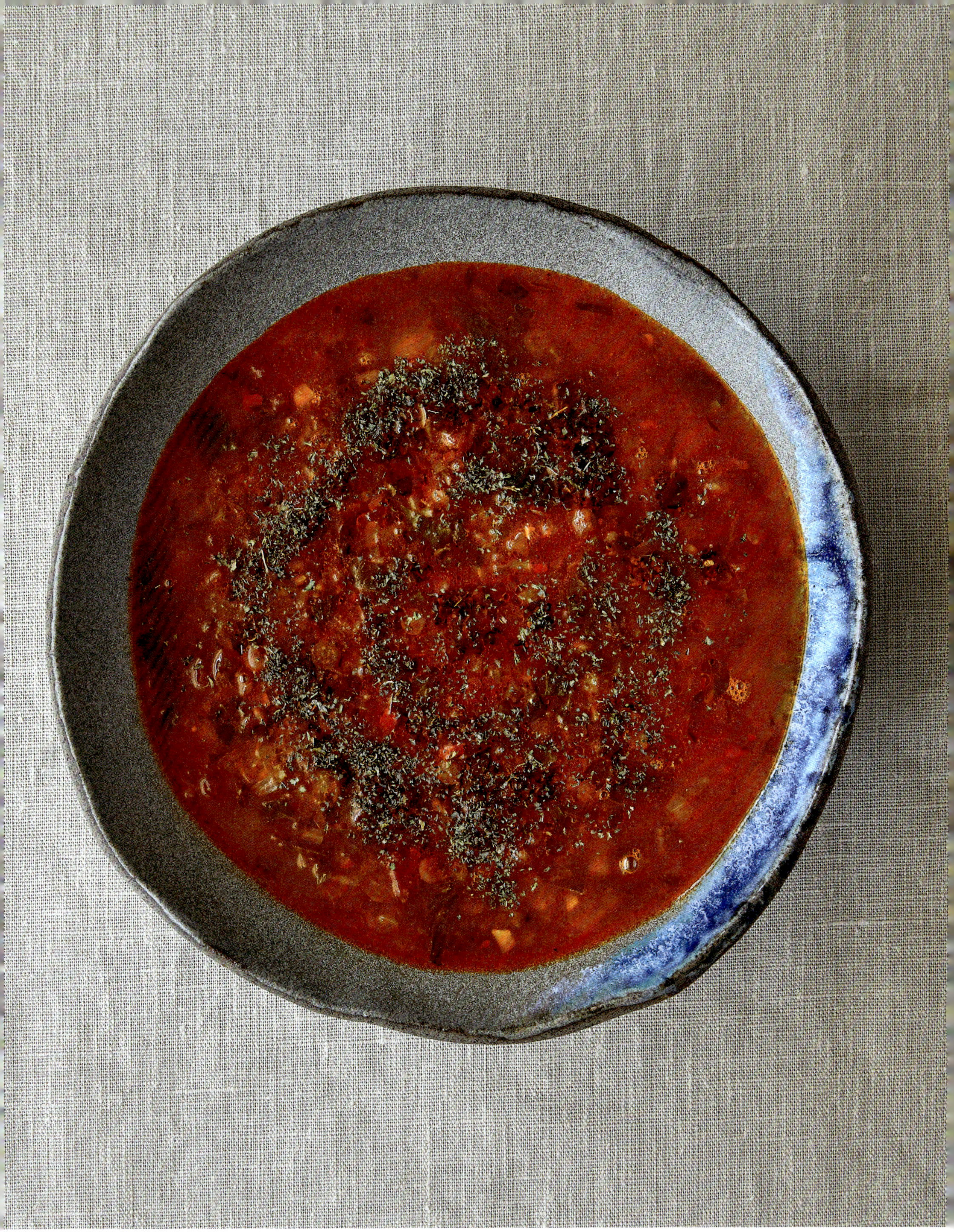

ASTARLI SÜTLAÇ
(RICE PUDDING)

6 servings

Every season, but especially during Ramadan Feast

Astarlı sütlaç is the combination of two puddings -- a plain one, called zerde, and a rice pudding, called sütlaç -- in the same serving dish. The ingredients are simple, preparation is easy, and the result is light. It's made especially during Eid, when it's common to receive many visitors, as it can be made and kept for several days. In olden times, it was kept under the sofa in the sitting room on winter days: When a visitor came, the hostess could serve them immediately by pulling out a tray-full of rice pudding bowls. (Quite practical!)

You can play around with the topping, adding lightly toasted pine nuts, fresh fruit, such as sliced bananas or strawberries, or grated coconut. If you want to add a boost of flavor to the zerde, add 1 teaspoon rose water, 1 teaspoon vanilla powder, or a pinch of lemon rind after it is cooked. Serve astarlı sütlaç with one slice of baklava or kurabiye (shortbread cookies) -- especially during Eid.

INGREDIENTS:

For the sütlaç:
4 ⅔ cups (1120 milliliters) milk
⅓ cup (60 grams) white medium-grain rice, rinsed and drained

For the zerde:
½ tablespoon safflower (optional)
5 ½ cups (1375 milliliters) water
⅓ cup (60 grams) rice
1 cup (200 grams) sugar

To garnish:
½ cup pistachio nuts (50 grams), preferably Turkish Antep, chopped
½ cup (40 grams) pomegranate seeds

Note: *To help the sütlaç and zerde set more quickly, you can make a slurry from 8 grams of cornstarch and 100 milliliters of water for the sütlaç and 12 grams of cornstarch and 100 milliliters of water for the zerde. Add these slurries at the very end of cooking and whisk thoroughly.*

METHOD:

For the sütlaç: Bring the milk to a boil in a medium pot. Add the rice, reduce heat to maintain a simmer, and cook for about 1 hour, stirring occasionally, until the mixture thickly coats a wooden spoon. Remove from the heat and half-fill six individual serving bowls with the rice pudding. Let cool.

For the zerde: Soak the safflower in ½ cup of the water for 10 to 15 minutes, then strain and reserve the liquid. Bring the remaining water to a boil in a medium pot, then add the rice and ⅓ cup of the sugar. Lower the heat to maintain a simmer and cook for about 20 minutes, stirring occasionally. Then add the strained safflower liquid and another ⅓ cup of the sugar. Continue cooking until it has a creamy texture. Add the remaining sugar and boil for another 5 minutes.

Ladle over the cooled rice puddings. Let cool slightly, then garnish with the pistachio nuts and pomegranate seeds.

FİLİZ HÖSÜKOĞLU

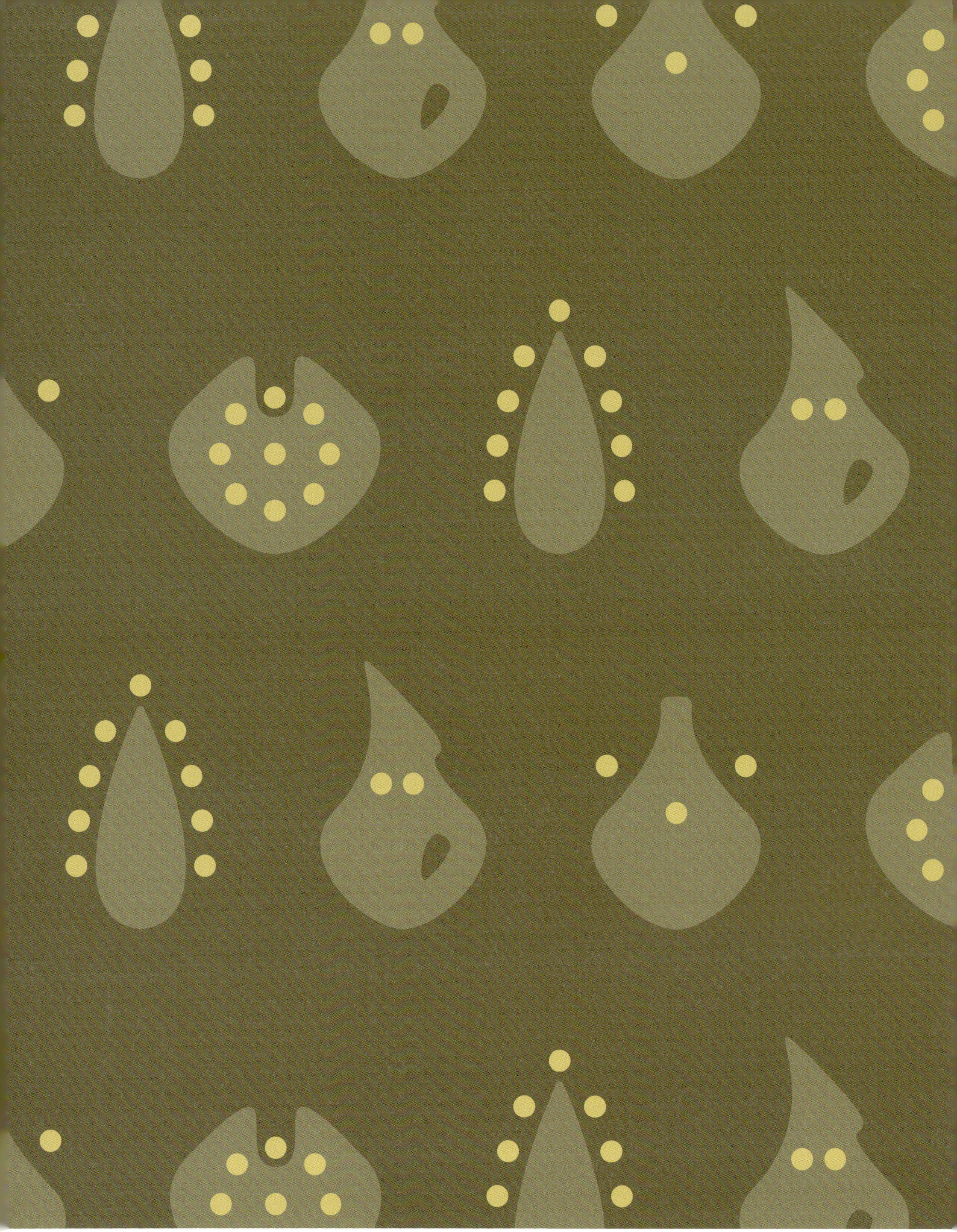

MSA for LIFE

Cem Erol

As a professional culinary school, the main responsibility of MSA is to deliver the internationally accepted cooking techniques, foundational principles, chemistry, and outcome behind every recipe in a professional kitchen. But at MSA we also believe that today, where culinary boundaries cross so many national borders in matters of food, it is also our duty to find practical ways to educate tomorrow's chefs about the notion of food diversity and what we can learn from it.

That is why when Filiz Hösükoğlu first came to MSA to tell us about the LIFE Project, my colleagues and I knew immediately that we wanted to be an integral part of it. There was no other way of describing our excitement that day as we learned of the possibility to support this important gastrodiplomacy program.

It has been a great opportunity for both our students and the MSA culinary team to test and experience these wonderful recipes. We learned about the contributor's regions, local food culture, ingredients, thinking, and creativity behind every recipe -- the soul of home cooking -- from a perfect source: the men and women who had carried these recipes from generation to generation. The work we did was to follow the exact recipes provided by their owners. We checked to see if they needed some fine-tuning for standardization. Our goal was to shape the recipes so that anybody can recreate these colorful, inspiring dishes in their own kitchen, wherever they may be.

Cem Erol is a graduate of the Tourism and Hotel Management Department of Bilkent University. He furthered his education in the United States, studying at Johnson and Wales and then working in hotels and clubs including the Loews Miami Beach Hotel, Marco Island Marriott, and Ritz Carlton Naples Golf Resort in Florida. He returned to Istanbul in 2004, where, as the sous chef at Hotel Les Ottoman, he specialized in Ottoman and Turkish cuisine. Mr. Erol went on to helm the kitchen at Banyan Restaurant, then continued as executive chef at the W Hotel, where he was responsible for overall kitchen operation, including the management of the W Kitchen concept and Spice Market designed by chef Jean-Georges Vongerichten. Mr. Erol is the executive instructor chef at MSA, a position he has held since January 2010.

In this fast-moving world, it is very difficult -- yet more essential than ever -- to keep alive any cultural heritage, traditions, valuable stories, or habits. They must be told, shared, practiced, and handed down to new generations. These recipes are not only for cultural preservation in books, but are a valuable reference and inspirational foundation for creating tomorrow's culinary ideas and innovations.

A cookbook carries history and living memories within its pages. It is a perfect tool for understanding the foodways of our heritage. We believe this book will be one of those timeless examples of shared regional food culture that will shed light on the complexity of recipes and stories that will inform those who seek to understand our culinary heritage.

We want to not only recognize, but also thank all of the wonderful recipe contributors and the team that allowed us to be part of this important venture. We are very proud to be part of the LIFE Project.

FATIMA FOUAD

Fatima, who comes from Sa'da, Yemen, has been a passionate baker since childhood. She was always an avid reader of cookbooks and food magazines and honed her technique by experimenting with different cake recipes. She and her husband had four children, but Fatima did not work and had no source of income -- so when her husband left them, she needed to support herself and her children on her own. Fatima explains that her culture made it difficult to be a woman who owns a business, but she nevertheless recognized that she had a valuable service to provide and opened her own pastry shop.

Once the war started, and resources and electricity became scarce, Fatima closed her shop and moved with her children to Turkey. She was able to tap into a network of fellow Yemenis in Istanbul, but she knew that there were resources available -- even willing investors -- that she, as someone unfamiliar with the Turkish business climate, did not have access to. Fatima joined the LIFE Project's first cohort and soon got the training, feedback, and contacts to continue pursuing her baking business. (She even won the business pitch competition at the end of the training.) Fatima is currently selling baked goods through her online platforms and a coffee shop in Istanbul.

Follow Fatima on Instagram: @koop.tr.

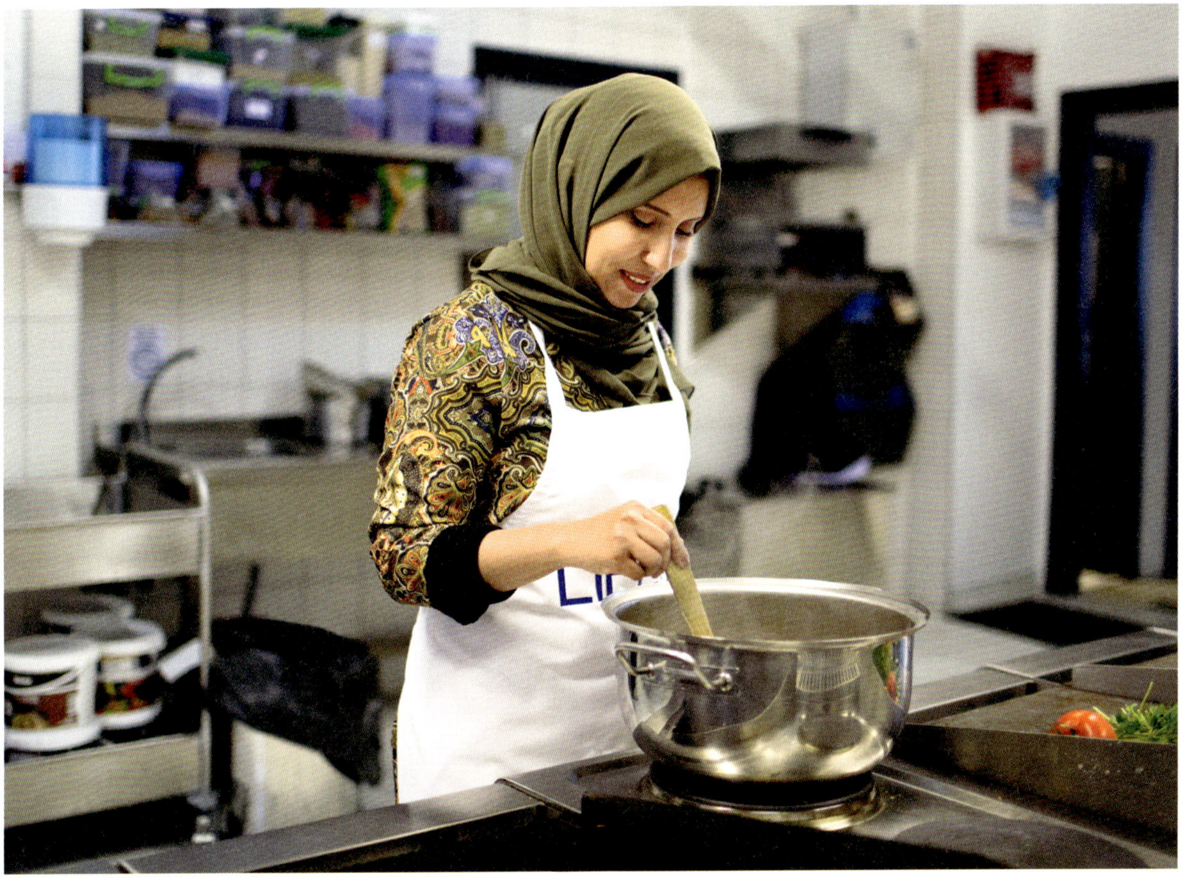

SHURBET KHUDAR W DAJAJ

(VEGETABLE SOUP WITH CHICKEN)

4 servings

Every season

This soup is an easy way to include more vegetables into your diet. The vegetables are left chopped, but they can also be blended into a puree, as Fatima did when her children were young. She also adds parsley and fresh coriander to give color and flavor.

Use whichever seasonal vegetables you have at home. Some cooks add rice, vermicelli, or dumplings to the soup to give a different flavor and thick texture.

INGREDIENTS:

5 tablespoons olive oil
1 onion (220 grams) finely chopped
1 carrot (150 grams), diced in 1-cm (½-inch) cubes
1 zucchini (250 grams), seeded and diced in 1-cm (1/2-inch) cubes
1 tomato (200 grams), peeled and roughly diced
1 large bone-in, skin-on chicken breast (100 to 120 grams)
1 ½ teaspoons spice mix (see note)
1 chicken stock cube (optional)
5 cups (1180 milliliters) hot (just-boiled) water
1 scallion (40 grams)
½ cup chopped parsley (10 grams), plus more for garnish
1 tablespoon chopped cilantro (5 grams), plus more for garnish
1 ½ teaspoons salt
2 tablespoons (30 milliliters) fresh lemon juice (optional)

METHOD:

Warm the oil in a large pot set over medium-high heat. Add the onion, carrot, and zucchini, increase the heat to high, and cook, stirring often, for 5 to 7 minutes. Add the tomato, chicken breast, spice mix, and chicken stock cube, if using, then add the water. Bring to a boil, then reduce the heat to maintain a simmer for about 20 minutes (uncovered), or until the chicken is tender. Remove from heat.

Remove the chicken breast and shred, then add it back to the pot. (Discard the skin and bones or save for another use.)

Add the scallion, parsley, cilantro, salt, and lemon juice, if using. Taste and adjust seasonings as needed.

Serve warm, garnished with chopped parsley and cilantro.

Note: *To make the spice mix, grind 5 tablespoons cumin seed and 1 tablespoon cardamom seed in a spice grinder or mortar and pestle, then transfer to a small bowl. Add 3 tablespoons curry powder and 1 tablespoon turmeric. This mix can be used with any meat and vegetable dish -- store leftovers in a glass jar.*

FATIMA FOUAD

ZURBIAN

(RICE WITH LAMB)

10 servings

During weddings and festivals

Yemeni Zurbian is related to biryani, the flavorful Indian rice dish. This style of cooking rice is embraced by many nations and eaten throughout the Arabian Peninsula. Some say it originates in Persia -- the word biryani is derived from the Persian words birian, meaning fried before cooking, and birinj, meaning rice. It came to Yemen through the southern port city of Aden, the site of many cross-cultural developments. It was originally called Adeni Zurbian before spreading to the rest of the country. Zurbian is one of the main dishes served at weddings and festivals. Its white rice, brown caramelized onions, and yellow and red saffron make for a rich tableau of colors. Serve it for your next happy occasion, with plenty of zahawiq (green chile sauce, page 62).

INGREDIENTS:

- 5 tablespoons (75 milliliters) olive oil
- 3 large onions (600 g), sliced in half moons
- 1 kilogram bone-in lamb (top round or chuck), cut into 6- to 7-cm (2- to 2 ½-inch) cubes (ask your butcher to cut it, with its bones; may substitute beef)
- 1 onion (200 grams) finely chopped (to be cooked with meat)
- 1 teaspoon ground cumin
- 1 teaspoon freshly ground black pepper
- 1 teaspoon plus 2 tablespoons rice spice mix (see note)
- 2 cloves garlic
- 3 teaspoons coarse sea salt, plus more to taste
- 2 cups (470 milliliters) plus 8 ½ cups (2 liters) just-boiled water, plus more as needed
- 1 kilogram (2.2 pounds/5 cups) basmati rice
- 1 cup (250 grams) yogurt
- 1 tablespoon chopped cilantro
- 3 large potatoes (600 grams), peeled and quartered
- 2 tablespoons raisins
- 3 tablespoons almonds or cashews
- ¼ cup clarified butter or olive oil
- 1 teaspoon saffron (optional)
- 2 spicy green peppers, such as jalapeño, sliced in rounds for garnish (seeds removed)

METHOD:

Warm the olive oil in a large (5 ½-liter/6-quart capacity) pot over medium-high heat, then add the sliced onions. Cook, stirring often, until the onions begin to soften, about 5 minutes. Lower the heat and continue cooking, stirring occasionally, until the onions are golden and lightly caramelized, about 30 to 40 minutes. Take care not to burn the onions; if you do, start over.

Meanwhile, place a large, heavy-bottomed pot over medium-high heat and sear the meat (with the bones) on all sides. (Fat will render out, so you shouldn't need to add oil.) Add the finely chopped onion, cumin, black pepper, 1 teaspoon of the spice mix, chopped garlic and 1 teaspoon of salt; cook, stirring, for about 10 minutes, until the onion softens. Once the liquid evaporates, add 2 cups (470 milliliters) of just-boiled water. Put the lid on and bring to a simmer over high heat; reduce to low and cook until the meat is tender, approximately 45 minutes.

While the meat is simmering, bring the 8 ½ cups (2 liters) of water to a boil in a medium saucepan. Add the rice and 1 teaspoon of salt, then turn off the heat. Let sit for 20 minutes, then drain and rinse.

Puree the yogurt, cilantro and 1 tablespoon of the caramelized onions in a blender. (You can finely mince the cilantro and onions and stir into the yogurt, but the result will not be as smooth.)

Add the quartered potatoes to the caramelized onions and cook, covered, over medium-high heat for 10 minutes (the potatoes will finish cooking later).

›

MSA for LIFE 58

FATIMA FOUAD

ZURBIAN
(RICE WITH LAMB)

When the meat is finished, add it to the caramelized onions and potatoes, along with the remaining 2 tablespoons rice spice, the raisins, nuts, remaining 1 teaspoon salt, the clarified butter, and the drained and rinsed rice. If there is any liquid left from cooking the lamb, pour it into a liquid measuring cup and add water to reach 4 cups. Spread the yogurt mixture over top of the rice, then pour in the 4 cups of liquid/water.

Mix the saffron with 2 tablespoons of hot water and drizzle over the mixture. Put the lid on. Bring to a full boil, reduce the heat, and simmer for 20 minutes on low heat, until the rice has absorbed the liquid. Let rest for 10 minutes, give a gentle stir, then adjust seasonings to taste and garnish with sliced green peppers.

> Spices play a key role in the varieties of zurbian -- this one includes the basics, but professional chefs add their own twists. Lamb is the meat of choice; a little lamb fat could be used to caramelize the onions. The rice is colored with the superior-quality Isfahani saffron, which also lends a distinct flavor. Since saffron is expensive, some cooks use food coloring powder. If zurbian is prepared without a special occasion at hand, then it is common to replace the lamb with bone-in chicken pieces.

Another way to add flavor: smoke. Fatima places the outer layers of the onion in the middle of the cooked dish like a nest, and pours 3 tablespoons of olive oil inside. She then heats a 4-centimeter cube of fehim (natural coal) over a stove until it reddens, drops the hot coal into the oil-filled onion, and covers the dish with a layer of foil and the lid, allowing the smoke to permeate the zurbian for about 10 minutes.

Note: *To make the rice spice mix, grind 5 tablespoons cumin seed, 2 teaspoons black peppercorns, 1 tablespoon whole cloves, 1 teaspoon cardamom seeds (from about 15 to 20 cardamom pods), and 1 teaspoon broken cinnamon sticks. Store leftovers in a tight-sealing jar at room temperature for up to 3 months.*

ZAHAWIQ

(GREEN CHILE SAUCE)

Makes 1 cup

Every season

This hot sauce is very popular in Yemen. It is served with rice in the south and with bread in the north. It can be eaten with cheese and lavash bread, especially for breakfast. In the old times, zahawiq was ground with stone grinders, which were found in every Yemeni house -- a practice some people still prefer today.

INGREDIENTS:

1 large tomato (200 grams), peeled and halved
8 spicy green chile peppers (such as jalapeño or serrano), stemmed and roughly chopped
1 ½ teaspoons (2 grams) chopped cilantro (from 2 to 3 sprigs)
2 cloves garlic
Salt, as needed

METHOD:

Blend everything until mostly smooth. Taste and add salt if needed. Store in the refrigerator for up to 2 weeks.

Note: *There are many versions of zahawiq. If you do not like spice, use mild peppers. For different flavor and texture, add chopped parsley, olive oil, and lemon juice. To make red zahawiq, add 2 more tomatoes to the mix and blend until creamy.*

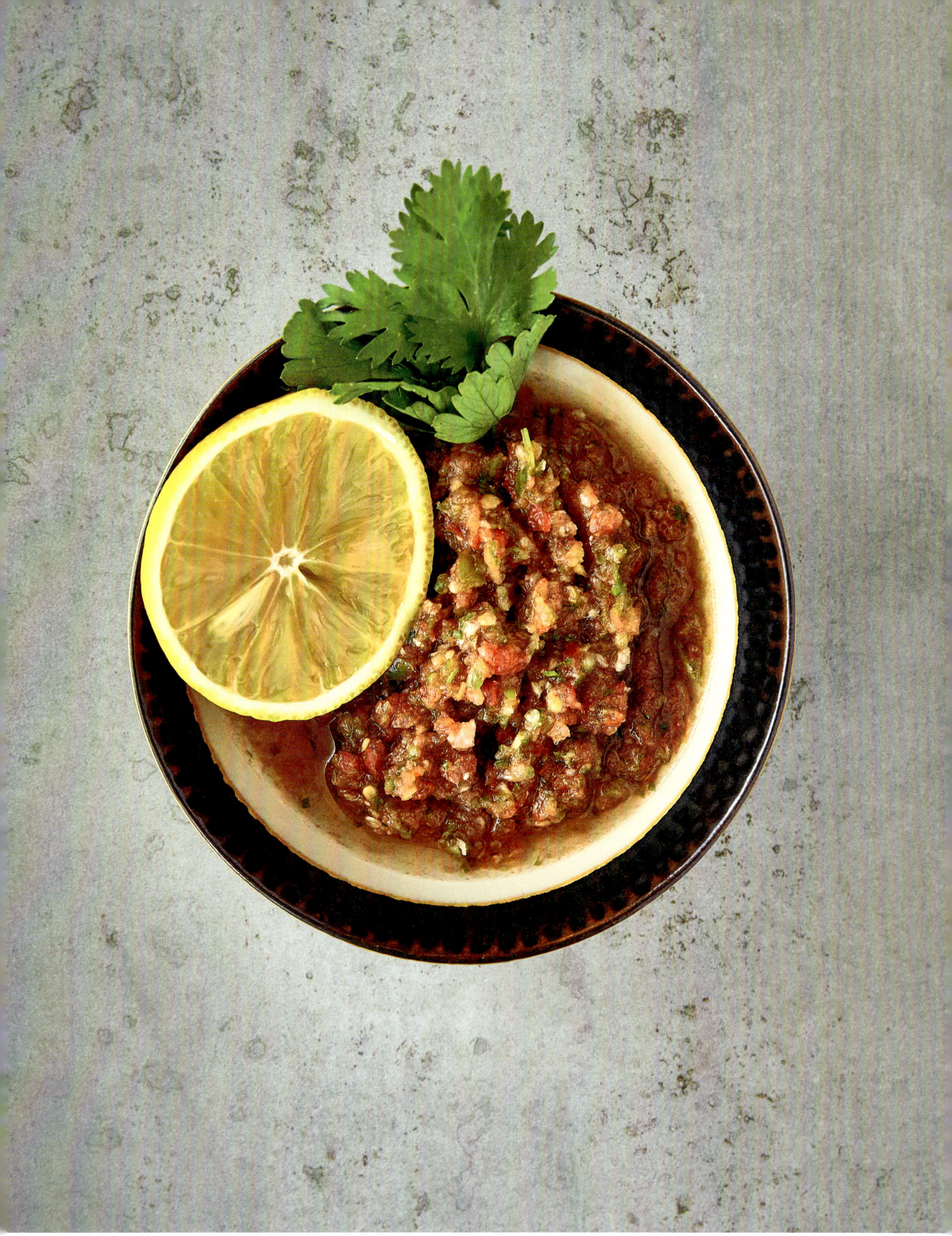

HARISSA/HARISA
(PEANUT DESSERT)

4 servings (makes 10 to 12 pieces)

Every season

Traditional sweets such as this harissa are popular in southern Yemen -- but since it's not available in Turkish markets, Fatima started to make her own. Harissa is typically served after lunch with qisher, a type of unsweetened coffee prepared from coffee peels.

INGREDIENTS:

- 4 cups (600 grams) shelled and peeled peanuts
- 5 whole cloves, crushed with the side of the knife
- 2 cups (400 grams) sugar
- 1 cup (230 milliliters) water
- 1 tablespoon (14 milliliters) fresh lemon juice
- 1 tablespoon wheat starch
- 2 teaspoons rose water
- ½ teaspoon vanilla powder
- 1 teaspoon ground cardamom, a pinch reserved for garnish
- 2 ½ tablespoons (40 milliliters) vegetable oil
- Blanched almonds, for garnish (optional)

METHOD:

Grind the peanuts and cloves into a powder in a food processor. Combine the sugar, water, lemon juice and wheat starch in a saucepan and bring to a strong simmer, whisking to dissolve the sugar and starch. Simmer for 10 minutes, to thicken. Add the ground peanuts, rose water, vanilla powder, and ground cardamom to the saucepan, stirring to combine.

Pour the oil into a 24-cm (9- to 10-inch) round baking dish, using your fingers or a brush to coat the bottom and sides, then pat the peanut mixture evenly inside. Put in the refrigerator to set for at least 30 minutes.

Cut the harissa into 10 to 12 diamond shapes. Sprinkle over the reserved cardamom and decorate with blanched almonds, if using.

Note: *Harissa can be prepared with orange blossom water instead of rose water. For a slightly more sturdy harissa, semolina can be added to the sugar and water mixture (during cooking). Peanuts can be substituted with other nuts, such as walnuts, hazelnuts or pistachios. Some cooks add food coloring to brighten the appearance.*

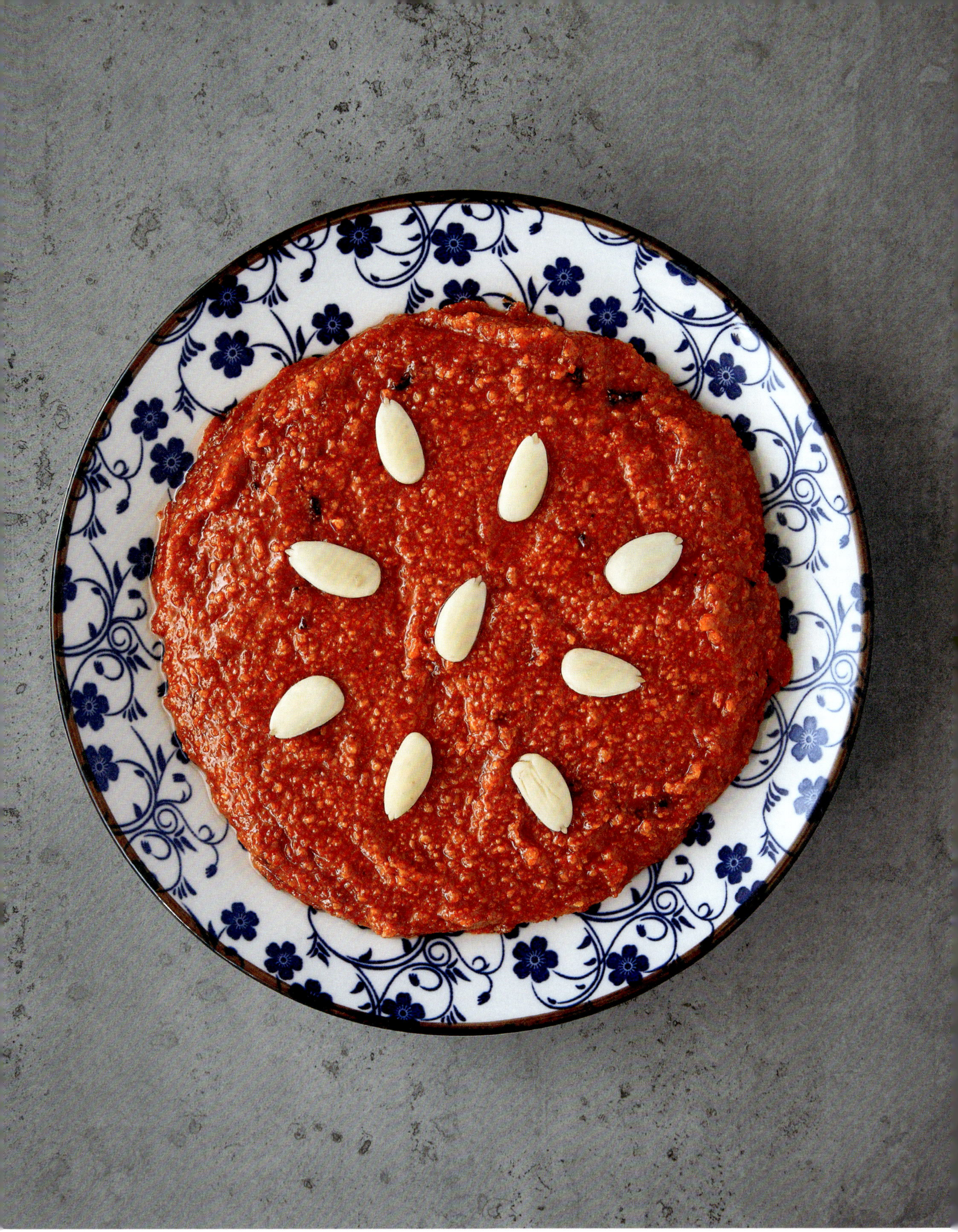

MUZ FATTAH

(BANANA BREAD)

4 servings

During winter and for new mothers

In some areas of Yemen this is called arikeh. It is a popular and comforting dish mostly eaten during winter, because it is full of calories. It is also served to sick children and new mothers.

Muz Fattah is best served hot, with honey on the side for extra drizzling. If lavash bread is not available, you can use any other bread. You can also substitute other fruit (even plump dates and raisins) for the bananas.

INGREDIENTS:

7 tablespoons (100 grams) butter or oil

2 lavash or pita breads (120 to 140 grams), cut into 1- to 1.5-cm (about ½-inch) pieces

4 ripe bananas, sliced

2 tablespoons (50 grams) honey, plus more for serving

4 tablespoons cream (may also use 80 grams clotted cream or mascarpone)

1 tablespoon (10 grams) nigella seeds (see page 22)

METHOD:

Warm the butter in a large skillet set over medium heat, then add the lavash and sliced bananas. Cook, stirring occasionally, for 8 to 10 minutes, until everything is toasted and golden brown in spots. Transfer to a serving dish, drizzle with the honey and cream, and sprinkle with nigella seeds.

FATIMA FOUAD

FATIMA HAMMO

Fatima studied arts, crafts, and sewing in Aleppo, where she ran a beauty salon and made and sold ballgowns. She moved to Turkey, with her husband and seven children, to escape the war. Around the same time, Fatima developed asthma and couldn't continue working in salons as she had planned to do. She needed to help pay for her children's university educations though, so Fatima -- already an excellent cook -- decided to make sweets and pastries to sell to university students. It didn't take long for people in her neighborhood to recognize the quality of her cooking, and Fatima received more and more orders -- so much so that she decided to develop her business management skills and turn her side job into a full-fledged catering business. Her specialty, kibbeh, features a combination of lamb, bulgur, nuts, and spices that make for a magnificent harmony of flavors.

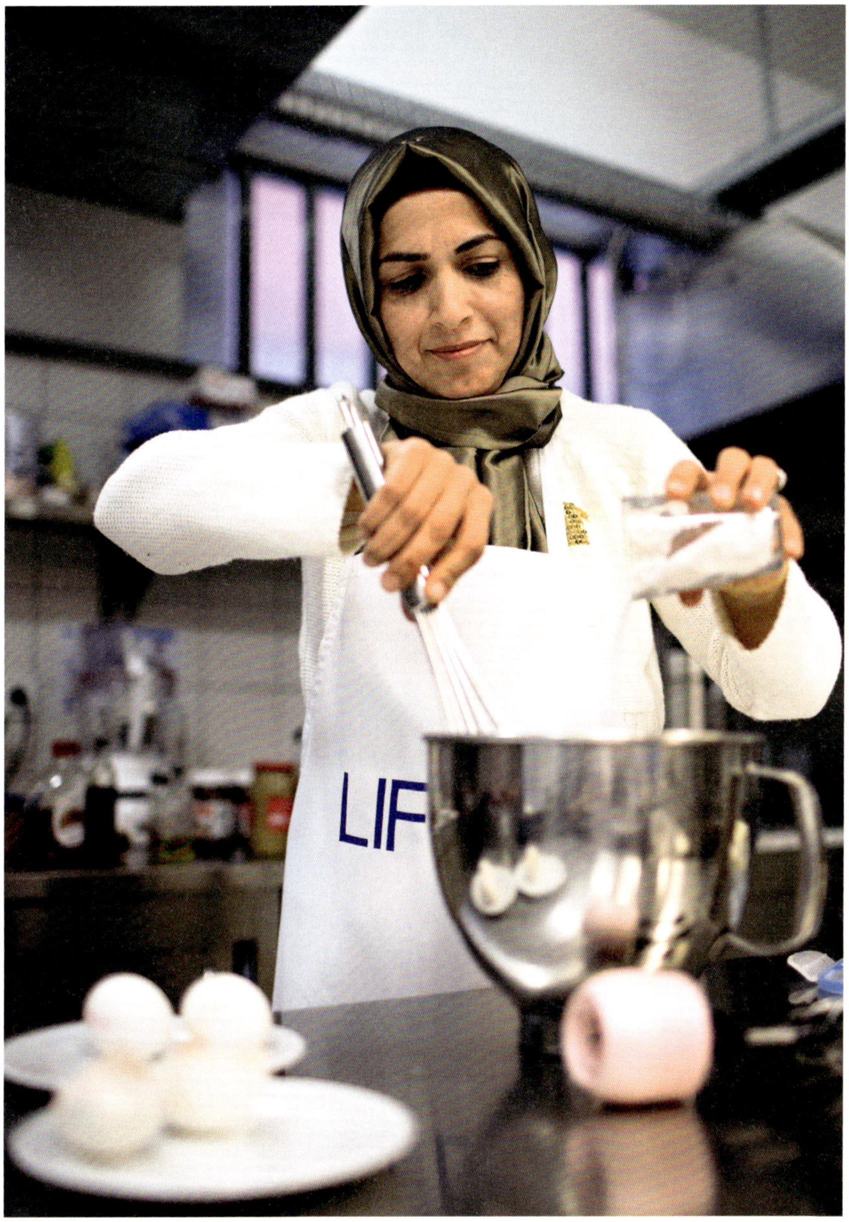
LIF

KIBBEH BIL SANIEH

(KIBBEH IN A TRAY)

8 servings (makes 16 kibbeh diamonds)

Winter and every season

This style of kibbeh, baked in a dish, is popular in Syria and Lebanon. It is easy and practical, and, unlike other ways of making kibbeh, there is no deep frying.

Note that you'll need to prepare the filling in advance, as it needs to be cold when you assemble the dish. Pistachios can be added to the filling, in addition to the walnuts; you can use olive oil instead of butter, or even decrease the amount of butter or oil if you like. If the circular tray is used, instead of square or rectangular one, you can score the kibbeh into flower designs. Serve with laban bi khiar (yogurt, cucumber, and dried mint salad; see Maha Al Tinawi's recipe on page 142).

INGREDIENTS:

For the filling:
1 tablespoon butter
100 grams walnuts, coarsely ground or chopped
750 grams ground lamb (10 percent fat)
500 grams onion, finely chopped
1 teaspoon salt
1 teaspoon freshly ground black pepper
½ teaspoon ground allspice
1 egg

For the bulgur paste:
2 ½ cups (500 grams) fine grain bulgur
2 cups (500 milliliters) water
500 grams lean ground lamb or beef
1 onion, quartered
1 teaspoon salt
1 teaspoon freshly ground black pepper

For assembly and baking:
Water, for your hands and sprinkling
½ cup (120 grams) butter, at room temperature
½ cup blanched almonds

METHOD:

Prepare the filling: Melt the butter in a large skillet set over medium heat, then add the walnuts and cook, stirring occasionally, for 10 to 15 minutes, until toasted. Remove from skillet and add the ground lamb, onion, salt, pepper, and allspice. Cook, stirring often, until the juices evaporate, about 30 to 40 minutes. Remove from heat and stir in the toasted walnuts. Set aside to cool slightly, then add the egg and mix thoroughly.

While the filling is cooling, make the bulgur paste: Put the bulgur in the bowl of a food processor, then add the water. Stir well with a fork and let sit for 15 minutes.

Add the lamb or beef, onion, salt, and pepper, then pulse about 3 times, or just until you have a malleable paste.

Butter a 40-by-25-cm (15-by-10 inches) baking dish and preheat the oven to 180°C (350°F).

Spread half of the bulgur paste into the dish, patting with moistened hands to make it as even as possible. Next spread the filling, again making it as even as possible. Finish with the rest of the bulgur paste, pressing down with your hands to ensure that it sticks to the filling.

Cut into 16 diamond shapes, make a small indentation in the center of each diamond, and press one almond in each dimple. Use your hands to spread the butter over the kibbeh and bake for 30 minutes, until the top is browned. Remove from the oven and sprinkle some water over top with your fingers, then serve.

FATIMA HAMMO

FOR LONG-TERM REFUGEES, SUSTAINABLE LIVELIHOODS
REPRESENT MORE THAN SURVIVAL

FOR LONG-TERM REFUGEES, SUSTAINABLE LIVELIHOODS REPRESENT MORE THAN SURVIVAL

Kathleen Newland

When today's international system for dealing with refugees was set up in the aftermath of World War II, it was assumed that refugee status was temporary: since the guns had fallen silent, displaced people would either be able to return to their homes or, for the minority unable or unwilling to do so, would find new homes in other countries. Problem solved! Today, solutions for refugees are elusive. Conflicts drag on for years or decades. Many conflicts that finally end leave behind destroyed communities and irrevocably fractured polities.

Refugee status in the 21st century is, increasingly, a life sentence. The UN Refugee Agency, UNHCR, estimates that half of all refugees live in what the agency calls "protracted situations'—lasting five years or more. As I write, the civil war in Syria is in its ninth year and has impelled more than 6 million refugees to seek safety in other countries. South Sudan's civil war is entering its seventh year, with 1.2 million refugees. A third generation of Afghans and Somalis are growing up as refugees. Of 32 protracted refugee situations in the world today, 23 have lasted for more than 20 years.

Added to the reality that so many refugees have no prospect of going home in the foreseeable future is another hard fact: for the past many years, international donors have contributed only about half the money needed to meet the needs of refugees as identified by UNHCR. Almost 85 percent of refugees live in low- or middle-income countries. Shortfalls in humanitarian funding and the limited resources of even the most generous host countries means that there is little alternative to self-reliance to pull refugees out of desperate poverty and secure their futures.

Kathleen Newland is a senior fellow, trustee, and co-founder of the Migration Policy Institute, where she focuses on the relationship between migration and development, the governance of international migration, and refugee protection. She serves or has served on the boards of directors of the International Rescue Committee, USA for UNHCR, the Stimson Center, Kids in Need of Defense (KIND), the Foundation for The Hague Process on Migrants and Refugees, and the Women's Refugee Commission. She is also a member of the LIFE Project Advisory Council. Ms. Newland has authored or edited several books, as well as numerous reports, policy papers, articles, and book chapters.

But self-sufficiency is more than a practical imperative. It also restores to refugees a sense of self-respect and security. Sustainable livelihoods are the key to people's confidence that they can control their own prospects and build a life for their families. That is why initiatives like the LIFE Project mean so much more than an income—although that aspect is hugely important.

Food entrepreneurship as a source of sustainable livelihoods taps into perhaps the most basic thing that human beings have in common—the need to eat, and the sense of well-being that can come from eating well. Food is not only a necessity of life, but a key to culture, a bridge across social divides, and a means of outreach to others. It reinforces the commonality of the human experience. As a basis for refugee self-reliance, it can sustain the soul as well as the body.

FATMA HÜLYA TEK

Fatma has long dreamt of opening a restaurant of her own, where she can make home-style, traditional dishes. And thanks to business training through the LIFE Project, she is now more prepared to do so. Fatma was born in Bolu, the administrative center of the Bolu Province that lies between Ankara and Istanbul. The area is known for its dense forests, hot springs, and good cooks. Much of Fatma's family, in fact, works in food-related businesses -- some are retired hotel restaurant chefs, and her sister is a nutritionist. Fatma plans to open her restaurant near the Bakirkoy hospital in Istanbul, as hospitals often do not have healthy options near them. While today more restaurants are opening, Fatma hopes to stand out from the rest by recruiting her family members as well as recent Bolu Culinary School graduates, thus providing a space for tradition and innovation to flourish in the same pot.

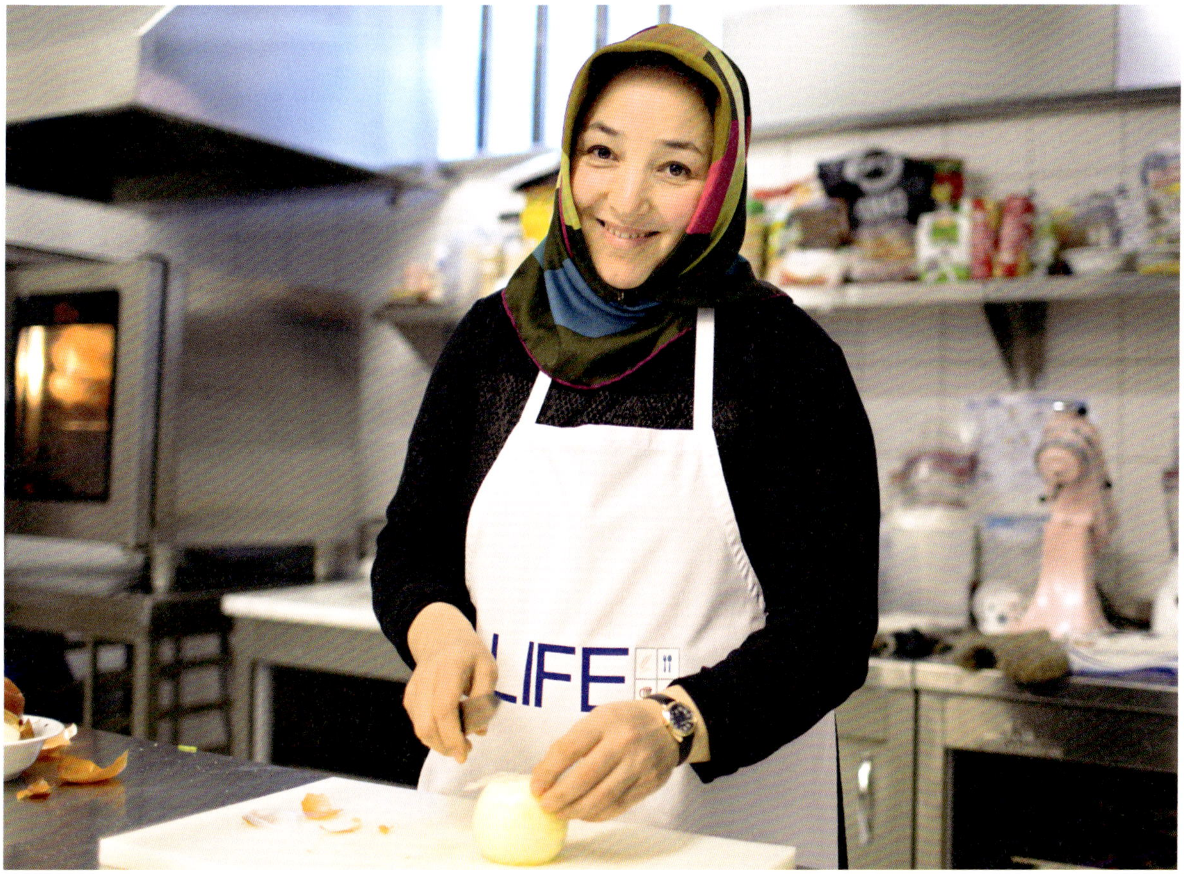
LIFE

TAVUKLU PAZI SARMA

(SWISS CHARD STUFFED WITH CHICKEN)

8 servings (makes about 20 sarmas)

Winter (when Swiss chard is available)

These stuffed chard rolls are a food for mourning: Meskhetian Georgians prepare rolled Swiss chard for the guests who travel from afar to pay their respects at a funeral; friends and relatives similarly prepare the dish to bring to those at the funeral parlor. Fatma first tried them when she visited a friend -- she loved the dish so much that she now regularly makes them at home.

INGREDIENTS:

1 ½ kilograms Swiss chard
500 grams chicken drumsticks
6 tablespoons olive oil
2 large onions (500 grams total)
2 cups (300 grams) orzo
1 teaspoon salt
1 teaspoon freshly ground black pepper
1 ½ cups (50 grams) dill, finely chopped
2 cups (200 grams) canned mixed vegetables (potato, carrot, and green peas; see note)
½ cup (100 milliliters) olive oil (or any vegetable oil)
3 cups (700 milliliters) water
2 cups (325 grams) tomato puree

Note: *If canned vegetables are not available, substitute with cooked green peas, cubed potatoes, and carrots. Substitute rice or bulgur for the orzo, or use cabbage instead of Swiss chard. Lamb, beef, or even mushrooms can take the place of the chicken. The filling itself can be served as a main dish accompanied by some salad or pickles -- no stuffing of leaves required.*

METHOD:

Bring a large pot of water to a boil. Trim the chard leaves away from their stalks, reserving the stalks for another use (such as Siliq Mutabal, page 196). Cut the leaves into 12-by-17-cm (4 ¾-by-6 ½-inch) rectangles or 14-cm (5 ½-inch) squares. Drop into the boiling water and blanche for 20 seconds, then use a slotted spoon to transfer to a bowl of ice water. (Reserve 4 cups/945 milliliters of hot water for the next step.) Remove from the ice water and lay flat to drain on several kitchen towels. Cut chicken into 1-cm (½-inch) cubes, reserving the bones. Boil the chicken cubes and bones in the reserved water for 40 minutes, then strain, reserving 2 cups (500 milliliters) of this chicken stock for the filling. Discard bones (keep remaining stock for another use). Warm the oil in a large skillet over low heat, add the onion and cook for about 10 minutes, until softened. Add the orzo and continue cooking for another 8 to 10 minutes, until lightly toasted. Add the reserved 2 cups chicken stock and the salt and pepper. Cook, uncovered, until the orzo is plump and the liquid evaporated, 15 to 18 minutes. Remove from heat and let cool, then add the dill, chicken, and canned mixed vegetables. This is your filling. Preheat the oven to 170ºC (325ºF).

Line a short cup or dish (8- to 9-cm/3- to 3 ½-inches in diameter) with 1 or 2 Swiss chard leaves. Put 1 heaping tablespoon of the filling in the center, then fold over the edges of the leaves to enclose. Press with your fingers, so the leaves cover the filling and take the shape of the cup. Turn the cup upside down, and place the stuffed leaves on a tray, flat side down. Repeat with the remaining leaves and filling. Stir ½ cup of olive oil into 3 cups of water, then pour over the stuffed leaves. Drop 1 tablespoon of tomato puree over each of the bundles. Dampen a sheet of parchment paper and place over the stuffed leaves. Bake (middle rack) for 15 to 20 minutes, until the water is almost completely absorbed and the Swiss chard has darkened. Serve hot or cold.

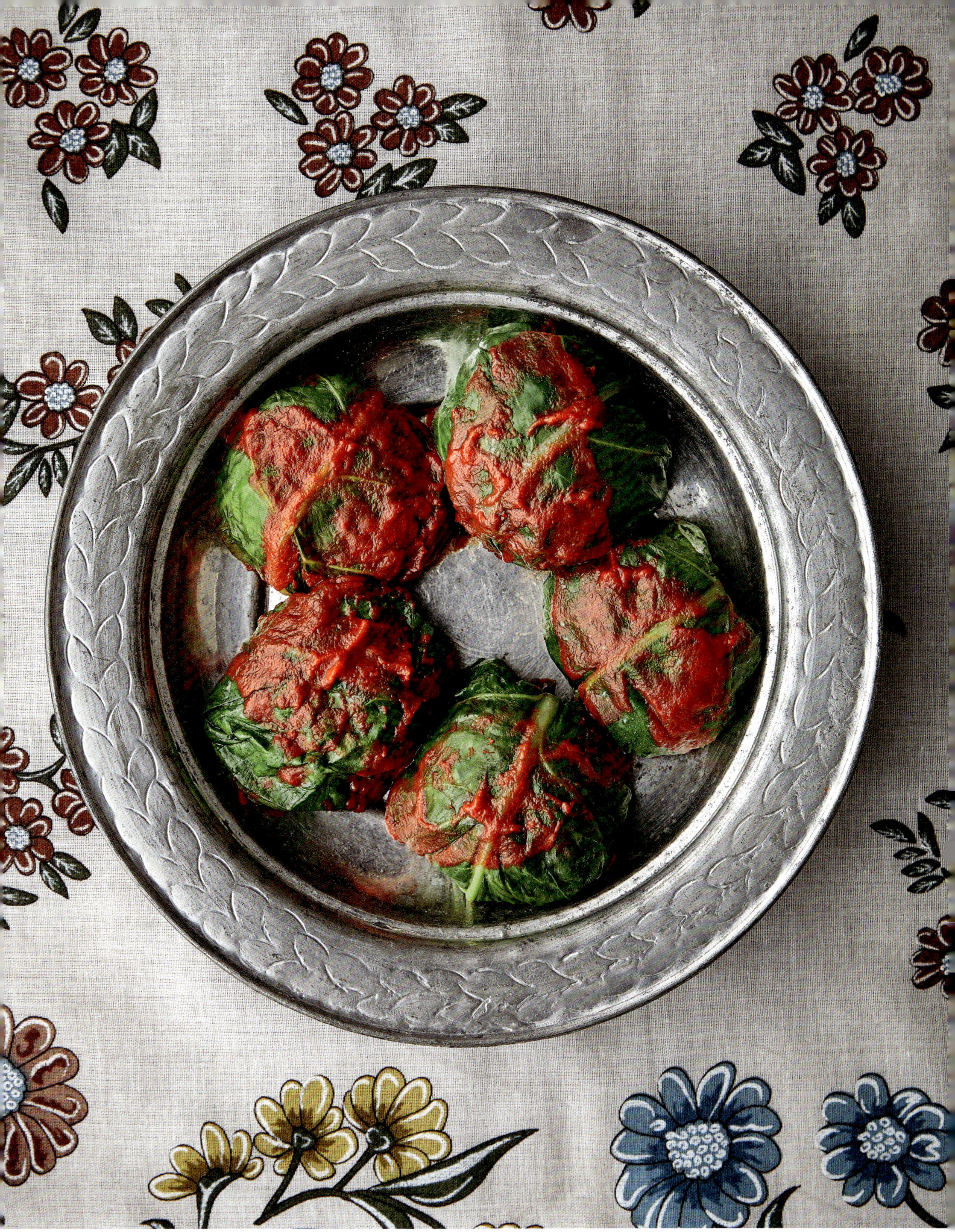

GONCA GÜL TATLISI
(ROSEBUD COOKIES)

15 servings (makes 30 cookies)

Every season

Fatma learned how to make this sweet from her friend who lives in Rize, a province in northeast Turkey. According to the story, two lovers would make this dessert when they were at odds with each other, in hopes of reconciling. Gonca gül tatlısı are also prepared at every stage of a courtship -- during the proposal, to celebrate the engagement, and to eat during wedding parties, as a symbol for happiness and love.

INGREDIENTS:

For the syrup:
3 ½ cups (800 milliliters) water
3 cups (540 grams) sugar
2 tablespoons (25 grams) lemon juice

For the dough:
1 cup (250 grams) yogurt
½ cup (75 grams) melted butter or margarine
1 cup (170 grams) olive oil (or any other oil)
1 egg
1 cup (170 grams) semolina
4 cups (550 grams) flour
1 tablespoon (10 grams) baking powder
2 tablespoons (15 grams) vanilla powder
300 grams walnut halves (may substitute pistachios, hazelnuts, or almonds)

METHOD:

Prepare syrup by combining the water and sugar in a medium saucepan over medium heat. Boil for 20 minutes, then remove from heat, stir in the lemon juice, and let cool.

Mix the yogurt, butter, oil, and egg in a large bowl with a wooden spoon. Stir in the semolina, flour, baking powder, and vanilla powder, mixing to make a dough as soft as an earlobe.

Preheat the oven to 170ºC (325ºF). Pinch off a walnut-sized ball of dough. Flatten the ball into a circle about 1 cm (⅓ inch) thick. Use a small, sharp knife to cut the dough into four pieces, but keep the center of the dough intact. Place a walnut half so that it stands up in the center (the bottom should be perpendicular to the dough). Fold over two opposite pieces around the walnut, then fold over the remaining two pieces, to make a rosebud shape. Repeat with the remaining dough and walnuts, placing the shaped pieces on a greased baking sheet as you go.

Bake (middle rack) 25 to 30 minutes, until golden. While the cookies are still hot, ladle the syrup over them over a period of 10 to 15 minutes, until they absorb the syrup and become glossy. It is always tastier if the dessert is prepared in advance and rests overnight, as the taste develops.

FATMA HÜLYA TEK

GÜLHAN SALCAN

Gülhan loves to cook -- she grew up with her mother's stories and delicious food, and now teaches her own children local and traditional dishes. One method of passing these traditions on to the next generation is to take part in a custom seen throughout Turkey: many people who move to large cities like Ankara or Istanbul return to their hometowns each summer, to visit family and prepare a variety of preserves to eat throughout the year. Gülhan and her children return to Elazığ -- a city and province in Central East Anatolia -- for about two months. They make jams and pickles, brine vine leaves, and dry vegetables for the winter, bringing them back to enjoy in Istanbul.

It's this strong connection to her mother that Gülhan credits as key to her own success in food. For four years, she ran a cafe in Istanbul's Fatih district, serving local dishes. After receiving entrepreneurship training through the LIFE Project, Gülhan hopes to open a new cafe in the Bakırköy district of Istanbul, this time serving gluten-free dishes to better cater to those with celiac disease -- such as herself.

Watch Gülhan's cooking on YouTube at Gülhanla Glutensiz Lezzetler.

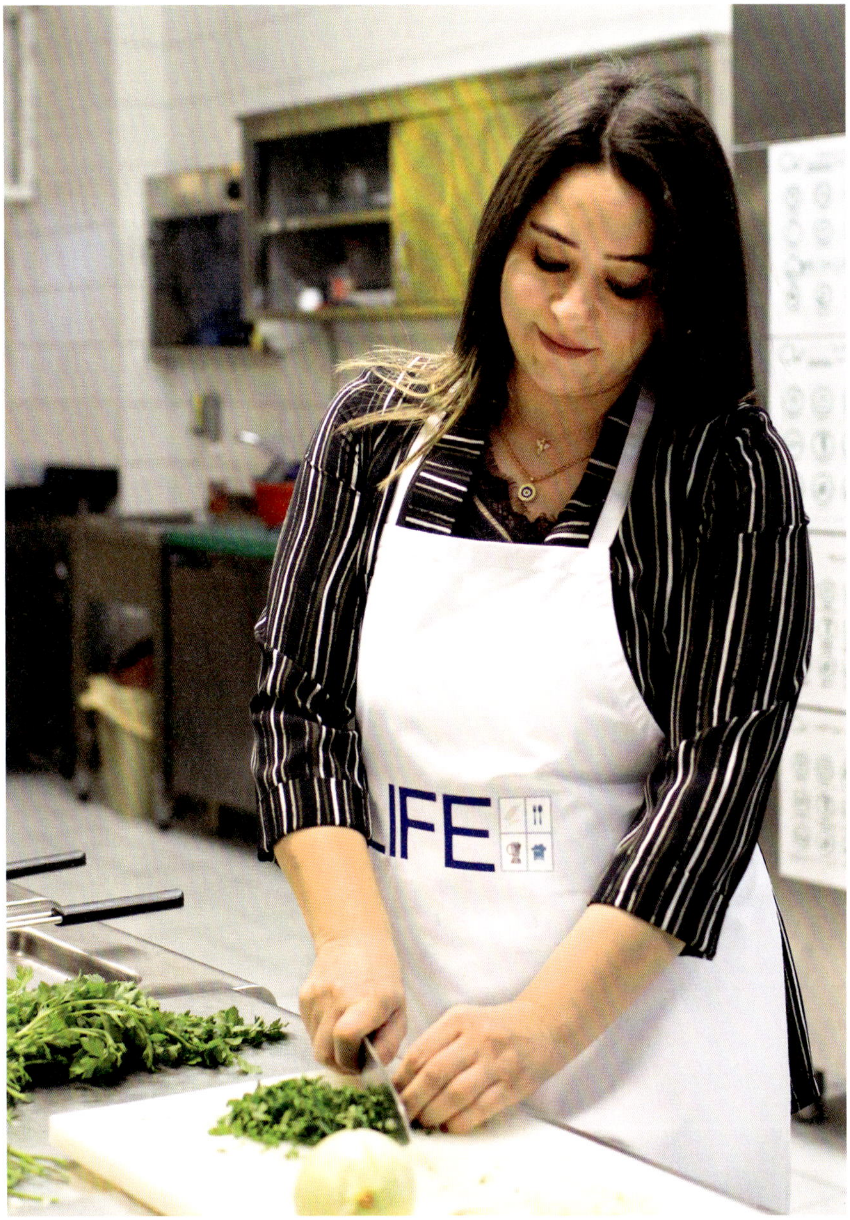
LIFE

HARPUT KÖFTESİ

(BULGUR KOFTES IN TOMATO AND PEPPER PASTE SAUCE)

4 servings

Autumn, winter, and spring

Harput Köftesi -- kofte named for Harput, a highly elevated town about five kilometers from Elazığ city -- are an indispensable part of Elazığ cuisine, frequently decorating tables during festivals and weddings. There is a saying about this type of köfte: "I prepared Harput Kofte, rolled (or 'gındırlamak' in a local language) it from Harput to Elazığ, and it did not disintegrate." Therefore, they're shaped like tires. Gülhan's mother would often cook this dish with dried basil, a common ingredient in Elazığ. Rub the dried basil between your fingers and palms before adding it to a dish, as Gülhan's mother taught her -- this helps release oils left in the leaves and increases the flavor of your final dish.

INGREDIENTS:

For the sauce:

1 tablespoon (30 grams) butter
2 tablespoons (30 milliliters) olive oil
1 tablespoon (25 grams) tomato paste
1 tablespoon (25 grams) pepper paste (see page 22)
5 cups (1250 milliliters) water (see note)
½ teaspoon salt

For the köftes:

500 grams ground lamb (20 percent fat)
1 onion, finely chopped
½ cup (10 grams) finely chopped parsley
1 tablespoon dried basil (see note)
1 tablespoon crushed red pepper flakes
½ teaspoon freshly ground black pepper
½ teaspoon salt
1 cup (200 grams) fine grain bulgur (see page 21)
3 to 4 tablespoons plus ½ cup (125 ml) water
1 to 2 tablespoons semolina, if needed
1 egg, if needed

Note: *Fresh basil can be used in addition to the dried to provide a stronger aroma. For the sauce, 1 or 2 cups of meat stock can be added to substitute water for richer taste.*

METHOD:

For sauce: Melt the butter with the olive oil in a large saucepan over medium heat, then add the tomato and pepper pastes. Cook, stirring to break up the pastes, for about 10 minutes, then add the water and salt. Bring to a boil, then reduce heat to maintain a simmer. Cook, covered, for another 10 minutes.

Meanwhile, make the köftes: Put the lamb, onion, parsley, dried basil, red pepper flakes, black pepper, and salt in a large bowl. Knead well with your hands for 5 minutes. Add the bulgur and knead well, until all ingredients are incorporated, about 10 minutes more. Add up to 4 tablespoons of water during kneading to help moisten the bulgur. (Kneading for a longer period helps the entire aroma and flavors from the ingredients to get integrated, and is vital to ensure the köftes hold together.)

Pour the 1/2 cup of water into a small bowl and wet your fingers. Pinch off a walnut-sized (2-cm/ ¾-inch diameter) piece of the mixture, then mold it by pressing your thumb and middle finger into the center of the ball, to make a tire-like shape of even thickness all around. Put this first little tire into the water bowl; if it does not disintegrate, then the mixture is properly prepared and you can continue shaping the köftes. (If it does disintegrate, knead in 1 or 2 tablespoons semolina or 1 whole egg and test again.)

Slide the köftes into the simmering sauce, cook (at a gentle boil) for 15 minutes, then serve right away. If you are not going to serve right away, remove the köftes from the liquid, as they may disintegrate if left in the warm sauce.

GÜLHAN SALCAN

HEDİK/ DİŞ BUĞDAYI

(WHEAT BOILED WITH CHICKPEAS)

Serves 6 people

Every season

At the end of harvest, women in Anatolian villages used to boil freshly harvested wheat with chickpeas to make hedik. Walnuts from the autumn harvest can add a unique flavor, but any nuts can be used to garnish, including pistachios, almonds, and hazelnuts. Some serve hedik with its liquid while others prefer to strain and serve it like pilaf. You can make it more savory or sweet, depending on your garnish.

INGREDIENTS:

- 2 cups (220 grams) wheat berries, soaked overnight
- 1 cup (220 grams) dry chickpeas, soaked overnight
- 9 cups (2250 ml) water
- 1 cup (120 grams) walnut halves, to garnish
- Sugar and ground cinnamon, to garnish (optional)
- Salt, to garnish (optional)

METHOD

Drain the wheat berries and chickpeas, then put in a pressure cooker with the 9 cups of water.

Put the lid on and follow the cooker's directions to bring to high pressure. Let cook for 45 minutes, then remove from heat and allow the pressure to release naturally.

Garnish with walnuts, and serve either with sugar and cinnamon or salt depending on the guest's preference.

Note: *If you don't have a pressure cooker, you can cook the hedik in a covered pot -- it will take about 2 hours, on low heat.*

Hedik is traditionally prepared to celebrate a baby's first tooth, as wheat symbolizes the hope that the teeth will grow as straight and uniform as a wheat's head. The mother or the grandmother of the baby prepares huge quantities of hedik to give to neighbors; in turn, the neighbors are expected to put little presents or little gold coins in the hedik plate when they return it. Some families prefer to invite the relatives to celebrate the first tooth arrival with a party where they serve hedik. The mother puts a pencil, pair of scissors, piece of gold, a comb, book, and similar objects on a tray or in a bag. The baby then chooses one of the objects to determine their profession -- pencil for teacher, scissors for tailor, and so on. Such hedik preparations and first tooth rituals have been practiced in much of Anatolia for ages, each differing from region to region.

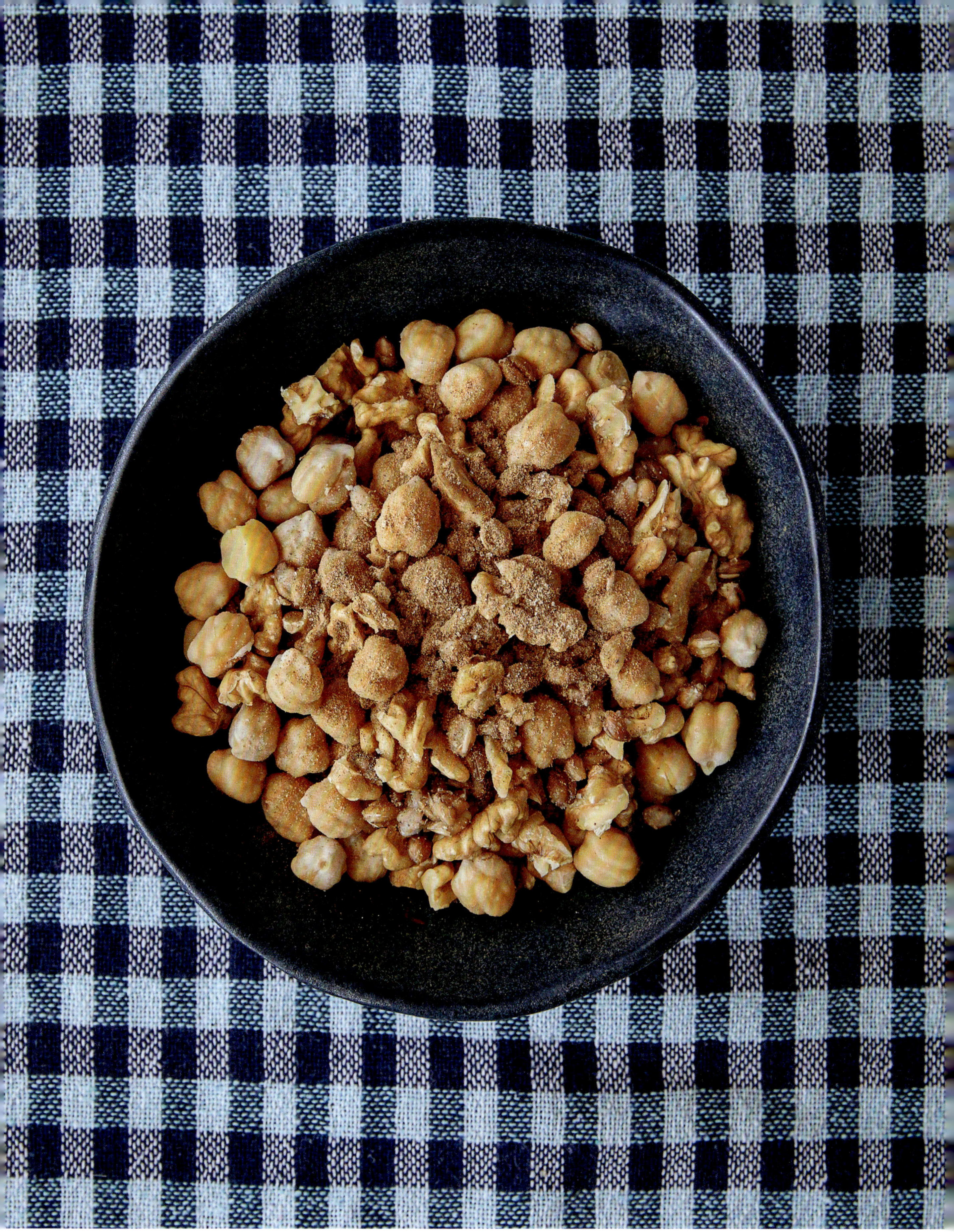

TURKEY'S FOOD ENTREPRENEURS

TURKEY'S FOOD ENTREPRENEURS

Yigal Schleifer

In late 2002 I arrived in Istanbul, for what turned out to be an eight-year adventure in that magical city. My first night there, while staying in the hilly Gümüşsuyu neighborhood, I heard the mysterious ringing of a bell followed by a long, one-word call -- "booooo-zahhh." He was a roving street vendor selling boza, a lightly fermented drink made out of millet or other grains, with a consistency somewhere between porridge and runny applesauce. Dating back to Ottoman times (or even earlier) boza quickly goes sour. It is traditionally sold and consumed in the winter, when cooler weather keeps the drink's fermentation in check.

This vendor opened my eyes to the incredible world of small-scale food entrepreneurship in Istanbul. His is a micro example -- one person selling a seasonal product on foot -- but Istanbul was filled with similar stories, from a man who carted around a steaming copper samovar of sahlep, a drink made out of a tuber related to the orchid, to a vendor who sold freshly peeled and salted cucumbers from a little cart set up near the Galata tower.

In 2009, a friend and I started a blog about our favorite local food spots and street vendors to introduce a broader audience to Istanbul's vibrant, enchanting neighborhoods. A few years later the endeavor turned into Culinary Backstreets, a company that covers the neighborhood food scene and offers small group culinary walks in more than a dozen cities around the world. As I see it, these food entrepreneurs are part of Istanbul's human infrastructure. We tend to portray infrastructure in physical terms: roads, transportation, housing, public works -- all essential elements of city life -- but we often overlook the human element of what makes a city and its neighborhoods livable and dynamic.

Small-scale food entrepreneurs are a particularly important part of this human infrastructure. Take away the boza seller or a small spot that's been serving the same dish to locals for generations, and the integrity of the neighborhood is damaged, along with the larger urban fabric. These are people and places that not only serve affordable food to locals, but also act as a repository of neighborhood and city history.

Documenting and celebrating the work and the stories of these makers is one way of ensuring that they can keep doing what they do. And bringing a new audience to these entrepreneurs, particularly visitors from outside Turkey, helps develop a new language of international understanding. Turkish cuisine, history, people, and culture become something human, made up of the stories and lives of street vendors, restaurant owners, bakers, butchers, and countless others. Culinary Backstreets may be a "food tour" company, but time and time again, our guests come for the food and end up staying for the people.

Yigal Schleifer, a LIFE Project Council Advisory member, is the co-founder of both Culinary Backstreets and its predecessor, the blog Istanbul Eats. Between 2002 and 2010 he lived in Istanbul, where he worked as a correspondent for the Christian Science Monitor, Eurasianet, and the English-language service of the German Press Agency (DPA). He is also one of the authors of the 2009 Fodor's guidebook to Turkey. He has worked for the New York Post, New York Times, and Vanity Fair, and written for various other publications. Mr. Schleifer lives in Washington, D.C

HANADDY KHEAWE

Hanaddy believes in "nefes" in cooking, which means that you must put your soul into cooking -- and that the outcome will reflect how you feel. For Hanaady, a good cook is neat, tidy, and works without causing too much chaos in the kitchen. She learned these traits from her mother, elder sister, and aunt, who taught her traditional Syrian recipes as well as dishes from around the world. The ability to cook is important to Hanaddy; as she was learning, Hanaddy put together a notebook of recipes to pass down to her own children, so that they would learn at a younger age than she did.

While cooking is a meaningful and central part of her life, Hanaddy's business is centered around design. Born and raised in Damascus, she studied fine arts and worked as an art teacher before moving to Turkey five years ago. She now works as an events designer, preparing decorations for parties and other special occasions. Hanaddy hopes to expand the services that she can provide to her clients by finding a business partner who specializes in sweets; she joined the LIFE Project for its networking opportunities and to learn about accounting and marketing. The recipe she shares, below, is perhaps the perfect one to illustrate her cooking and art background -- it requires skill, confidence, and a little bit of soul.

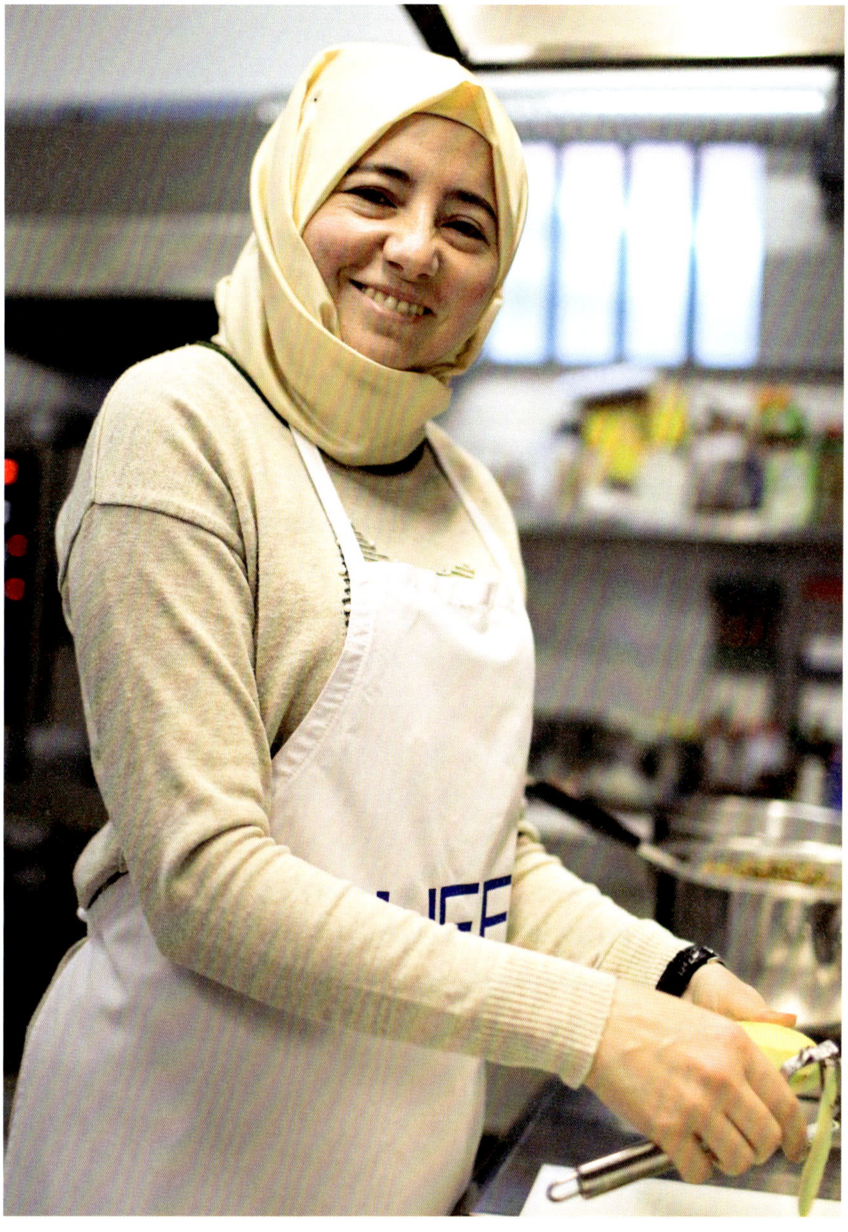

MAKLOUBEH

(UPSIDE-DOWN RICE WITH EGGPLANT AND LAMB)

8 servings

Summer, when sweet eggplants are in season

Makloubeh -- with fried eggplant, meat, spiced rice, and nuts -- is widely prepared around the Middle East. Some cooks add cubes of lamb or other meat over the eggplant, while others use ground meat (or both).

Presentation is what makes this special, and shows off the skill of the cook: the ingredients must be piled gently, so as to cook evenly and allow flavors to mingle, but also firmly, so that when the finished dish is flipped onto its serving platter, the makloubeh shows its artful layers.

Serve with laban bi khiar (see recipe, page 142).

INGREDIENTS:

2 cups (350 grams) rice
5 tablespoons (70 milliliters) oil
500 grams ground lamb
1 ½ teaspoons salt
½ teaspoon freshly ground black pepper
½ cup (20 grams) pine nuts
½ cup (60 grams) blanched almonds
½ cup (40 grams) cashews
½ cup (100 grams) butter
1 kilogram thin eggplants, preferably 10 to 12 cm (4 to 5 inches) long
2 ½ cups (670 milliliters) water
1 tablespoon ground dry vegetable spice (baharat hudar muceffefe), if available (may substitute with black pepper and allspice)

Note: *To lower the fat, brush eggplant slices with oil and roast for 20 to 30 minutes at 180ºC (350ºF), until golden brown. If the dry vegetable spice is not available, use turmeric or saffron for flavor and color, if you like. In southeast Turkey, green pistachio nuts are used in addition to other nuts for garnishing. Roasted cauliflower florets can be used if eggplant is not available. Some cooks garnish the finished dish with chopped parsley or cilantro.*

METHOD:

Soak the rice in a bowl of water for 30 to 40 minutes.

Warm 2 tablespoons of the oil in a large pot set over medium heat, then add the ground lamb, ½ teaspoon of the salt, and the pepper. Cook, stirring frequently, until the juices evaporate. Pour into a mixing bowl, then toast the pine nuts in 1 tablespoon of oil in the same pot. Once they're toasted, add to the lamb, then toast the almonds and cashews with the remaining 2 tablespoons of oil, transferring them to the lamb bowl once done. (This is your garnish.) Remove the pot from the heat, then drain and reserve any excess oil.

Peel and stem the eggplants, then cut them in half lengthwise. If they are more than 10-cm long, divide them in half widthwise, so that the eggplant slices will be 10- to 12-cm long. Melt the butter in the pot, then add the eggplant slices and cook for 10 to 12 minutes over medium heat, until soft and golden. Remove from heat and arrange the eggplant slices on the bottom of the pot, in any pattern that you like.

Strain the rice and layer it over the eggplant. Add the water, dry vegetable spice (if using), and remaining teaspoon of salt. Drizzle over any excess oil from the sautéd nuts. Bring to a boil over medium-high heat, then lower to medium and simmer, covered, for 20 minutes. Turn off the heat once the rice absorbs all the liquid. Flip the pot onto a serving dish, and carefully remove the pan.

Garnish with the lamb and nuts.

HANADDY KHEAWE

HAYAT ALI NAJI AL-LAITH

Hayat Ali Naji Al-Laith is a person of many interests. She holds a masters in business administration and loves to cook, a skill she learned from both of her parents. In 2018, Hayat, her husband and children moved from Sana'a, Yemen, to Istanbul. Adjusting to her new home was difficult -- she found it particularly challenging to enter the workforce, and she joined the LIFE Project to learn more about the Turkish business climate.

Hayat is eager to share her culture through its food -- she constantly updates and tweaks traditional Yemeni recipes, always striving to make the perfect version of the dish. Although she prefers a home-cooked meal over one from a restaurant, she's always had a dream of opening and running a restaurant of her own, where she could serve traditional, home-style dishes. She's working towards that goal by catering, making her versions of asida, shafoot, bint al-sahn, and the other classic recipes that she has shared in these pages.

HAYAT ALI NAJI AL-LAITH

SHAFOOT/SHAFUT

(BREAD IN YOGURT SAUCE)

4 to 6 servings

During Ramadan

The main ingredient of the shafut is lahuh, a spongy pancake-like bread made of wheat or corn. (Similar to Ethiopian injera, but not as sour.) The bread is soaked with an herbed yogurt sauce, rendering the whole thing almost like a savory custard -- it's the perfect dish to eat in warm summer months, and a good way to use up leftover flatbread if you don't have any lahuh. In some regions of Yemen, shafut is practically required when breaking the fast during Ramadan. You can even tell a family's financial status based on the type of shafut they prepare.

INGREDIENTS:

3 cups (750 grams) yogurt
1 cup milk
1 tablespoon chopped Persian leeks (tareh, available in Middle Eastern markets, or substitute with 1 scallion)
1 scallion
1 teaspoon finely chopped parsley
1 teaspoon chopped dill (optional)
1 tablespoon chopped cilantro
1 clove garlic, crushed with a pinch of salt
1 tablespoon chopped fresh mint
1 small green hot pepper (optional)
½ teaspoon ground thyme
½ teaspoon cumin seed
1 ½ teaspoons coriander seed, crushed
½ teaspoon salt
2 lahuh, cut into small 1-cm squares (may substitute with any type of flatbread)
Pomegranate seeds, grapes, or herbs to garnish

METHOD:

Blend all of the ingredients (except for the lahuh and garnishes) until smooth. Arrange the bread on a platter or large plate, then pour the sauce over top. Chill for 3 to 4 minutes, then serve garnished with pomegranate seeds, grapes, or herbs.

Note: *Shafut can be garnished with whichever fresh vegetables are available, including cucumber, tomatoes, lettuce, and carrots.*

TURKEY'S FOOD ENTREPRENEURS

HAYAT ALI NAJI AL-LAITH

FAHSA

(BEEF STEW)

4 to 6 servings

Every season

Fahsa is a traditional Yemeni stew often prepared with spiced beef or lamb. It's served boiling hot in a stone dish called a harda, topped with a hulba, a whipped fenugreek sauce, and eaten with bread, especially for lunch. Fahsa is particularly famous in Sana'a. If you have a stone pot, that is ideal here, as it retains heat and keeps the fahsa boiling hot. If not, use a heavy-bottomed pot, such as cast-iron or a Dutch oven. Start the hulba first -- the ground fenugreek needs to soak for 2 hours before it's whipped. You will have leftover stock -- keep it to make soup or pilav.

INGREDIENTS:

For the hulba:

2 tablespoons ground fenugreek
½ cup (120 milliliters) water
1 to 2 tablespoons green zahawiq (see recipe, page 62)

For the stew:

1 ½ kilogram beef stew meat, cut into 2-cm cubes
2 tablespoons vegetable or olive oil
1 ½ cups (150 grams) chopped green onions
1 tablespoon Yemeni spice (see note)
5 cloves garlic
1 medium tomato (300 grams), cut into 1-cm cubes
5 cups (1180 milliliters) water

To serve:

2 tablespoons olive oil
1 onion, chopped
1 green bell pepper, seeded and chopped
1 red pepper (hot or sweet), seeded and chopped
1 cup (240 milliliters) chicken stock
Red zahawiq (see note, page 62)

METHOD:

For the hulba: sprinkle the fenugreek over the water in a large bowl. Let sit for two hours (the fenugreek will clump a bit), then tip the bowl over a sink to drain away the excess water (while keeping the soaked fenugreek in the bowl). Whisk the mixture by hand until the mixture thickens and turns a creamy white color, about 5 to 8 minutes. Stir in one or two tablespoons of green zahawiq (to taste).

For the stew: soak the meat in salted water for 5 minutes, then drain and rinse. Warm the oil in a large pot set over medium-high heat. Add the green onion and cook for 2 minutes. Add the meat and cook for 5 minutes, turning to lightly brown the meat on all sides. Stir in the spice blend, then the garlic, and finally the tomato. Add the water, bring to a boil, then cover, lower the heat, and simmer for 2 hours, or until the meat is very tender. Shred the meat.

Warm the 2 tablespoons of olive oil in a stone pot (or Dutch oven) set over medium-high heat, then add the onion and peppers. Cook, stirring often, for 5 to 10 minutes, until the vegetables begin to soften. Ladle in the shredded meat and 2 cups of the stock, plus the chicken stock. Simmer over low heat until the peppers are completely softened. Pour the hulba over top and serve directly from the pot, or transfer the fahsa to a serving bowl and serve the hulba and red zahawiq on the side.

Note: *To make the Yemeni spice, toast 1 tablespoon cumin seeds, 1/2 tablespoon black peppercorns, 1/2 tablespoon green cardamom pods, 1 tablespoon turmeric powder, and 2 tablespoons dried onion, then grind to a powder. You can also substitute the spice with a pinch of cumin, black pepper, crushed cardamom seeds, and turmeric powder. Fahsa can also be served in the middle of a table, with green or red zahawiq and hulba on the side.*

TURKEY'S FOOD ENTREPRENEURS

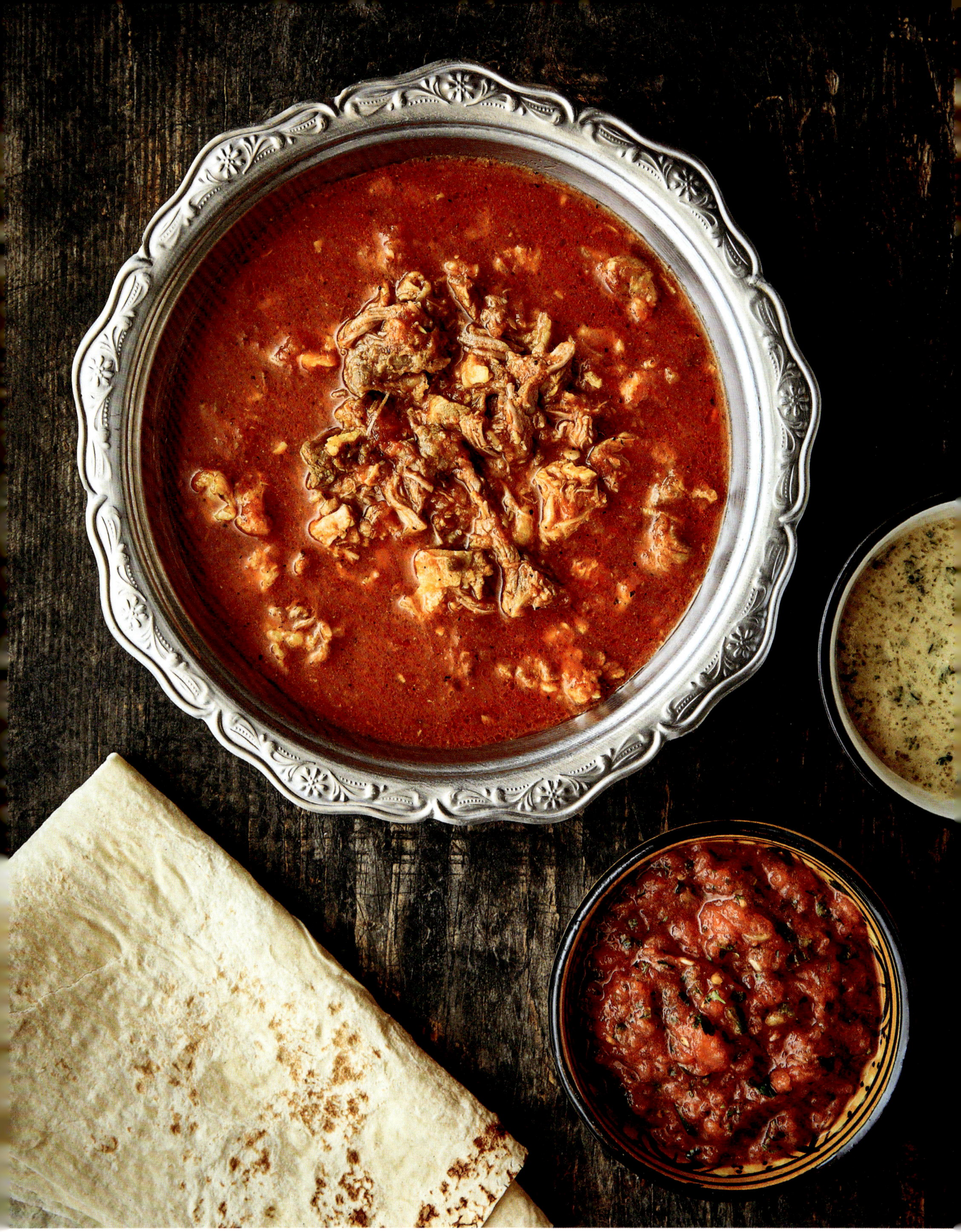

SHORBET LAHME

(WHEAT AND LAMB SOUP)

4 to 6 servings

During Ramadan

This soup is well-known in Yemen, where its hearty and filling qualities make it a fine choice to serve during Ramadan.

Hayat's aunt cooks the green pepper with the onion, but Hayat prefers to keep it as a garnish at the end, as her father taught her. You can also make the soup with chicken instead of lamb.

INGREDIENTS:

2 tablespoons olive oil

1 onion, diced

250 grams lamb shoulder chop, cut into 1-cm (½-inch) cubes

1 teaspoon ground turmeric

1 teaspoon ground cumin

1 teaspoon freshly ground black pepper

1 teaspoon Yemeni spice mix (see fahsa recipe, page 96)

Seeds from 3 cardamom pods

1 small piece cinnamon stick (3 to 4 cm/ 1 to 1 ½ inches) long

1 dried bay leaf

2 cloves garlic

1 small tomato, chopped

1 teaspoon tomato paste (optional)

5 cups water

1 cup coarsely ground/cracked wheat berries (bulgur or rice can be substituted)

1 tablespoon chopped parsley

1 tablespoon chopped cilantro

1 spicy green pepper, seeded and chopped (may substitute with a mild pepper)

METHOD:

Warm the oil in a large pot set over medium-high heat, then add the onion. Cook, stirring occasionally, until golden brown, about 15 minutes.

Add the lamb, spices, bay leaf, garlic, tomato and the tomato paste, if using. Add the water, then bring to a boil. Reduce the heat to maintain a simmer; cook until the meat is tender, 30 to 45 minutes.

Add the coarsely ground wheat and simmer for 30 minutes. Remove from heat and garnish with the parsley, cilantro, and green peppers.

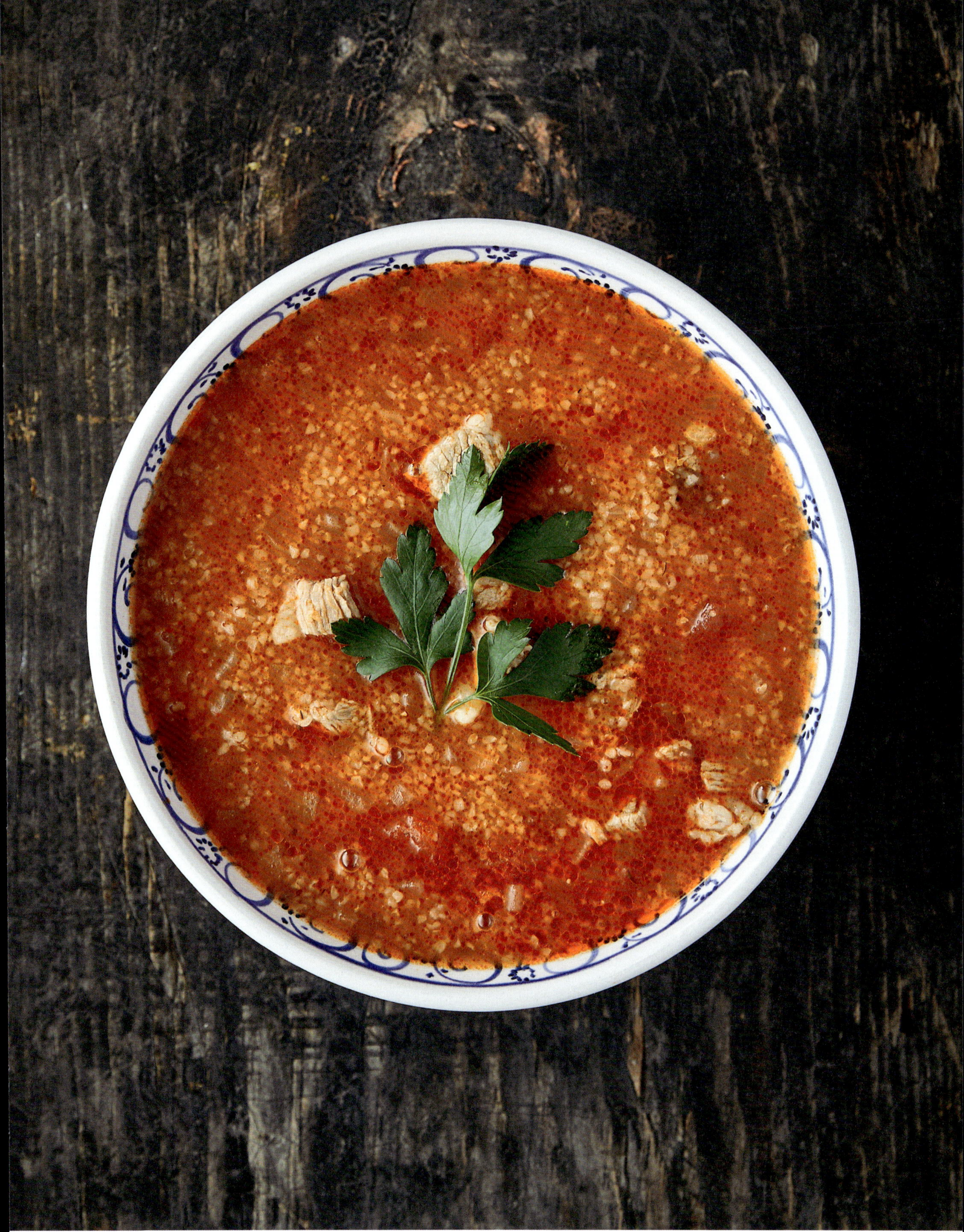

BINT AL-SAHN

(THE DAUGHTER OF THE PLATE)

4 to 6 servings

Every season, during special events

Hayat learned to make this special-occasion dessert from her mother -- it features thin layers of dough slathered with butter or margarine, then baked until golden and flaky.

Honey in Yemen is a sign of wealth and social status, making it the most important ingredient. It is said that bint al-sahn shows how capable a person is as a cook -- if it is properly prepared then she or he passes the test.

Bint al-sahn is traditionally baked in a round baking dish with short edges. You can use a round 26-cm (10-inch) diameter metal cake pan.

INGREDIENTS:

- 4 cups (520 grams) flour, plus more for dusting
- 1 tablespoon instant yeast
- ½ teaspoon salt
- 2 tablespoons milk powder
- 3 eggs, plus 1 egg yolk
- ¼ cup (60 milliliters) vegetable oil
- 1 cup (236 milliliters) water
- 1 cup (227 grams) margarine or unsalted butter, at room temperature, plus melted butter for serving
- 3 tablespoons nigella seeds
- 1 cup (236 milliliters) honey

Note: *You can use a rolling pin to stretch the dough, but your layers won't be as thin as when you use your hands.*

METHOD:

Put 2 cups of flour, the yeast, salt, milk powder, 3 eggs, oil, and water in a stand mixer with the dough hook attached. Beat on low, then increase to medium and gradually add the remaining flour, kneading until you have soft dough. Keep kneading the dough until it's elastic and not too sticky -- it shouldn't stick to your fingers when pressed. Don't worry about overworking the dough -- the more you beat, the better.

Add 2 tablespoons of margarine to the dough and knead with your hands in a circular motion to help shape the dough into a ball. (This makes taking pieces of the dough easier.) Spread a little of the margarine in a deep bowl, then cover with a towel and let rest in a warm place for 15 minutes (and no longer!).

Grease a baking sheet with some of the margarine, then sprinkle with a little flour.

Break off 12 equal pieces of dough, about the size of a walnut. (Experienced cooks can make 15 to 20 balls.) Put the balls on a baking sheet, cover lightly with a towel, and let rest until the balls double in size, about 20 minutes (depending on how warm your kitchen is).

Melt the remaining margarine, then use a little to grease the bottom (not sides) of the cake pan.

Take a ball of dough and start stretching the dough with your fingertips until it's about the size of your hand.

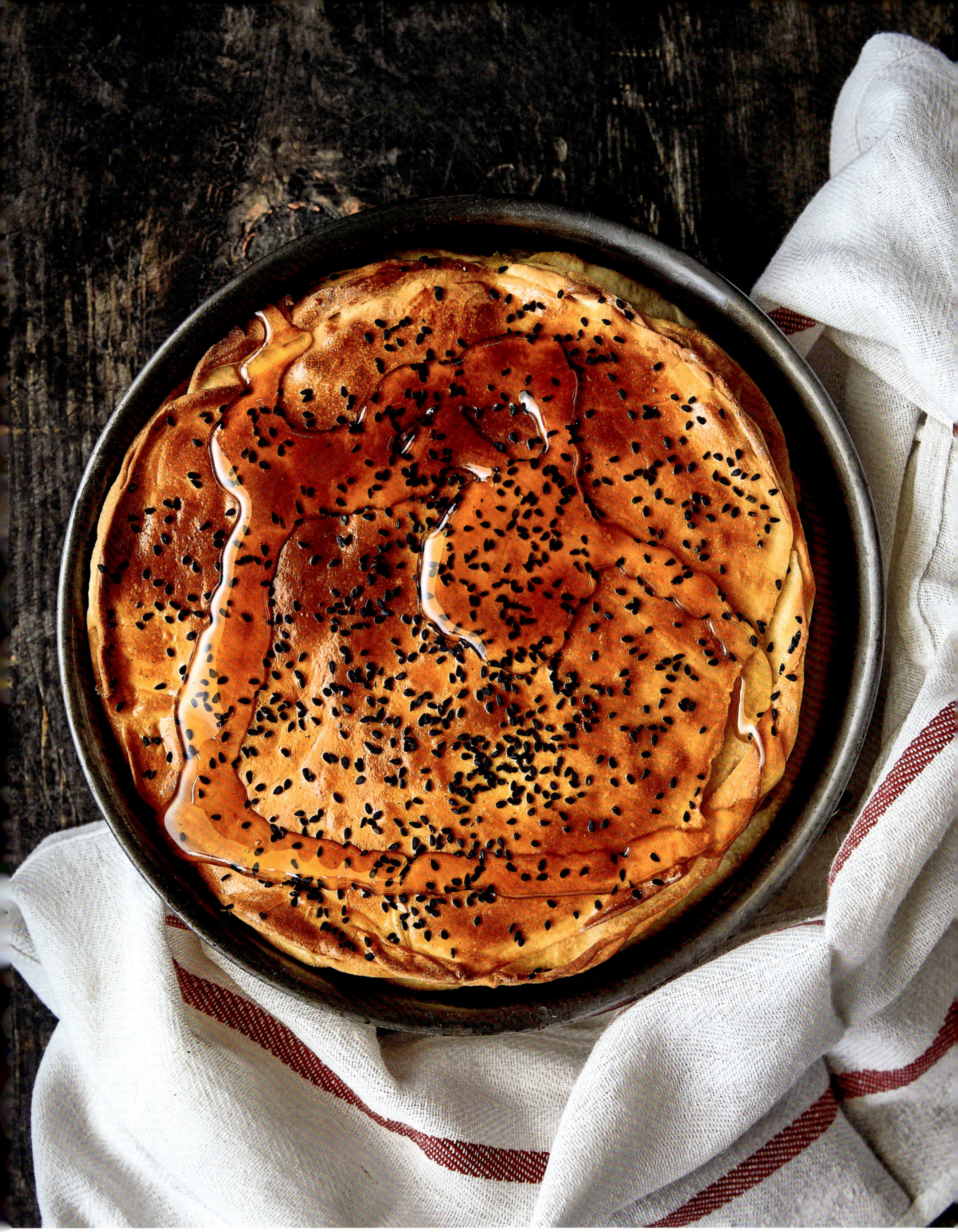

BINT AL-SAHN
(THE DAUGHTER OF THE PLATE)

TURKEY'S FOOD ENTREPRENEURS

Then, use the palms of your hands to continue stretching the dough, moving the dough in a circular motion between your hands to make a thin, round piece of dough. (If you were to throw the dough from one hand to another, the dough would become more rectangular in shape.)

Put the dough in the prepared pan and carefully stretch it even more, until all the edges reach over the side of the pan's edges (it is the secret for making thin layers). Press the dough onto the outside edges of the pan, then spread 2 tablespoons of the melted margarine over top. Repeat the same method with all the dough balls and trim away the excess dough from the edges.

Spread the egg yolk on the last layer and sprinkle the nigella seeds over top. Cover the pan loosely with plastic wrap and let rest until it's risen, about 15 to 30 minutes. Preheat the oven to 200°C (400°F).

Bake (middle rack) for 30 minutes, or until the top is light golden. Drizzle with some of the honey, then serve with the rest on the side along with extra melted butter for more drizzling.

ASIDA

(CORN PORRIDGE)

4 servings

Every season

Asida is a staple food that can be served as a dessert (see note) or with savory main dishes such as soups and stews, where it takes the place of rice, bulgur, potatoes, and other starches. Although its ingredients are basic, technique is required to ensure a lump-free porridge: adjust the heat as you're cooking, to be neither too high nor too low. A stainless steel pot works best. Pay attention as you go -- it's easy to over or undercook.

The asida can be prepared with wheat or corn flour, or both. The traditional way to eat asida is to take a small morsel with your fingers, press in the middle to create an indent, then use it to scoop stew and eat both dishes in one bite.

INGREDIENTS:

2 cups (240 grams) corn flour (see page 21)

1 cup (120 grams) flour

4 cups (945 milliliters) water, at room temperature

½ cup (125 grams) yogurt

1 tablespoon butter

1 teaspoon salt

METHOD:

Oil a serving dish. Whisk 1 cup of the corn flour with the flour in a small bowl. Put 2 cups (473 ml) of the water, the yogurt, butter and 3 tablespoons of the flour mix in a medium pot over medium heat. Bring to a boil, stirring with a wooden spoon, then gradually stir in the rest of the flour mix, followed by the remaining cup of corn flour.

Cook, stirring thoroughly to prevent lumps, until the flour absorbs the water. Gradually stir in the remaining 2 cups of water. Continue cooking at a gentle boil for 20 to 30 minutes, until it reaches the consistency of thick peanut butter.

Remove from heat and pour into the prepared serving dish, using a greased wooden spoon to shape it into a smooth dome shape. Make an indent in the middle with the spoon. If serving with stew, such as the fahsa (page 96), pour some of the broth into the middle.

Note: *To serve asida as a dessert, spoon honey or fruit molasses (such as date, grape, or fig) into the center and drizzle generously with melted clarified butter.*

HAYAT ALI NAJI AL-LAITH

FOOD, THE ULTIMATE SOCIAL MEDIATOR

FOOD, THE ULTIMATE SOCIAL MEDIATOR

Mert Fırat

Learning how to make a recipe from your family -- honing a technique to then pass it down to later generations -- is one of the oldest traditions of mankind. This is what makes food so special: it is at the center of all cultures, friend and family gatherings, special events and celebrations. Many of our biggest moments in life are centered around either preparing or sharing a meal. Memories are often made while sitting around the dining table.

It is within a framework of sharing and gathering that world leaders adopted the 17 Sustainable Development Goals at the September 2015 United Nations Summit. The goals call all countries to work together to end all forms of poverty, achieve food security, fight inequalities, combat climate change, promote inclusive and sustainable economic growth, and more. Food is a powerful tool to help achieve these goals: cooking with friends, family, and even strangers brings people together to exchange ideas and share their culture and heritage through food. Coming together and sharing a meal is a communal tie that binds almost everyone, the world over -- when that meal includes foods from other cultures, the opportunity for social cohesion is even stronger.

The LIFE Project empowers its members to communicate and learn from others. Participants share knowledge, experiences, and emotions, while using food as a tool to meaningfully connect and understand each other. These acts of cooking and eating together are about more than sharing a meal. It is a chance to discuss critical issues and show that everyone -- no matter their gender or birthplace -- can be an advocate for positive change.

Mert Fırat is an actor, social entrepreneur, and volunteer. He is the co-founder of Ihtiyac Haritası (Needs Map), an online platform to connect people in need with those who want to support. He also co-founded the arts and theatre organizations SanatMahal, DasDas, and InogarArt. He is the first Goodwill Ambassador of the United Nations Development Programme Turkey. Mr. Fırat is on the LIFE Project Advisory Council.

IMAN BATIKH and MOHAMAD YAHYA KAWAKIBI

Iman and Mohamad Yahya, both from Aleppo, Syria, came to Istanbul with their two children. From a young age, Mohamad Yahya was in the kitchen with his mother, watching, tasting, and learning how to cook. She always encouraged him to experiment and try new recipes -- he particularly likes recreating restaurant dishes at home, and is known for his spiced chicken. These qualities in turn were passed along to Iman, who calls Mohamad Yahya her trainer in the kitchen. Cooking is a science to Iman, and she credits her husband's constructive feedback with making her a better cook. The two work well together -- both collaborating and listening to each other's ideas.

Before they moved to Turkey, Iman studied theology in the university and Mohamad Yahya worked in interior design with his father, a job that was interrupted at age 22 by military service. Upon return to civilian life, Mohamad Yahya apprenticed in a friend's restaurant; once in Turkey, he became the general manager of a Syrian restaurant. Now that the two have completed their LIFE Project training, they are more equipped to pursue their next goal: opening a restaurant of their own.

IMAN BATIKH and MOHAMAD YAHYA KAWAKIBI

MAHSHI BETINCAN MA FITIR

(MUSHROOMS COOKED WITH STUFFED EGGPLANTS)

6 servings

Winter and spring (when desert truffles are available)

Iman learned this dish from her grandmother, who would make it with terfeziaceae (desert truffles -- kamaa in Arabic, keme in Turkish). Since there is a shortage of terfeziaceae, Iman uses mushrooms instead.

In Gaziantep, Turkey, there is a similar technique where dolma with fresh vegetables are cooked in the same pan with cubed meat and green beans, while various stews and lahmacun (thin rounds of dough topped with ground lamb, vegetables, and herbs) are prepared with keme.

INGREDIENTS:

3 tablespoons (40 milliliters) plus ¼ cup (60 milliliters) olive oil

500 grams lamb sirloin chop, cut into 1-cm (½-inch) cubes

1 ½ kilograms mushrooms, such as cremini, halved

30 dried eggplants for stuffing (kuru dolmalık patlıcan)

1 cup (175 grams) rice, soaked in cold water for 30 minutes

500 grams ground lamb

1 teaspoon salt

1 teaspoon freshly ground black pepper

3 tablespoons (40 milliliters) room temperature water, plus 2 cups (470 milliliters) hot water

METHOD:

Warm 3 tablespoons of the oil in a large pot over medium-high heat, then add the cubed lamb and cook, stirring, until browned on all sides and the juices have evaporated. Add the mushrooms, cover, and cook for 10 minutes.

Meanwhile, bring a large pot of water to a boil, add the eggplants, and cook for 10 minutes, until they are partially soft. Drain, rinse, and let rest in a colander. Drain the rice. Combine the rice, ground lamb, salt, black pepper, and remaining ¼ cup olive oil in a large mixing bowl, then add 3 tablespoons of water.

Stuff eggplants two thirds of the way full with the rice filling, leaving space at the top for the rice to expand. Press the edges to enclose the filling, then arrange the stuffed eggplants over the cooking meat and mushroom mixture. Put a plate over the stuffed eggplants to keep them tight in the pan and add the 2 cups of hot water. Reduce the heat to medium-low and cook, covered, for 90 minutes. Serve the stuffed eggplant either on a separate serving dish or over the meat-mushroom mixture.

Note: *You can also use dried peppers for stuffing (dolmalık kuru biber) as a substitute for eggplants. When Iman prepared this in the LIFE Project kitchen, she also stuffed fresh red bell and kapia peppers (kapya biber) and cooked them together with the stuffed dried eggplants. For the rice filling, you can add other spices, garlic, and finely chopped onion to make more of a traditional Turkish dolma.*

IMAN BATIKH and MOHAMAD YAHYA KAWAKIBI

DALAE MAHSHI BIL-RUZZ

(STUFFED RACK OF LAMB)

6 servings

Every season, for events and festivals

It may sound complicated, but this is a simple dish, with many possible variations. Mohamad Yahya learned this from his grandmother, improved his technique with his mother, and added his own twists -- such as rubbing the ribs with vinegar and cinnamon -- on his own.

INGREDIENTS:

- 8 tablespoons (120 milliliters) olive oil
- 50 grams pine nuts
- 150 grams ground lamb (leave some fat on for more flavor)
- 1 cup (150 grams) rice
- 1 teaspoon salt, plus more for rubbing the lamb
- 1 ½ kilograms rack of lamb
- 2 tablespoons vinegar
- 5 grams freshly ground black pepper
- 7 grams grated nutmeg
- 3 grams cinnamon
- 2 cups (470 milliliters) water
- ½ cup finely chopped parsley
- 1 sweet red pepper, sliced

METHOD:

Preheat the oven to 200°C (400°F). Warm 2 tablespoons (30 milliliters) of the oil in a small skillet over medium heat, and toast the pine nuts for 5 minutes, or until golden.

Combine the ground lamb, rice, toasted pine nuts, and 1 teaspoon of salt in a mixing bowl; this is your stuffing.

Cut a deep incision along the bottom length of the rack (along the loin), making it deep enough to stuff in the filling. Rub the inside and the outside of the lamb with vinegar. Sprinkle with some salt and rub in the black pepper, nutmeg, and cinnamon.

Place the stuffing in the cavity and fold over the meat to enclose; secure with kitchen twine and put in the baking dish. Mix the water with the remaining 6 tablespoons (90 milliliters) of olive oil and pour over the lamb. Cover the baking dish with foil and bake for 2 hours, then check to make sure the water has not all evaporated. If it has, add some more, then recover and continue roasting for 1 hour more, or until the ribs develop a caramelized crust.

Let rest for 10 minutes before slicing. Serve garnished with the parsley and sliced peppers.

Note: *Finely chopped dill and onion can be added to the filling, as well as dried currants.*

IMAN BATIKH and MOHAMAD YAHYA KAWAKIBI

MAMUNIYEH

(SEMOLINA HELVA)

6 servings

Every season

This is Iman's recipe for semolina helva, a very popular treat in the Balkans, Turkey, and various Middle Eastern countries. In Aleppo it is served with salty cheese -- such as cubes of jebne keab (antep peyniri in Turkish) or braided jebne meshallaleh (örgü peynir) -- and bread to balance the sugar in the helva. In Turkey, it is served as a dessert at the end of the meal. It is also prepared on the seventh, 40th and 52nd days of a funeral and distributed to neighbors.

INGREDIENTS:

1 cup (100 grams) semolina
½ cup (120 milliliters) oil
4 cups (945 milliliters) water
2 cups (400 grams) sugar
1 tablespoon (30 grams) butter
½ cup (50 grams) pistachio nuts, ground (may use any type of nut; leave some whole if you like)
1 teaspoon ground cinnamon

METHOD:

Cook the semolina and oil in a medium pot set over medium-high heat for about 20 minutes, or until the semolina is golden and nicely fragrant.

Combine the water, sugar, and butter in a medium saucepan set over medium-high heat, stirring to dissolve the sugar. Bring to a boil, then add the semolina and reduce the heat to low. Cook, stirring constantly, until the mixture thickens, about 10 minutes.

Garnish with the pistachio nuts and cinnamon. Serve hot or cold; leftovers are great with ice cream.

Note: *You can also make this with milk instead of water. In Gaziantep, unsalted cheese is cut into 2-cm (¾-inch) cubes and added to the cooking helva, resulting in a deliciously stringy texture. Pine nuts can also be added while the semolina is cooking. If you'd like a thicker or thinner helva, use less or more water.*

IMAN BATIKH and MOHAMAD YAHYA KAWAKIBI

UNLIKELY ENTREPRENEURS

UNLIKELY ENTREPRENEURS

Dalia Mortada

Wherever Syrians settled, scattered across Turkish cities such as Istanbul, Gaziantep, Ankara, and Mersin, so did their culinary culture. They started opening restaurants, bakeries, butcher shops, and groceries. Long-standing institutions from Aleppo and Damascus migrated with their communities. Those nostalgic for home would make the pilgrimage to those stores to find fresh ice cream and halawet el jibn from Salloura, spiced beef sausage sandwiches from Syrjeia, and, from Buuzecedi, a hearty bowl of fatteh -- a layered casserole of fried pita, warm chickpeas, and cool garlic-yogurt sauce, all doused in olive oil or ghee and topped with toasted cashews and pine nuts.

And then came the unlikely entrepreneurs -- often women who never worked outside the home in Syria. Forced to become breadwinners and armed with exceptional culinary skills, these women are now translating their expertise into a living.

I think of Inam, the mother of four displaced by Syria's war to Egypt, then Dubai, and finally Istanbul. Like many women in Syria, cooking lunch or dinner at home was her full-time job. But in Istanbul, she needed work that paid. "Why shouldn't I make a living out of Syrian cooking?" Inam thought, so she began selling her falafel at a local farmers market.

The LIFE Project provides invaluable support to people like Inam. Through four months of entrepreneur incubation, LIFE graduates have a path to formalize their ventures and develop long-term and sustainable businesses. Just as important, they have a network of like-minded people across cultures and genders who share the same experience, creating a unique and valuable support system. These new entrepreneurs have the confidence to take their new skills to create and keep building their communities through food. Rising from the ashes of tragedy are businesses owned by once-reluctant entrepreneurs, now fully embracing their roles as culinary innovators and managers.

Dalia Mortada serves on the LIFE Project Advisory Council. She is an editor for NPR's Morning Edition and previously worked as an independent journalist and consultant, with work appearing in such publications as The New York Times, The Nation, NPR, BBC, and PRI's The World. She lived in Istanbul from 2011 to 2018, reporting on Turkish politics and society, the refugee crisis throughout the region, maternal health in Ethiopia, and more. In 2015, she founded Savoring Syria, an interactive story-telling project that uses food to connect people to Syria and Syrians. Ms. Mortada lives in Washington, D.C.

INAM AL-SHAYEB

Inam has an infectious and ever-present smile, despite upheavals and troubles that she has been through. Along with her husband and four children, Inam fled Damascus in 2012; they lived in Egypt for one year, Dubai for another, and settled in Istanbul in 2014. (Just a few years later, one of Inam's sons migrated to Germany, through the Mediterranean, to continue his college education -- the move was a risky and nerve-wracking experience.)

To stay connected with and share her Syrian culture, Inam turns to food. This passion, she realized, could be used to support her family, and she started selling Syrian-style falafel at a local farmers market, quickly gaining fans. During her time with the LIFE Project, Inam not only learned skills necessary to grow her business but the confidence to use them -- no small feat for someone accustomed to falafel being something traditionally made by men.
She plans to open her own small kiosk in Istanbul's Uskudar district, where she can serve Syrian breakfast and sell falafel (a recipe that, alas, is a closely guarded secret).

Find Inam on Instagram: @inam_mutfakta.

INAM AL-SHAYEB

BABA GANOUSH

(SMOKY EGGPLANT SALAD/DIP)

4 servings

During spring and summer

Baba Ganoush is the father of eggplant salads and a sister to hummus, with minimal ingredients. There are various stories around the origins of this smoky dip, found throughout the Levant. In one history, there was a widely loved priest (papa) named Gnug. One day a student wanted to present a gift for him; he cooked Papa Gnug a meal composed of eggplant and vegetables. Gnug invited the village people to share in this meal. Impressed by his generosity, the people named the dish after him, "Papa Gnug." But baba ghanoush translates as "pampered papa" in Arabic -- in another story, there was a lovely girl who dearly loved her father who, as he was quite old, had almost no teeth. The girl created a smooth and comforting food by mashing the eggplant to feed and please her father.

No matter the origin, its enduring popularity is a testament to its taste. Serve baba ganoush with kebabs and other main dishes, or eat it simply with warm pita or other breads. Inam garnishes the dip with pomegranate seeds, walnuts, and pomegranate molasses. Some recipes call for tahini, others add a pinch of sugar, or a tablespoon of plain yogurt. The key to them all is to keep it simple.

INGREDIENTS:

2 medium globe eggplants (500 grams)
Pinch salt
2 cloves garlic (8 grams)
1 tomato (about 250 grams)
1 large green bell pepper (about 100 grams)
10 tablespoons (50 grams) chopped flat leaf parsley, plus more for garnish
¼ cup pomegranate molasses
Juice of ½ lemon
2 tablespoons (30 milliliters) olive oil (optional)
1 tablespoon toasted and chopped walnuts, for garnish
2 tablespoons pomegranate seeds, for garnish

METHOD:

Preheat the oven to 200°C (400°F). Prick the eggplants with a fork, then place them on a baking sheet and bake for 30 to 40 minutes, turning a few times with tongs, until well charred on all sides and collapsed. Wrap the eggplants with foil and set aside for 15 to 20 minutes.

While the eggplants are cooling, add a pinch of salt to the garlic and crush in a mortar and pestle (or use the back of a knife on a cutting board.) Peel and seed the tomato, reserving the seeds for another use if you like, and then dice the flesh. Seed and dice the green pepper.

Carefully remove and discard the charred eggplant skin, then finely chop the flesh and transfer to a medium mixing bowl. Add the garlic, tomato and pepper, using a fork or wooden spoon to mash and stir the ingredients into the eggplant. Mix in the parsley, pomegranate molasses, and lemon juice, then taste and adjust the seasoning. Place in a serving dish and garnish with a drizzle of olive oil and pomegranate molasses and a scatter of parsley and walnuts. Garnish with the pomegranate seeds.

INAM AL-SHAYEB

BABA GANOUSH
(SMOKY EGGPLANT SALAD/DIP)

Note: You can char the eggplants over the flame of a gas stove (or on a gas or charcoal grill), using tongs to turn occasionally, until the outside is blackened and the flesh has collapsed.

Some cooks prefer mashing the eggplants with a wooden spoon in a wooden bowl, as they believe that the eggplant does not lose its color. An older method was to crush the garlic in a large mortar and pestle, then add the charred and cleaned eggplants and continue to mash, resulting in a particularly creamy texture.

Fatima Fouad from Yemen (page 54) provided a recipe called "barteh," which is quite similar to baba ganoush. She used charred eggplants, tomato, scallion, green chile pepper, cilantro, parsley, dill, garlic, lemon juice, salt, black pepper, and cumin. Barteh is an appetizer and served with rice or bread. It is mainly famous in Aden, Yemen.

FATTOUSH

(BREAD SALAD)

4 servings

During summer, and Ramadan

This simple and tasty bread salad has many variations around the Mediterranean, including the Italian panzanella, Turkish omaç, and Catalan pa amb tomàquet. They each give new life to old, dry bread by toasting and then tossing pieces with bright and flavorful seasonal ingredients. Try adding chopped purslane, fresh mint, and lettuce to the mix. Fattoush is particularly satisfying on hot summer days.

INGREDIENTS:

- 100 grams flatbread (such as khubez suri, lavash, or pita)
- About 2 cups (500 milliliters) olive oil, for frying (see note)
- 1 yellow onion (200 grams)
- 1 tablespoon ground sumac
- Pinch of salt
- 3 tablespoons (45 milliliters) apple cider vinegar
- Juice of 1 lemon (30 milliliters)
- ½ cup (120 milliliters) olive oil
- 3 tablespoons (45 milliliters) pomegranate molasses
- 2 cloves (8 grams) garlic, crushed
- 2 medium tomatoes (500 grams), peeled and chopped
- 2 medium cucumbers (200 grams), seeded and chopped
- 20 grams fresh mint, coarsely chopped (including soft stems and leaves)

Garnish:
- 4 lemon slices
- ¼ cup pomegranate seeds
- Fresh mint leaves
- 6 black or green olives

Note: Once you've fried the bread, let the oil cool, then strain and reserve for another use, if you like. If you'd rather not fry, toast the bread pieces in a 175ºC (350ºF) oven for 15 to 20 minutes, or until golden brown and crisp.

METHOD:

Cut or tear the bread into 1.5- to 2-cm (½- to ¾-inch) squares. Heat the olive oil in a frying pan and fry the bread pieces in batches until golden brown. Transfer bread to a paper towel-lined baking sheet to drain.

Cut the onion in half from top to bottom, then slice into thin half moons. Use your fingers to rub the sumac and salt into the onions.

Whisk the apple cider vinegar, lemon juice, ½ cup olive oil, pomegranate molasses, and garlic in a large mixing bowl. Add the tomatoes, cucumber, and chopped mint, tossing to coat.

Transfer the tomato mixture to a serving dish, then garnish with the onion slices, lemon slices, pomegranate seeds, mint leaves, olives, and the fried bread squares.

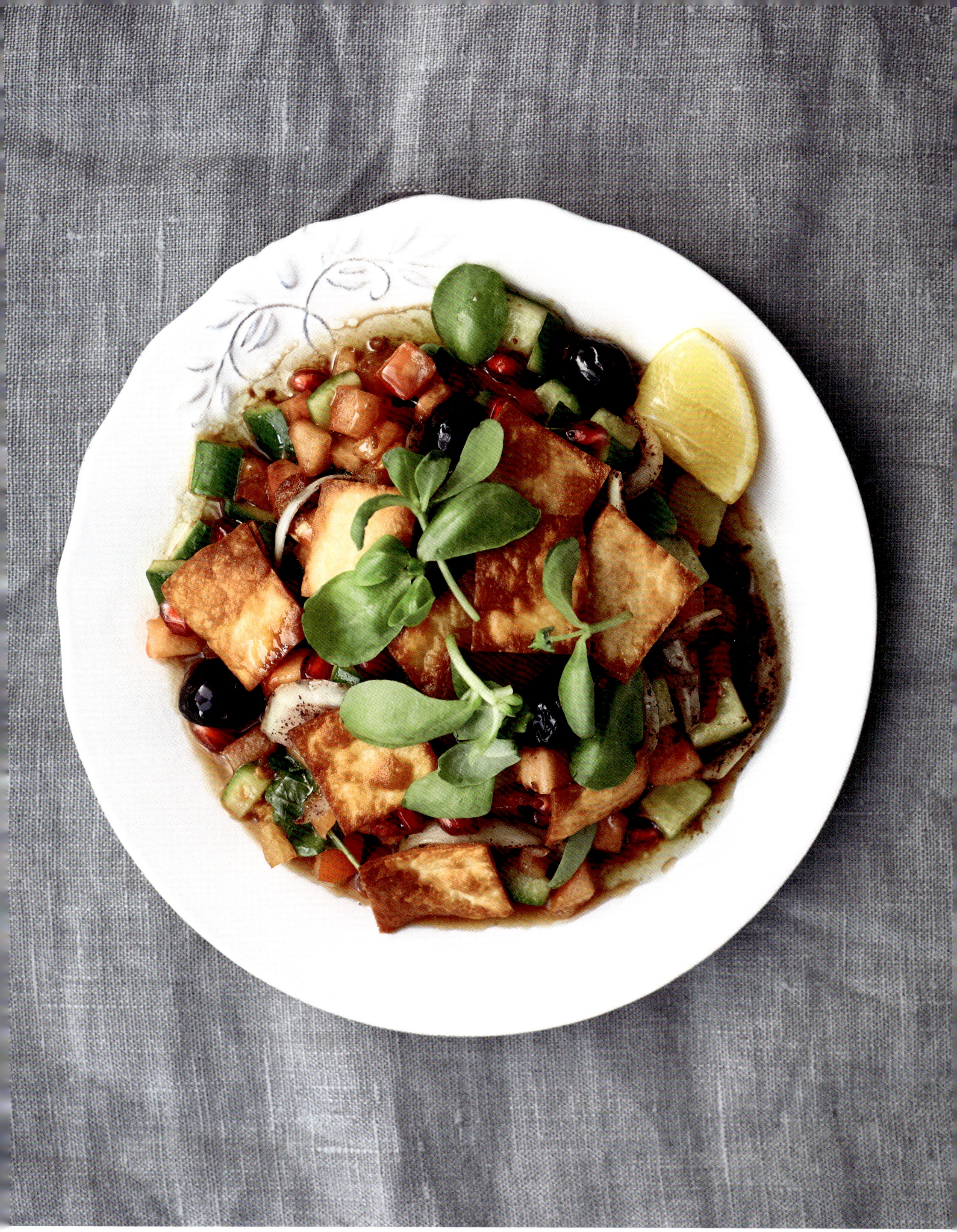

MUHAMMARA

(WALNUT AND PEPPER DIP)

4 servings

Every season

This versatile dish has a unique earthy, sweet, and sour flavor. It's served as a dip, spread for breakfast, or as a side dish with kebabs and chicken. In Damascus, this is one of the appetizers (muqabilat) prepared for feasts, alongside humus, baba ganoush, and fattoush, decorating tables for guests. Muhammara is prepared with one part sweet and one part hot peppers; in other regions such as Aleppo, it's prepared only with hot peppers. Muhammara is easy to prepare and enjoyed by almost everyone, so there are many versions of the dish -- see a few suggestions in the notes below.

Store the dip in the refrigerator for up to 4 days; its flavor improves after a day's rest.

INGREDIENTS:

- 100 grams ground red sweet bell pepper/ pepper paste (see page 22)
- 100 grams ground red hot pepper/ pepper paste (see page 22)
- Up to 1 cup (250 milliliters) water, as needed
- 2 3/4 tablespoons (40 milliliters) olive oil, plus more for garnish
- 2 tablespoons tahini, plus more for garnish
- 1 tablespoon fresh lemon juice
- 2 tablespoons pomegranate molasses
- ½ teaspoon salt
- 1 teaspoon brown sugar, if needed
- 200 grams ground/chopped walnuts, plus a handful of toasted walnut halves for garnish
- 100 grams fine bread crumbs (reserve 2 teaspoons for garnish)

METHOD:

Combine the pepper pastes in a medium mixing bowl, then stir up to 250 milliliters water if needed, until it is as thick as peanut butter. Stir in the olive oil, tahini, lemon juice, pomegranate molasses, and salt. Taste for a nice sweet/sour balance, adding the brown sugar if you'd like. Stir in the walnuts and bread crumbs, then transfer to a serving dish. Garnish with the walnut halves, 2 teaspoons of bread crumbs, and a drizzle of tahini and olive oil. Serve at room temperature.

Note: *Grind walnuts in mortar and pestle or in a food processor, or chop by hand. Each method/process adds a different flavor to the dip. Toast the walnuts and/or breadcrumbs with a little oil, either in a skillet or in an oven. Some cooks use roasted red bell peppers; others add a pinch of cumin and crushed garlic to the dip. Some add a few tablespoons of Aleppo pepper for a smoky flavor. And still others use red pepper flakes instead of pepper paste. Usually the cook garnishes the appetizers with the ingredients to inform the guest which ingredients were used.*

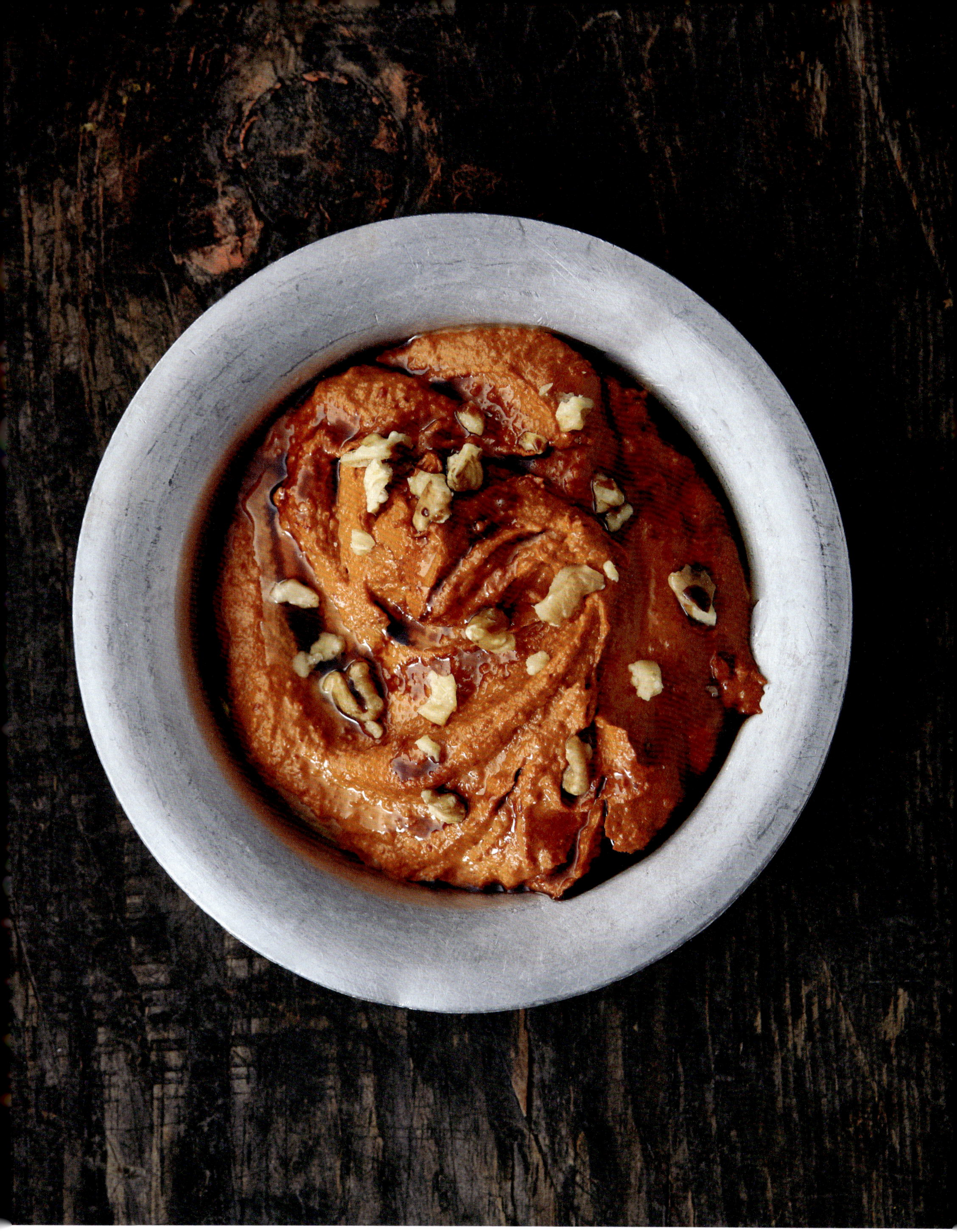

SHAKRIYEH

(LAMB STEW WITH YOGURT)

🍴 **4 serving**

During Eid al-Adha and Eid al-Fitr

Shakriyeh is prepared on the first day of Eid al-Adha and Eid al-Fitr; it is believed that the white color represents purity and optimism for a bright and prosperous future. This stew is always served with rice with vermicelli (see box on page 156), flavored with clarified butter.

INGREDIENTS:

- 500 grams boneless leg of lamb, trimmed of excess fat and cut into 2-cm (¾-inch) cubes
- 3 cups (700 milliliters) water
- 2 onions (400 grams), halved and peeled
- 2 bay leaves
- ½ teaspoon freshly ground black pepper
- 500 grams yogurt
- ½ teaspoon salt
- 2 tablespoons (10 grams) cornstarch

METHOD:

Give the meat a quick rinse, put in a 28-cm (4-quart) sauce pot, and add the water. Simmer over medium-high heat for about 15 minutes, skimming off any residue that forms on top. Add the onions, bay leaves, and black pepper, then lower the heat, cover and cook until the meat is tender, about 1 hour.

Remove the bay leaves and onions. Puree the onions in a food processor, using a bit of cooking liquid if needed. Return pureed onions to the pot and mix well.

In a separate saucepan, combine the yogurt, salt, and cornstarch, with one cup of the cooking liquid. Whisk thoroughly for 5 minutes, then bring to a simmer over medium-high heat.
Lower the heat to maintain a simmer for 15 minutes, stirring slowly all the while. Remove from heat and add it to the lamb onion mixture. Cook on low and stir constantly for 3 minutes, and serve.

Note: *Inam's mother used to grind the cooked onions using a special hand-held kitchen device. The Turkish version includes chopped onions (rather than boiled and pureed), cooked chickpeas, and a garnish of dried mint warmed in clarified butter.*

INAM AL-SHAYEB

LATIFA SMAILI

Latifa was born in Oran, a port city in Algeria. Although her mother taught her kitchen basics while Latifa was growing up and in college, she didn't embrace cooking, even after marrying and moving to Damascus. The war forced her and her husband to return to Algeria, where Latifa started working as an engineer at a biochemistry laboratory. They couldn't both get resident permits -- her husband is Palestinian -- so they moved to Turkey, where they were able to live together. Unfortunately, faced with health problems, Latifa could no longer work as an engineer. This was a difficult time for Latifa, who now stayed at home and didn't work. A friend suggested that she join a cooking group on Facebook, which proved fortuitous -- Latifa tapped into what she'd learned from her mother, made the recipes she saw, posted her results, and became part of a community. She then decided to start her own cooking-focused Facebook page and gained followers who enjoyed her creative ways with food. Latifa next plans to open a shop where she can sell French and Algerian sweets made with less sugar and fewer processed ingredients.

See Latifa's creations on Instagram at @sweet_cook_dar_latifa_cuisine.

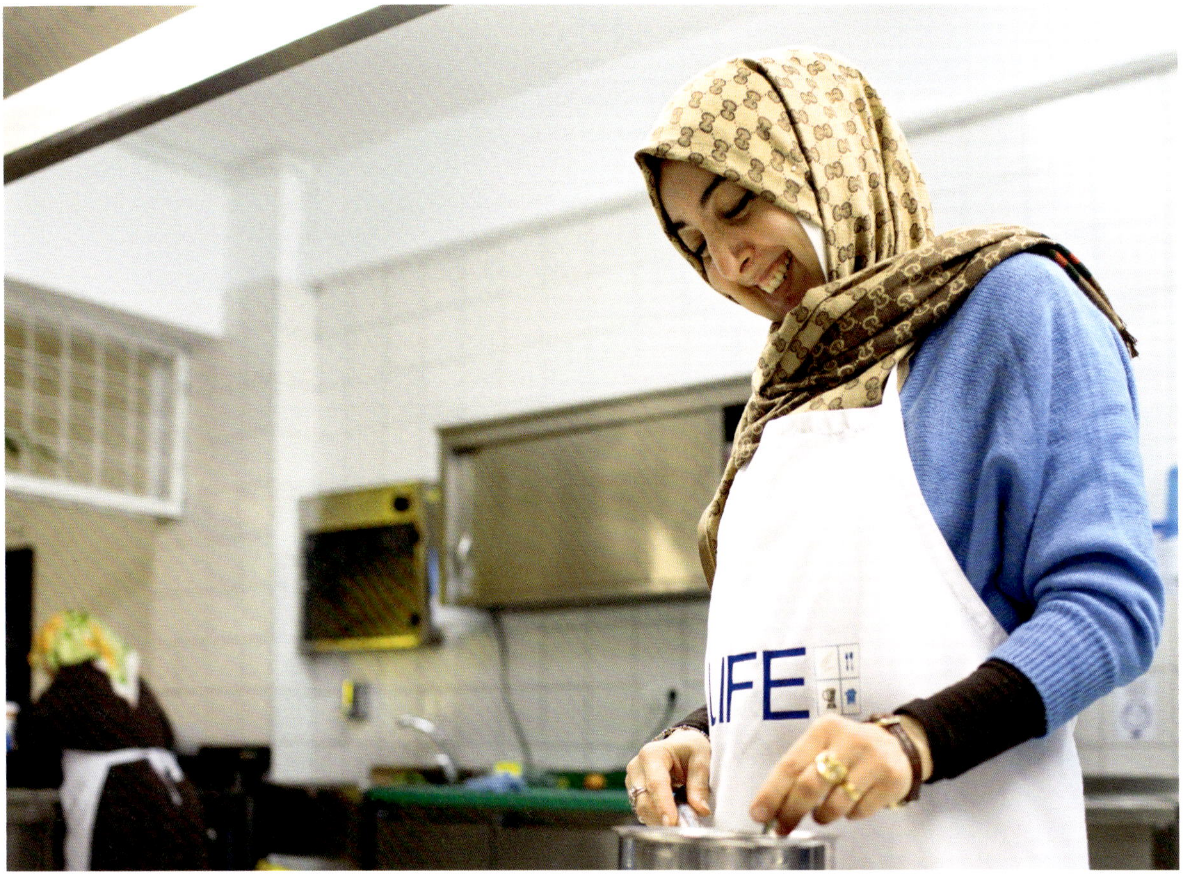

LIFE

MHAJEB/MAHJOUBA

(VEGETABLE AND CHEESE TURNOVERS)

6 servings (makes 6 turnovers)

Every season

Mhajeb are a typical street food, as well as a light meal or a children's snack enjoyed at home. Many women in Algeria are so skilled in making the dough that they handle and stretch the dough on their arms. According to legend, during the revolution, one woman was desperate to prepare food for her children and make a living as her husband was away. The only available ingredients at home were fine semolina, tomatoes, hot pepper, and onions. She made these turnovers, fed her children, and sent her son to the market to sell the rest. Her son returned with their earnings -- the turnovers were a success. The dish is named for this woman, as mahjouba means "hidden and unseen." She is a role model for those who make ends meet without the support of a partner.

INGREDIENTS:

For the filling:

½ cup (125 milliliters) olive oil
4 onions, finely chopped (700 grams total)
1 hot green pepper, finely chopped (30 grams)
4 tomatoes, peeled and finely chopped (800 grams total)
2 cloves garlic, finely chopped (5 grams total)
1 tablespoon (30 grams) tomato paste
1 teaspoon (2 grams) cumin
1 teaspoon (2 grams) black pepper
1 teaspoon (1 gram) sugar
200 grams cheddar cheese, grated

For the dough:

2 cups (500 grams) simit (fine semolina)
1 cup (150 grams) flour
1 teaspoon salt
1 cup (250 milliliters) water
½ cup (125 milliliters) oil

Note: *Cooks add grated carrot to the filling in the town of Biskra, where the shape is made into a half moon, rather than squares. A pinch of chopped parsley or dill can be sprinkled over the grated cheese, for extra flavor. These can also be made sweet with a sugar, cinnamon, and nut filling.*

METHOD:

For the filling: warm the oil in a large skillet over medium-high heat, then add the onion, green pepper, tomatoes, garlic, tomato paste, cumin, black pepper, and sugar. Cook for about 25 to 30 minutes, stirring often, until the mixture is creamy. Remove from heat and set aside to cool.

Meanwhile, make the dough: combine the simit, flour, salt, water, and oil in a large bowl, stirring with a fork and then your hands, until a dough forms. The more you knead, the more elastic it will become. Set aside for 15 minutes and knead again for a few minutes. Repeat this process three more times.

Lightly oil a work surface, divide the dough into egg-size balls, cover with a plastic wrap and let rest for one hour. Make a rectangle from each piece by stretching and flattening it with your hands. Put 2 tablespoons of the filling in the center, then spread it evenly over the dough. Sprinkle some cheese on top, and fold over the sides to make a square and completely enclose the filling.

Cook over lightly greased non stick pan set over medium heat until golden brown, about 10 minutes per side.

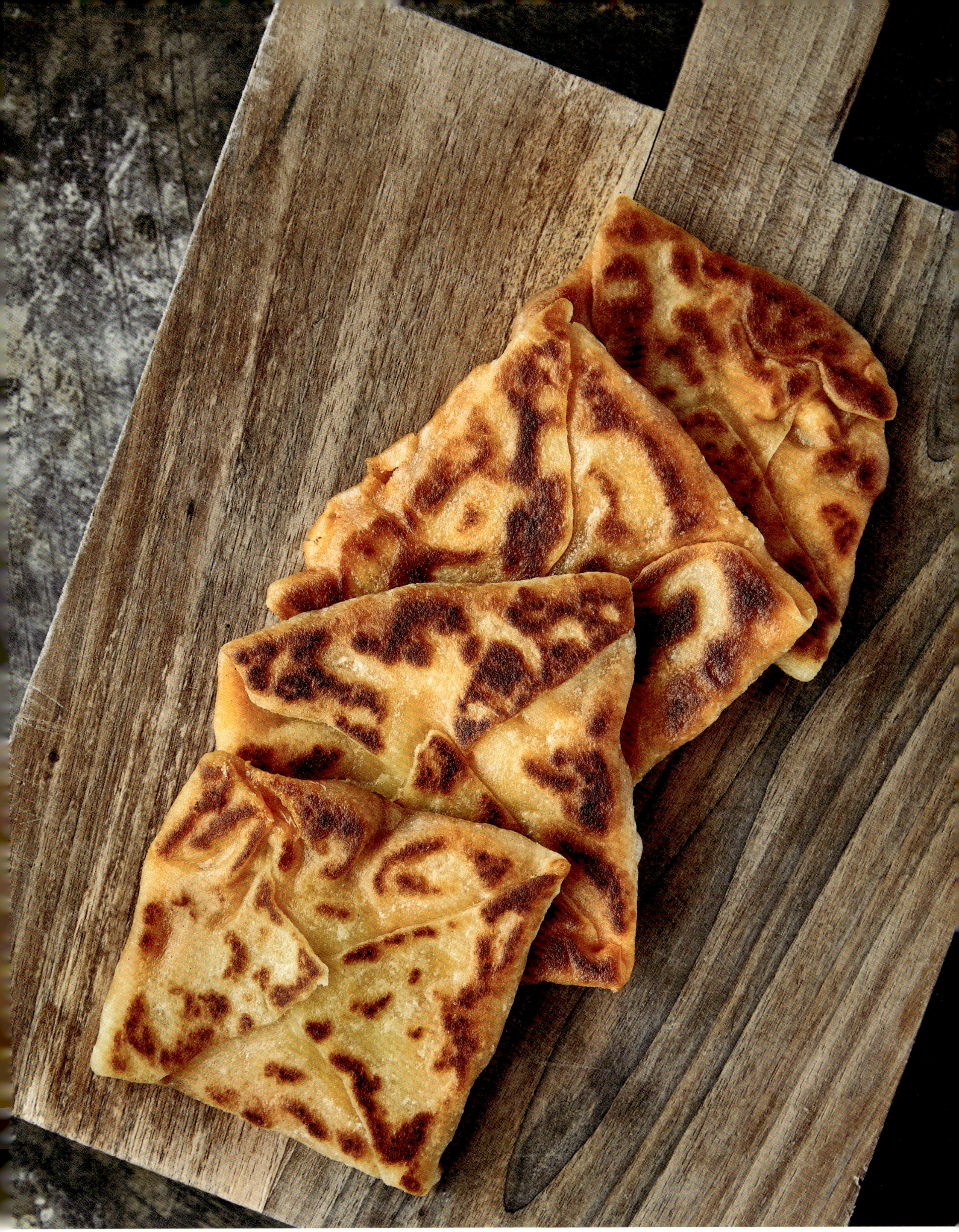

KUSKUS

(COUSCOUS WITH LAMB)

6 servings

Every season

Couscous is a staple food in Algeria, Morocco, Egypt, and Tunisia, and a way to test a young cook's skill. In order to have the ideal, perfect, fluffy couscous, you must steam it at three stages. Couscous in Algeria differs from city to city, as the geography and local crops determine what to add. In some regions, lentils, fava beans, sausage, or chicken are substituted for meat. Some add turmeric, ginger, coriander, and saffron to a meat sauce.

Serve as a main or side dish, or make it dessert by adding nuts, cinnamon, and sugar.

INGREDIENTS:

For the couscous:

2 cups (350 grams) couscous

2 tablespoons olive oil

3 cups (700 milliliters) water, plus more for sprinkling

2 tablespoons (40 grams) clarified butter

For the sauce:

¼ cup (55 milliliters) olive oil

500 grams boneless lamb loin chop cut in 2-cm (¾-inch) cubes (or 750 grams bone-in)

2 onions, finely chopped (440 grams total)

8 cloves garlic, finely chopped

3 tomatoes, peeled and finely chopped (750 grams total)

1 tablespoon (30 grams) tomato paste

3 cups (700 milliliters) hot water

3 potatoes, peeled and quartered (800 grams total)

3 zucchini, halved and quartered (730 grams total)

3 carrots peeled and quartered (500 grams total)

100 grams boiled chickpeas

Note: *The original recipe used bone-in meat, but cubed boneless works as well, and is slightly more convenient. Peeled and quartered turnips can be added with the vegetables, too.*

METHOD:

Rub couscous with 1 tablespoon of the oil, add 3 cups of water and drain immediately. Place the couscous in a steamer set over a boiling pot of water; steam for 10 minutes. (If you have a couscousiere steamer pot, now is the time to use it!)

Remove the couscous from the steamer, pour onto a baking sheet, and fluff it with a fork. Sprinkle with 3 tablespoons of water and the remaining tablespoon of oil. Wait for 5 minutes and transfer it back to the steamer. Repeat this process 3 times, with each steaming process lasting 15 minutes.

After the third round, after transferring it to the tray, add the clarified butter, stirring with a fork to distribute throughout.

In the meantime, start the sauce. Warm the ¼ cup of oil in a large skillet over medium-high heat, then add the lamb and onion and cook for 5 to 10 minutes, until lightly browned. Add the garlic, tomatoes, and tomato paste. Cook for 5 minutes over medium heat, then add the hot water and simmer, covered, until the meat is tender, about 45 minutes.

Add the potato, zucchini, and carrots and cook for another 15 to 20 minutes, until tender. Take care not to overcook the vegetables. Strain the meat and vegetables, reserving the sauce for serving.

Place the finished couscous in a large serving platter, then spoon the meat into the center. Arrange the carrots, zucchini, and potatoes around the meat, then pour the chickpeas around the edge of the couscous.

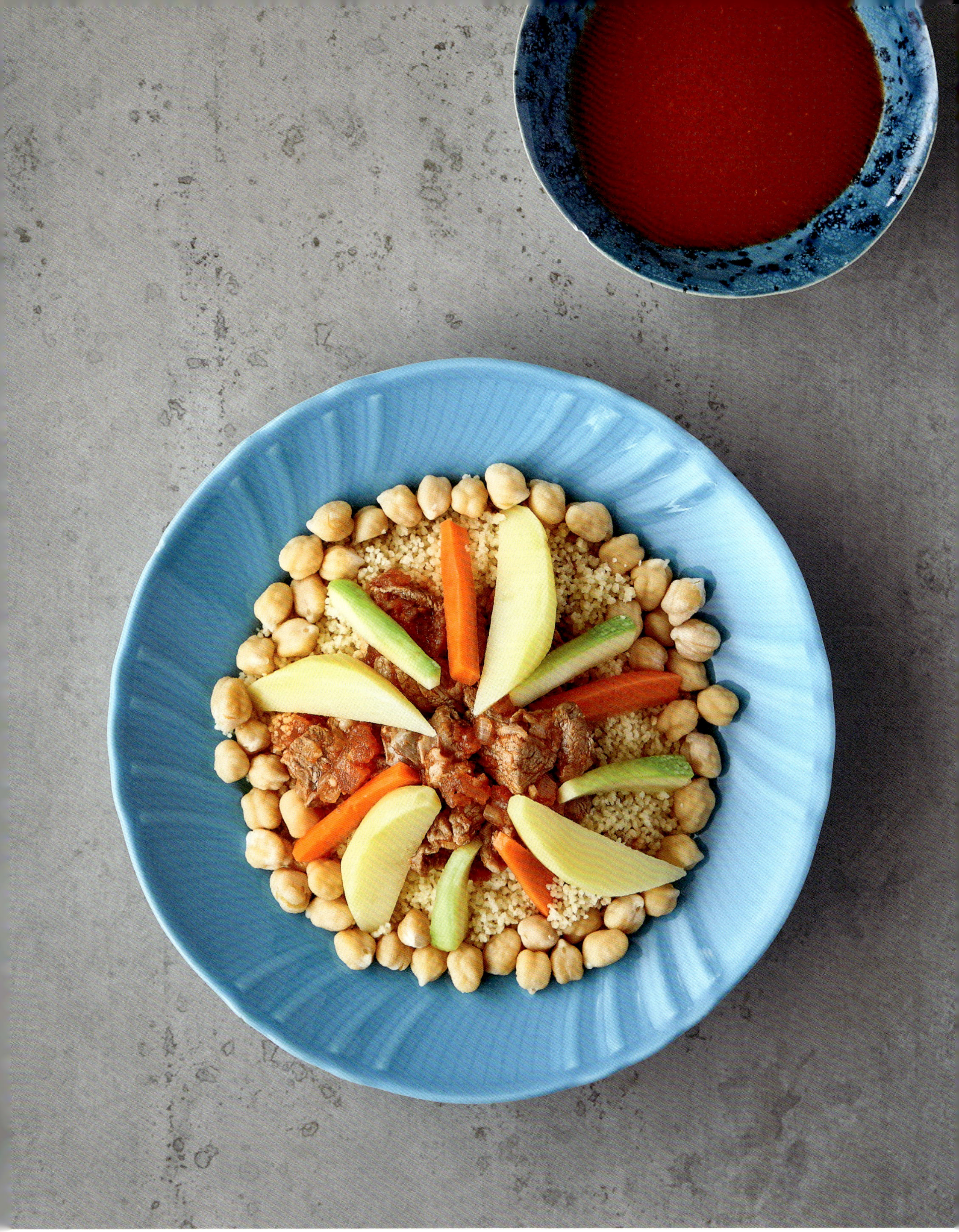

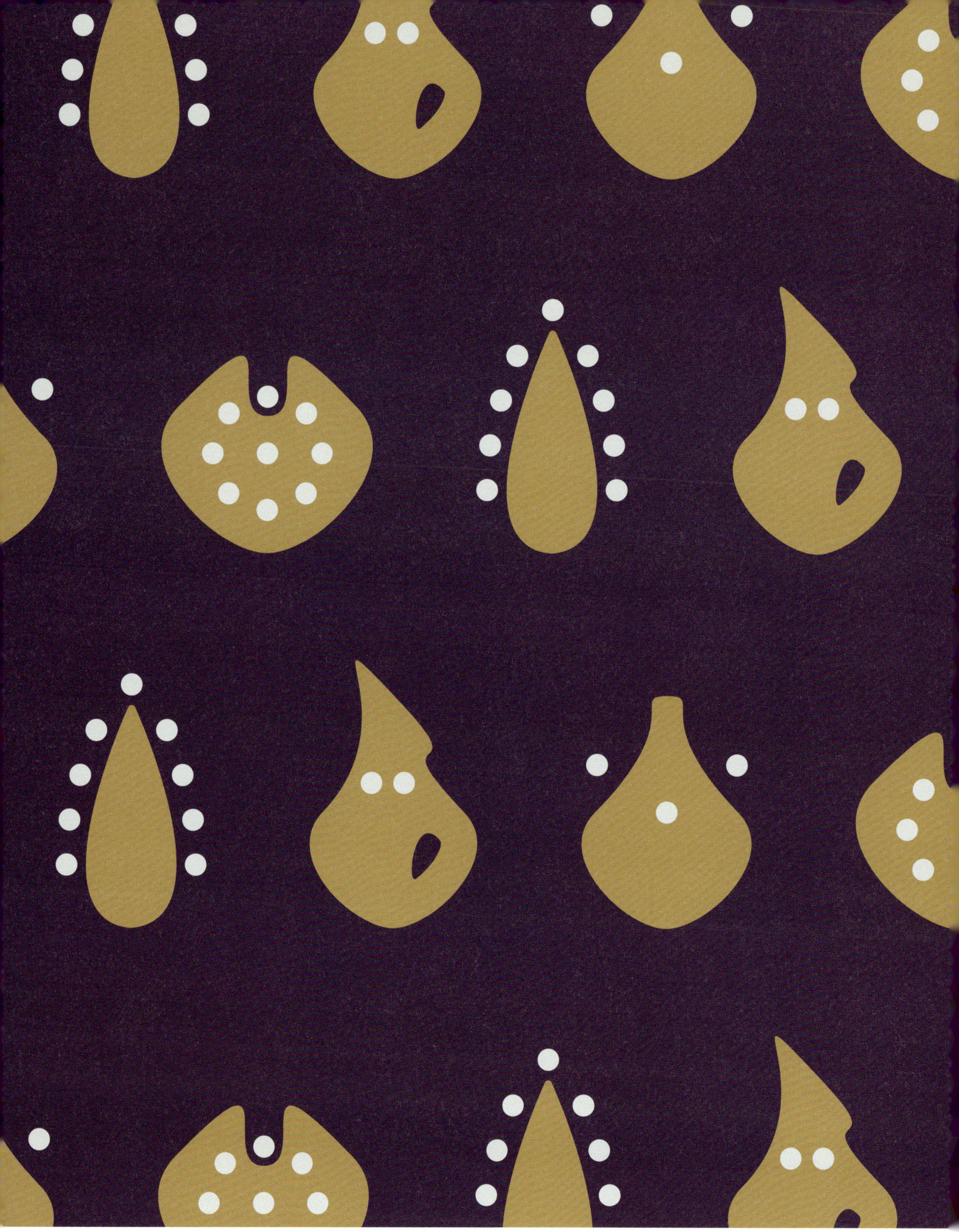

MIGRATION AND THE KITCHEN

Zeynep Kakınç

Cuisine is one of the most important indicators of culture, both socially and individually. Origin and belonging are important, but changes to a cuisine caused by immigration are undeniable. Globalization only makes these changes more complex: constant change inevitably affects culinary culture, as migration by its very nature implies adaptation.

I'm Circassian (Adyghea/Shapsug) and my ancestors are Caucasian immigrants. Our traditions have transformed over the last 150 years -- we do not serve dozens of dishes at once like our grandmothers did, but we still keep the scent and colorfulness from long ago. There is an old Adyghe saying: "Bisimir hesch'em yi 'wexwthebzasch'esch" -- the host is the guest's servant, meaning the host should strive to please their guest, adapting as necessary to accommodate them. The same could be said for the countries in which immigrants move to -- they must let new members of their society feel welcome. In return, newcomers will adapt and learn to live in their new home, set down roots and start businesses, and pass some of their culture on to new generations from a variety of backgrounds.

What types of changes in cuisine can we detect? On the one hand, as immigrants, we try to keep basic symbols of ethnicity but we also adapt to new conditions. No ethnic groups' culinary culture remains the same: new flavors, ingredients, and cooking techniques are added to those of the new home. And as local traditions grow and adapt, our tastes change and become more global.

If food is a kind of language, the discourse might change in shape, but its classic codes and traditions don't change easily. The important thing is to save our cultural heritage and to value changes at the same time -- to harmonize nostalgia with adaptation to new conditions.

Zeynep Kakınç has worked as a foreign news service manager, reporter, and editor. In 2000, she founded Mi Media Relations - Strategic Communications, Consultancy and Public Relations Agency. She has been a member of Mutfak Dostları Derneği (Friends of Kitchen Association) for 12 years, Turkey's oldest and most esteemed NGO in the field of gastronomy, and currently serves as president of the association. Ms. Kakınç is also president of the Logos Strategic & Gastronomic Communication Agency.

MAHA AL TINAWI

Maha's food is infused with memories and love for her father, who taught her and her brother how to cook when they were growing up in Damascus. She describes her father as her role model in life, work, and education -- Maha studied Sociology and Administrative Development at Damascus University and wrote several research papers and a book on contemporary intellectual studies. Maha moved to Istanbul in 2014 and works as a social consultant, but is still tied to food and plans to open a food truck specializing in Syrian food. As Maha prepared the following dishes for the LIFE cookbook, she remarked that she felt her father's soul in every step she takes -- and that her food tastes all the more special thanks to him.

MAHA AL TINAWI

OUZI

(LAMB AND RICE PILAF WRAPPED IN PHYLLO PASTRY)

10 servings (makes 10 pilaf-stuffed pastries)

During Eid al Adha and weddings

Ouzi is served during special occasions, such as weddings. For weddings, if ouzi wrapped in phyllo pastry is not served, then ouzi filling (rice, peas, and various nuts) is served with big chunks of roasted meat on top. It is a unique and tasty dish prepared for Eid and during Ramadan. Ghee and semn, types of clarified butter, may seem luxurious, but they are commonly used ingredients. This dish has another version, called Perde Pilavı (Drape Pilav), cooked in Turkey during weddings. Ouzi is always served with laban bi khiar (cucumber with yoghurt mixture) -- see recipe on page 142.

INGREDIENTS:

Filling:

1 cup (180 grams) long-grain rice
3 cups (700 milliliters) hot water
2 tablespoons (30 milliliters) olive oil
1/3 cup (50 grams) blanched almonds
1/3 cup (50 grams) pine nuts
1/3 cup (50 grams) cashews (optional)
¼ cup ghee or semn (clarified butter; see page 22)
250 grams ground lamb (20 percent fat)
250 grams peas (frozen or fresh)
½ teaspoon (2 grams) salt
½ teaspoon (2 grams) black pepper

To assemble:

½ cup (120 milliliters) olive oil
500 grams phyllo pastry (14 sheets, each 30-by-30 cm/12-by-12 inches)

METHOD:

For the filling: Soak the rice in 2 cups of hot water for about 15 minutes, then drain and rinse.

Warm the olive oil in a small skillet set over low heat, then add the almonds and cook, stirring often, for 3 minutes. Add the pine nuts and cashews, if using, and continue cooking for another 3 to 4 minutes, or until the nuts are golden.

Heat the ghee in a large pot and add the ground lamb. Cook, stirring from time to time, for 15 minutes. Add the peas and cook, covered, for another 15 minutes. Add the remaining 1 cup of hot water and the salt. Add the soaked rice to the pot. Cover and bring to a boil over high heat, then reduce to low and cook until the rice absorbs the liquid, about 15 to 20 minutes.

Preheat the oven to 175°C (350°F). Add the fried nuts and black pepper to the rice, then give it a good stir. Remove from heat and let rest, covered, for a few minutes.

To assemble, brush all sides of a small soup bowl or a big ramekin with some of the oil. Place 1 phyllo sheet inside. Fill it with 3 tablespoons of the rice filling and fold over the overhanging dough to completely enclose the filling. Tear off a piece of another phyllo sheet to reinforce the top, then press gently with the palms of your hands (to help hold it all together). Invert the filled phyllo onto a baking sheet, rounded side up. Remove the bowl, then brush the outside of the phyllo with some of the olive oil. Repeat to make a total of 10 ouzi, dividing the 4 extra phyllo sheets among them. (You will likely need to use multiple baking sheets.) Bake for 40 minutes, or until the outsides are slightly golden brown.

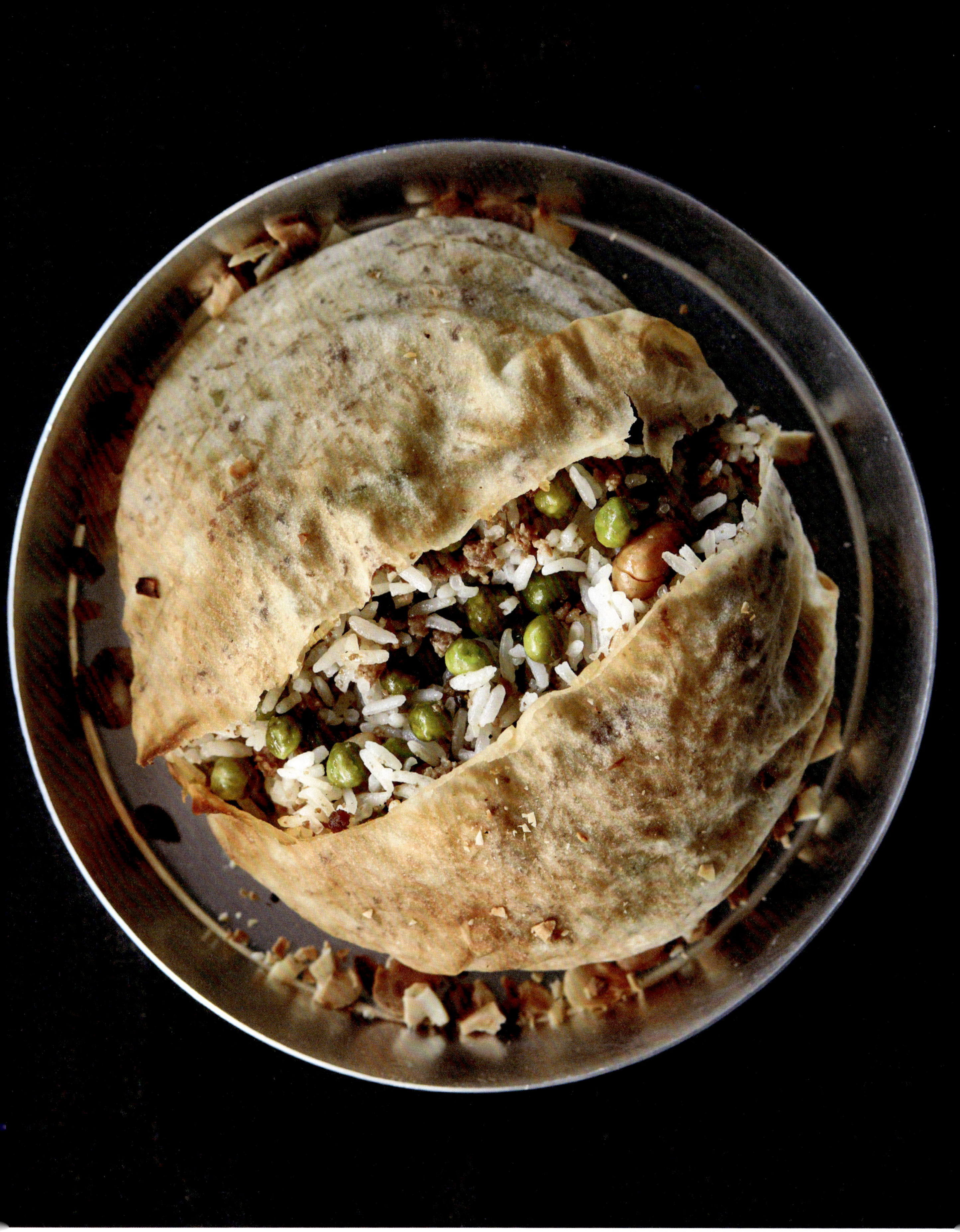

LABAN BI KHIAR

(CUCUMBER WITH YOGURT)

4 servings

Serve as an accompaniment to ouzi

Laban bi khiar is a dip or a cold sauce served with ouzi, as well as other main dishes, as it's believed to help digestion. It is also prepared in Turkey, Greece and Balkans in addition to Middle Eastern countries. (You may know it as tzatziki.)

This summer specialty is served cold -- prepare it in advance and store it in the refrigerator to help develop its flavors until serving. Laban bi khiar can be prepared with lettuce, fresh mint, parsley, or purslane, if cucumber is not available. Some cooks garnish it with a pinch of finely chopped dill and a few drops of olive oil.

INGREDIENTS:

- 1 tablespoon (15 milliliters) cold water
- 1 cucumber (about 300 grams)
- 1 clove garlic
- ½ teaspoon (2 grams) salt
- 250 grams strained yogurt (see note)
- 1 tablespoon (3 grams) dried mint

METHOD:

Peel and grate the cucumber. Peel and crush the garlic and a pinch of salt in the wooden mortar and pestle until you have a smooth paste. If a mortar and pestle is not available, crush the garlic with knife, chop finely, then add the salt and use the side of your knife to mash into a paste.

Add the cold water, grated cucumber, a pinch of dried mint and the garlic paste to the strained yoghurt. Mix thoroughly. Place in a serving bowl and sprinkle with the dried mint.

Note: *You can use Greek-style yogurt or strain your own -- put 2 ½ cups (625 grams) of plain yogurt in a towel- or cheesecloth-lined sieve set over a bowl, then let strain for 6 to 8 hours in the refrigerator. This will yield about 1 1/4 cups (300 grams) of strained yogurt. Save the strained liquid (whey) for another use, such as adding to brines, smoothies, or cold soups.*

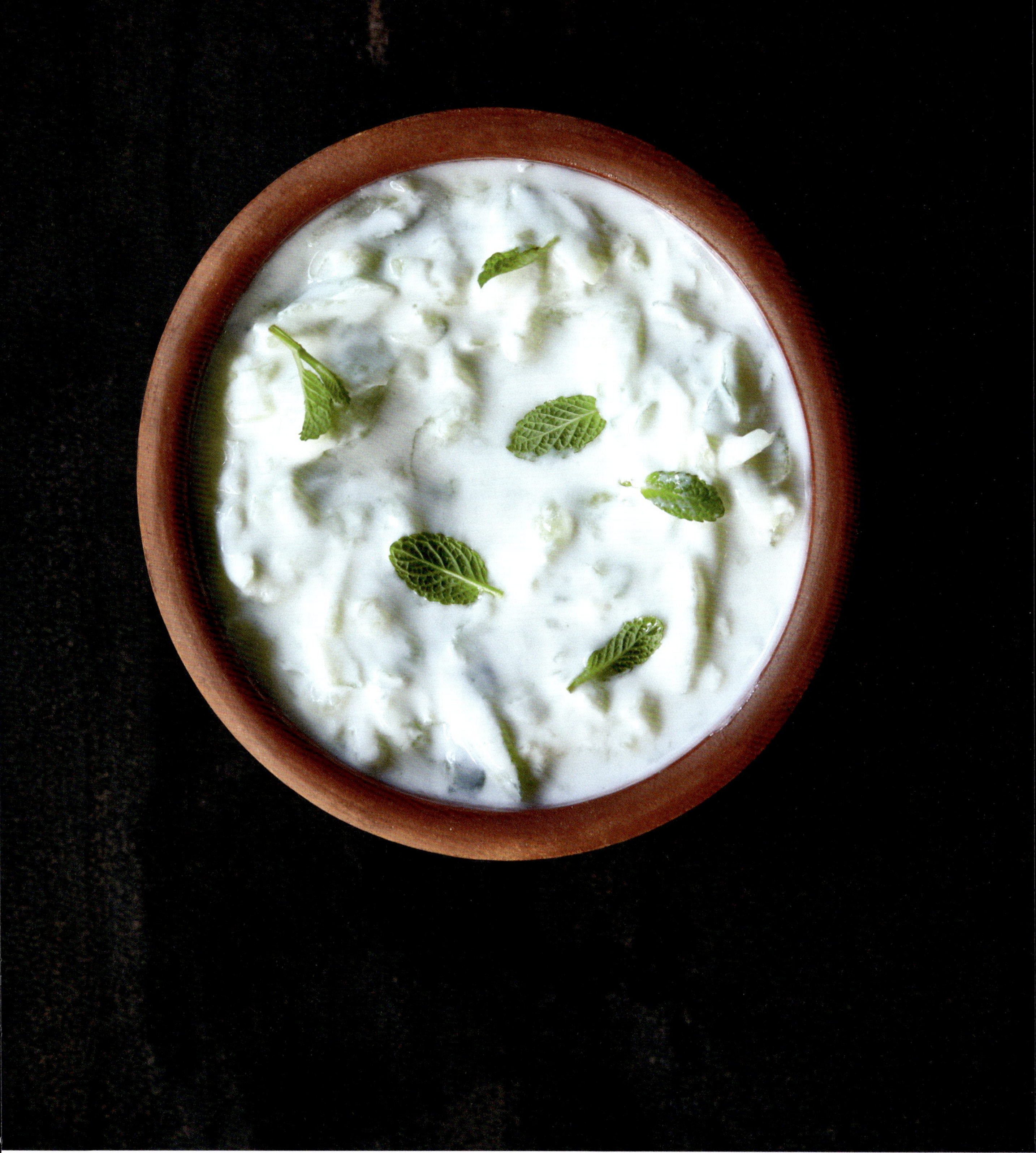

MUJADDARA

(LENTIL PILAF)

4 servings

During Spring and Summer

Mujaddara can be served at every meal, no matter the season. This vegetarian dish is easy and inexpensive to prepare; the lentils are a great source of iron and protein.

This version is made with bulgur, but rice is another common way to make it. Caramelized onion provides the signature flavor of mujaddara. According to Maha's father, mujaddara is a staple food for soldiers during their military service. It also makes for a versatile, pantry-friendly dish -- serve it with roasted vegetables, yoghurt, fried eggs, salads, or pickles.

INGREDIENTS:

3 large onions (1 kilogram total)
Scant ½ cup (110 milliliters) olive oil
1 cup (350 grams) green lentils, rinsed
½ cup (180 grams) coarse grain bulgur
1 tablespoon (4 grams) salt

METHOD:

Cut the onions in half from top to bottom, peel, and slice into thin half moons. Warm the olive oil in a large skillet set over medium heat, then add the onions. Cook, stirring from time to time, until the onions begin to sizzle, about 5 minutes. Lower the heat and continue cooking the onions, stirring occasionally, until they are lightly browned, about 20 to 25 minutes.

Put the lentils into a medium saucepan with 3 cups of cold water. Bring to a simmer over medium-high heat, then lower the heat to maintain a constant simmer and cook until the lentils are tender, about 30 to 45 minutes. Add more water if needed.

Add the bulgur and 2 tablespoons of the onions to the lentils, then continue cooking until all the liquid is absorbed, about 15 to 20 minutes. Season to taste with salt. Remove from heat and top with the remaining caramelized onions.

Note: *Mujaddara may also be seasoned with ground cumin, which is believed to promote digestion.*

MAHA AL TINAWI

TABBOULEH

(FINE GRAIN BULGUR SALAD)

4 servings

During summer

Tabbouleh tastes better when prepared a day in advance, but it can also be served right away. Almost every cook creates her or his own version, as it is easy to play with the ingredients.

Serve tabbouleh with kebabs and roasted vegetables, or by itself, as an appetizer. The real hero is parsley -- the bulgur is there to give a nutty dimension, not to be the main ingredient.

INGREDIENTS:

1/4 cup (100 grams) fine grain bulgur (see page 21)
3 tablespoons (45 milliliters) lemon juice
2 cups (100 grams) parsley
½ cup (10 grams) fresh mint leaves
13 to 14 (250 grams) scallions
2 tomatoes (about 400 grams total)
1 tablespoon dry mint
½ teaspoon (2 grams) salt
⅓ cup (80 milliliters) olive oil (preferably early harvest, extra-virgin)
Lettuce leaves, for serving

METHOD:

Mix the bulgur and lemon juice in a medium bowl and let soak for 15 minutes.

Finely chop the parsley, fresh mint, and scallions, then add to the bowl. Dice the tomatoes and add them (including their juices) to the bowl, then add the dried mint, salt, and oil, stirring to combine. Taste and adjust for seasoning. Serve on top of the lettuce leaves.

Note: *If scallions are not available, white or red onions can be used. You can also add chopped lettuce, cucumber, green, and red peppers.*

MAHA AL TINAWI

THE MIGRATION OF FOOD IN ANATOLIA

148

THE MIGRATION OF FOOD IN ANATOLIA

Nevin Halıcı

Anatolia has witnessed several waves of migration. Migrants in the 1920s, like my family, were part of a flow of people fleeing war, moving mostly on foot -- which took more than a year -- from Başkale in the east to Konya, in the west. They reached Mosul after two or three months, having mostly walked through the mountains, sometimes getting food from villages, often eating wild plants they found on their way, as it was dangerous to travel inside or through the cities.

The people of Mosul welcomed immigrants with stuffed meatballs. My mother, fighting back tears, explained to me how delicious the taste of the stuffed meatballs were, particularly considering that they had consumed only wild herbs for the several months of their journey. She was about five years old then, and gives her thanks to Allah that no one in her family has to go through such difficulties any more.

The immigrants who ended their journey in Konya found work in various sectors. They returned back to their normal lives in their new homes, their old foodways forming again. But where were the sirmo and mendü herbs of the Van mountains, to be used in cheese? They longed for flavors from their home and found suitable substitutes in thin leeks and mint, pressing their cheeses into earthenware jars and burying those jars upside down into wells, all efforts made in order to capture the flavor of their Van cheese. They used bulgur instead of dövme (hulled wheat). Only their lavash remained the same, baked in tandooris found in Konya.

My family's story offers a look into circumstances seen around the globe today. As we see in the LIFE Project kitchens, cooks continue to adapt to their new homes, even as increased migration and globalization has led to some ingredients being more broadly available. Take Muyassar Hamdan's Jordanian Mansaf (lamb cooked in yogurt, page 172): her original recipe uses jameed, dried and salted goat milk yogurt which is not always easy to find outside of Jordan. She suggests using plain yogurt instead -- the result is different from the original, but in the process a new dish is made (and perhaps, a new tradition).

So we see how people recreate recipes with local ingredients, forming a new cuisine that reflects the longing for flavors from the past.

Nevin Halıcı was born in Konya. She studied Home Economics and Nutrition at Gazi University in Ankara, before going on to get a PhD. Dr. Halıcı has traveled all over Turkey, province by province, to document regional recipes, resulting in 10 cookbooks. She has also curated exhibitions on Turkish Cuisine, done cooking demonstrations, and prepared menus for international food congresses and seminars.

MAYSAA ALGHERAWI

When Maysaa, newly married at 18, moved to Saudi Arabia from Syria, she didn't know how to cook. So her mother wrote a book of her own recipes and packed it with her luggage and other items bound for her new home. At a time when international phone calls were expensive -- and therefore limited -- it was her mother's recipe book that taught Maysaa how to cook. Maysaa speaks of her mother with great longing, or haneen (meaning a feeling of love and nostalgia); she taught Maysaa to trust her inner compass.

As she honed her cooking skills, Maysaa learned to follow her intuition, preferring to cook by sight, feel, and taste rather than rely on exact measurements. Today she is a precise, calm, and collected cook. She believes that the care you take in cooking conveys love, healing, and joy to the people you've cooked for. And, importantly, once you start something, you must finish it -- another skill passed down from mother to daughter.

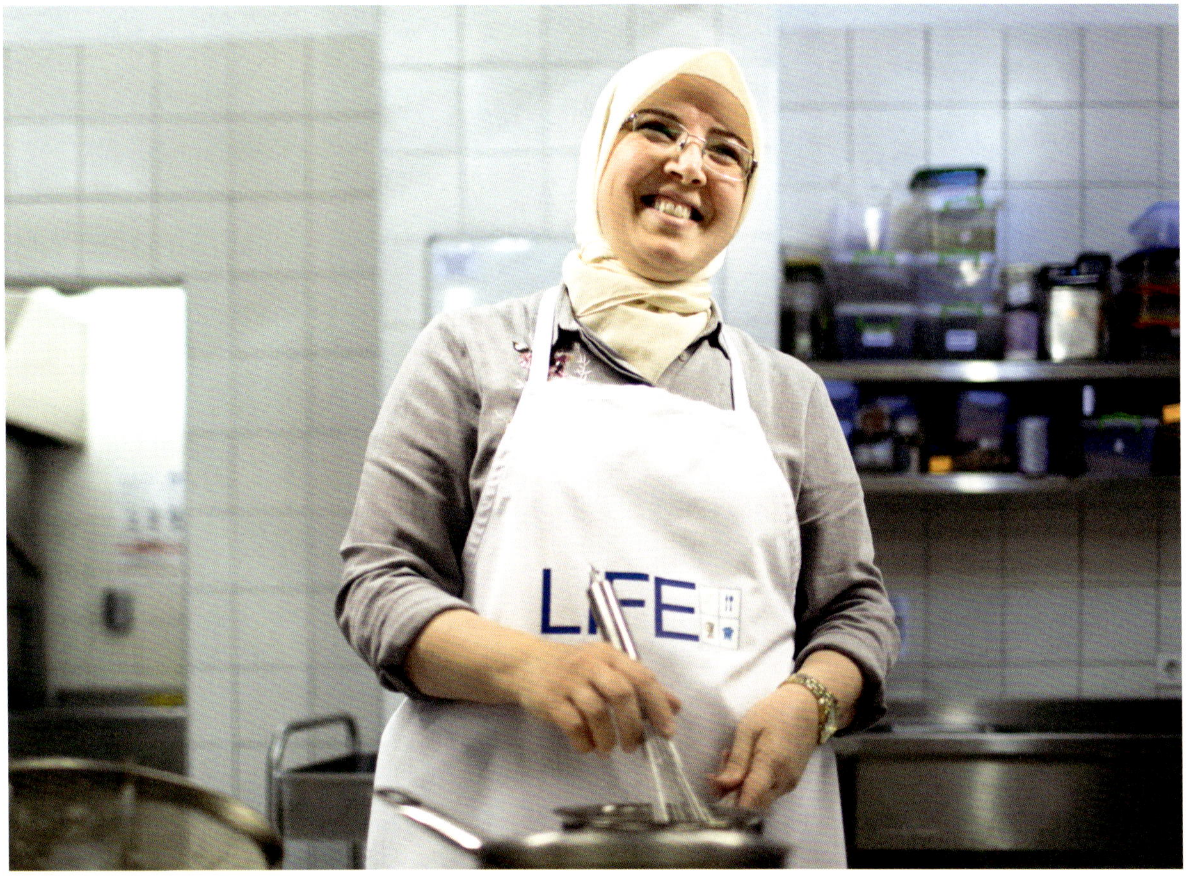
LIFE

SHISH BARAK

(DUMPLINGS COOKED IN YOGURT SAUCE)

2 servings

Every season, for festive occasions

INGREDIENTS:

For the dough:

2 cups (240 grams) flour

¼ teaspoon salt

1 ½ tablespoons (25 milliliters) olive oil, plus more for oiling the dough

1 cup plus 1 tablespoon (250 milliliters) water

For the filling:

250 grams ground lamb

1 onion, finely chopped (270 grams)

½ teaspoon salt

½ teaspoon freshly ground pepper

1 teaspoon seven spices (see note)

2 tablespoons (20 grams) finely chopped cilantro

1 tablespoon oil

For the sauce and to garnish:

2 kilograms plain yogurt

2 teaspoons wheat starch

3 tablespoons (30 milliliters) olive oil

5 cloves (40 grams) garlic, crushed

3 tablespoons (5 grams) finely chopped cilantro

It's said that these dumplings were originally called shish darak -- shish meaning helmet, darak meaning soldier -- since the shape of the dough resembles a soldier's helmet. It's unknown how they became shish barak. Prominent in the Ammara area of Damascus, the dumplings are the sister of mantı, a type of dumpling from Central Asia. Preparation is time consuming, thus home cooks prepare several portions of shish barak in one sitting, pack them in storage bags, and freeze for several months to have on hand for an easy meal or unexpected guests. Tiny shish barak are all the more enjoyable to eat -- try to make them so small that one sits comfortably in a tablespoon.

These dumplings are perhaps best in the spring, when local milk is more plentiful and takes on grassy, intense flavor thanks to the new abundance of plants and herbs for the animals to eat. Cooking with yogurt indicates a good future in Syrian cooking, due to its pure, white color. Other symbolic dishes include stuffed zucchini cooked in yogurt, shakriye (meat cooked and combined with yogurt), and kebbeh labaniye (kibbeh cooked in yogurt).

You'll have extra seven spice blend left over -- use it to season kababs, kibbeh, or other dishes featuring lamb.

METHOD:

Make the dough: mix the flour, salt, olive oil, and water in a large bowl until a soft dough forms, adding more water if needed. Brush a little olive oil on the dough, then cover with plastic wrap and let rest for about 10 to 15 minutes.

While the dough is resting, prepare the filling: use your hands to combine the lamb, onion, salt, pepper, spice mixture, and cilantro in a large bowl. Knead well to make sure the ingredients are well incorporated.

Preheat the oven to 180ºC (350ºF). Roll out the dough to an even 2-mm thickness. Cut 7-cm (2 ¾-inch) circles with a glass. Add 1 tablespoon of the filling to the center of each round, then fold to form half moons, pinching with your fingers to seal the edges. Pinch each pointed end together to form a hat-like shape. Place the dumplings a few centimeters apart on a greased baking sheet as you go. Reroll any scraps, let rest for 10 to 15 minutes, then repeat to use up the rest of the dough and filling.

THE MIGRATION OF FOOD IN ANATOLIA

MAYSAA ALGHERAWI

SHISH BARAK
(DUMPLINGS COOKED IN YOGURT SAUCE)

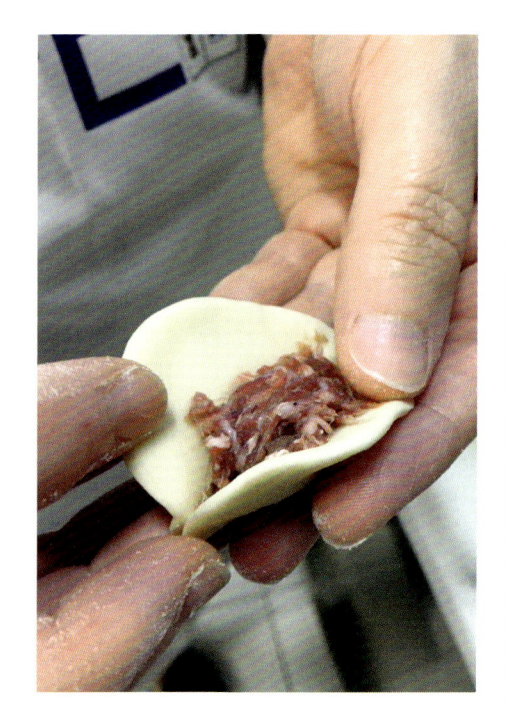

Brush the dumplings with the oil, then bake (middle rack) for 10 minutes.

To make the sauce, stir the yogurt, then strain through a fine mesh sieve into a into a large pot (to remove any lumps); stir in the wheat starch. Cook on low heat for about 30 minutes, stirring slowly, until the yogurt starts to boil. Add the dumplings to the yogurt mixture and cook until the dumplings are tender, about 25 minutes. Resist the urge to check the dumplings with a fork, as they might break apart. (If needed, shake the pan gently to mix the dumplings into the sauce a bit.)

Warm the olive oil in a small skillet over medium-high heat, then cook the garlic and cilantro for about 3 to 5 minutes, or until the garlic is golden. Drizzle the mixture over top of the dumplings and serve.

Note: *To make the seven spice blend, mix 2 tablespoons ground black pepper, 2 tablespoons paprika, 2 tablespoons ground cumin, 1 tablespoon ground coriander, 1 tablespoon ground cloves, 1 teaspoon ground nutmeg, 1 teaspoon ground cinnamon, and ½ teaspoon ground cardamom in a small jar. Shake well to combine.*

Some cooks add pine nuts to the meat filling, and others don't use starch with the yogurt, adding an egg instead to help keep the yogurt from curdling.

Maysaa's mother taught her that whoever begins mixing the yogurt should follow through to the finish -- no transferring the job to someone else. When boiling the yogurt, the mixture may stick to the pan and burn. In Idlib this is tolerated; in Damascus, the cook does their best to avoid this. If possible, the garlic is crushed in a copper or wooden mortar and pestle.

FAKHDET LAHMEH
(LEG OF LAMB)

🍴 5 servings

🌙❄ During winter and spring, and feasts

Fakhdet Lahmeh is a festive dish that seems particularly tasty in the spring, but also makes for a warm and comforting elixir in the winter. Bay leaves add a distinctive flavor and fragrance and are also said to help soothe the stomach. Serve with rice cooked with vermicelli.

INGREDIENTS:

- 3 tablespoons (30 milliliters) olive oil, plus more for frying the potatoes
- ½ kilogram boneless leg of lamb, cut into large 3- to 4-cm chunks
- 4 to 5 bay leaves (to taste)
- 6 to 7 green cardamom pods (to taste)
- 1 large onion, peeled but kept whole
- 5 cups (1250 ml) hot water
- 4 potatoes (1 kilogram total)
- 1 cup (150 grams) chopped mushrooms
- 1 teaspoon salt
- ½ teaspoon freshly ground black pepper

METHOD:

Warm the oil in a large, heavy-bottomed pot set over medium-high heat. Add the meat and cook, turning occasionally so that each side browns, about 15 minutes. Add the bay leaves, cardamom pods, whole onion, and water. Reduce the heat to low and cook, covered, until the meat is tender, about 50 minutes to an hour.

Meanwhile, warm 10 cm (4 inches) of olive oil in a large pan over medium-high heat, then add the potatoes. Fry until they're a light golden brown, then transfer to paper towels to drain.

Remove the onion, bay leaves, and cardamom pods (fish them out with a small sieve if necessary). Add the chopped mushrooms, salt, pepper, and fried potatoes to the meat stock and meat. Simmer, covered, for another 25 to 30 minutes, until the potatoes and mushrooms are tender. Serve with rice cooked with vermicelli (see box).

Note: *If you'd rather not fry the potatoes, you can add them directly to the lamb mixture.*

The ratio of the rice to vermicelli may differ; Maysaa uses 2 cups of short-grain rice for every ½ cup of vermicelli. Toast the vermicelli in ½ cup of olive oil for 15 minutes, until golden. Add the rice and toast for another 10 minutes, then add 3¾ cups of hot water and 1 teaspoon salt. Stir, cover, and cook for 18 to 20 minutes, until the liquid is absorbed. Remove from heat, add 1 tablespoon butter, then cover and let rest for 15 minutes. When it comes time to serve, the skilled cook is expected to create a dome shape when presenting the rice on a flat serving plate.

MAYSAA ALGHERAWI

SALATET JARJEER

(ARUGULA SALAD)

4 servings

Every season

A variety of appetizers and mezes are typically prepared when there is a meat or chicken dish on the table to accompany it, but Maysaa also prepares salads such as this to go with a big, hearty main dish, or kebabs, kibbeh, and boreks. Arugula's faintly bitter and peppery notes go very well with the tangy tart lemon and pomegranate dressing.

INGREDIENTS:

2 cups (150 grams) arugula
2 tomatoes (300 grams total)
2 scallions (40 grams), finely chopped
2 tablespoons (25 milliliters) olive oil
Juice of 1 lemon
1 teaspoon salt
2 tablespoons (30 grams) pomegranate molasses
½ cup (50 grams) walnut halves

METHOD:

Wash and dry the arugula leaves, then chop them into 2-cm (¾-inch) wide pieces and put in a large serving bowl. Peel the tomatoes, cut into 1-cm (½-inch) cubes and add to the bowl, along with the scallions. Mix gently with your hands.

Whisk the olive oil, lemon juice, salt, and pomegranate molasses in a small bowl, then drizzle over the salad. Garnish with the walnuts.

MAYSAA ALGHERAWI

FOOD, THE GREAT EQUALIZER

FOOD, THE GREAT EQUALIZER

Joan Nathan

I have studied how food connects us to culture and history throughout my entire life. This work was underscored in Istanbul, where I had the opportunity to reinforce a lifelong observation of my work as a journalist and cookbook writer: cooking together creates bonds across borders, religions, and cultures.

When I arrived at the LIFE kitchen, I noticed a woman carefully tucking orzo, chicken, and dill into a tiny porcelain teacup lined with a blanched Swiss chard leaf. Using the cup as a mold, she then turned it upside down and released it into a rectangular pan, spooning tomato sauce on top before baking. It occurred to me later that this may be the first time this dish, served in villages for generations during times of mourning, will be documented for the future. (See page 76 for the recipe.) Another woman was making a pilav with freekeh, a parched green wheat that has been around for centuries. Everyone discussed this dish because each person's family made it a different way, using oral recipes passed down through generations in every home and every village throughout the Middle East.

With the help of the LIFE staff I chose two dishes to make that we thought in some way would be familiar: a Jewish Macedonian leek and meat patty for the winter holiday, Hanukkah, and a Syrian Sabbath chicken that had been Americanized with noodles, rather than rice. When we finished cooking, we all shared these dishes with about 60 people. The food served was representative of their culture and mine, with familiar ingredients becoming a great equalizer.

After lunch, I spoke, through a translator, with the members about my life's work as a food writer and journalist. They were right with me as I talked about the struggle of being a woman who wanted my profession to be taken seriously by my husband, children, and the world. I told them how difficult it initially was to make a living with food. Afterwards, they said they thought American women had everything and didn't realize that we also had feelings of guilt and similar challenges that they faced every day.

The experience truly exemplified food as a universal language: by sharing recipes close and meaningful to us, we share our mutual humanity. Food breaks down human barriers, and food entrepreneurship -- especially by women -- is finally being taken seriously. This is a new generation of professional cooks helping themselves and their families survive -- and one day, thrive -- by profiting from what they already find fulfilling work: cooking.

Joan Nathan is the author of eleven cookbooks and a regular contributor to The New York Times and Tablet Magazine. Her work has earned numerous awards, including the James Beard Award for the best American cookbook and the IACP/Julia Child Cookbook of the Year Award. Her television series "Jewish Cooking in America with Joan Nathan" airs on PBS, and the documentary "Passover: Traditions of Freedom," of which she was a senior producer, won the prestigious CHRIS award. Ms. Nathan serves on the LIFE Project Advisory Council.

MOHAMAD SHADY KHAYATA

Shady was born in Kuwait, where his father was working at the time; once the Gulf War started, he and his family returned to their hometown of Aleppo. The Kuwaiti and Syrian school curriculums were quite different then -- so different that it was difficult for Shady to continue his education -- so at age 16 he stopped going to school and instead worked for several years in a sweets shop. Even when he joined the military, Shady wanted to improve his kitchen skills; he became the camp cook and, on his off weeks, kept working in another sweets-focused shop, learning all about such Eastern desserts as baklava and kunafe (see page 168). After his military time was over, Shady, at age 21, studied and taught himself in order to finally get his high school diploma.

The world was calling -- Shady moved to Dubai, where he was exposed to international cuisine, and then went on to Cairo, where he worked in a restaurant and learned to make Egyptian dishes and sweets. Once he returned to Aleppo, he married and opened a shop with a business partner. War forced him to move to Turkey in 2011, where he worked as head chef in a sweets production shop before opening a sweets-focused business of his own.
As more Syrians moved to Turkey and started their own food businesses, competition became too fierce for Shady's to survive. He now works for Koska, a large confectionery producer in Turkey. Through it all, Shady remains calm when working in the kitchen -- cooking is like meditation and keeps him focused.

MOHAMAD SHADY KHAYATA

KIBBEH MABRUMEH

(ROLLED KIBBEH)

10 servings (makes 12 to 13 kibbeh rolls)

Fall, Winter, Spring

INGREDIENTS:

For the filling:

200 grams walnuts

200 grams pistachio nuts

1 kilogram ground lamb (10 percent fat)

1 teaspoon salt

100 grams pine nuts

3 eggs

100 grams clarified butter, for baking

For the crust:

1 kilogram fine grain bulgur (see page 21)

1 cup (230 milliliters) water, plus more as needed

1 tablespoon (10 grams) salt

1 tablespoon (10 grams) allspice

2 tablespoons (50 grams) pepper paste (see page 22)

1 kilogram lean chunks of boneless lamb

1 onion, peeled and quartered

Note: The filling can be prepared without meat: use sauteed onion and pistachios or walnuts, then add pomegranate molasses for a pleasantly tart flavor. For the crust, red pepper flakes can be substituted for the pepper paste. Use lean ground beef for the crust if lean lamb meat is not available.

This rolled kibbeh is very practical and not as time consuming as kibbeh shaped into balls or patties. Instead of deep frying, as in the case of kibbeh balls, these are baked.

METHOD:

For the filling: crush the walnuts and pistachios with a rolling pin (traditionally a mortar and pestle would be used; you can also grind in a food processor). Warm a large skillet over medium-high heat, then add the meat and cook, stirring, until it's browned. Add the salt, pine nuts, and the ground walnuts and pistachios. Remove from heat and let cool to room temperature, then add the eggs and mix well.

For the kibbeh: put the bulgur in the bowl of a food processor and stir in the water with a fork. Add the salt, allspice, pepper paste, lamb pieces and onion, then pulse several times to mix well and form a dough. If the mixture seems too stiff, add water, a tablespoon at a time, until it's malleable.

Preheat the oven to 170ºC (325ºF). Divide the dough into six equal portions and roll them out into rectangles that are ½-cm (¼-inch) thick. Put a rectangle onto a sheet of plastic wrap that is slightly larger, then spoon ¾ cup of the filling along the entire length of the rectangle. Roll it up lengthwise, using the plastic wrap to help keep it all together and prevent the dough from sticking to your fingers. Continue rolling until you have a cylinder with a diameter of 6 to 8 cm (2 ¼ to 3 inches).

Wet your fingers with cold water and press gently to seal the edges, then transfer to a baking sheet. Repeat with the remaining dough and filling, adding the cylinders to the baking sheet as you go. Dot the clarified butter over the kibbeh and bake for 25 to 30 minutes, until they are golden and crispy on the outside. Once cool enough to handle, slice them into pieces 4 to 5 cm (1 ½ to 2 inches) long, place in a serving dish, and garnish with slivered pistachio nuts.

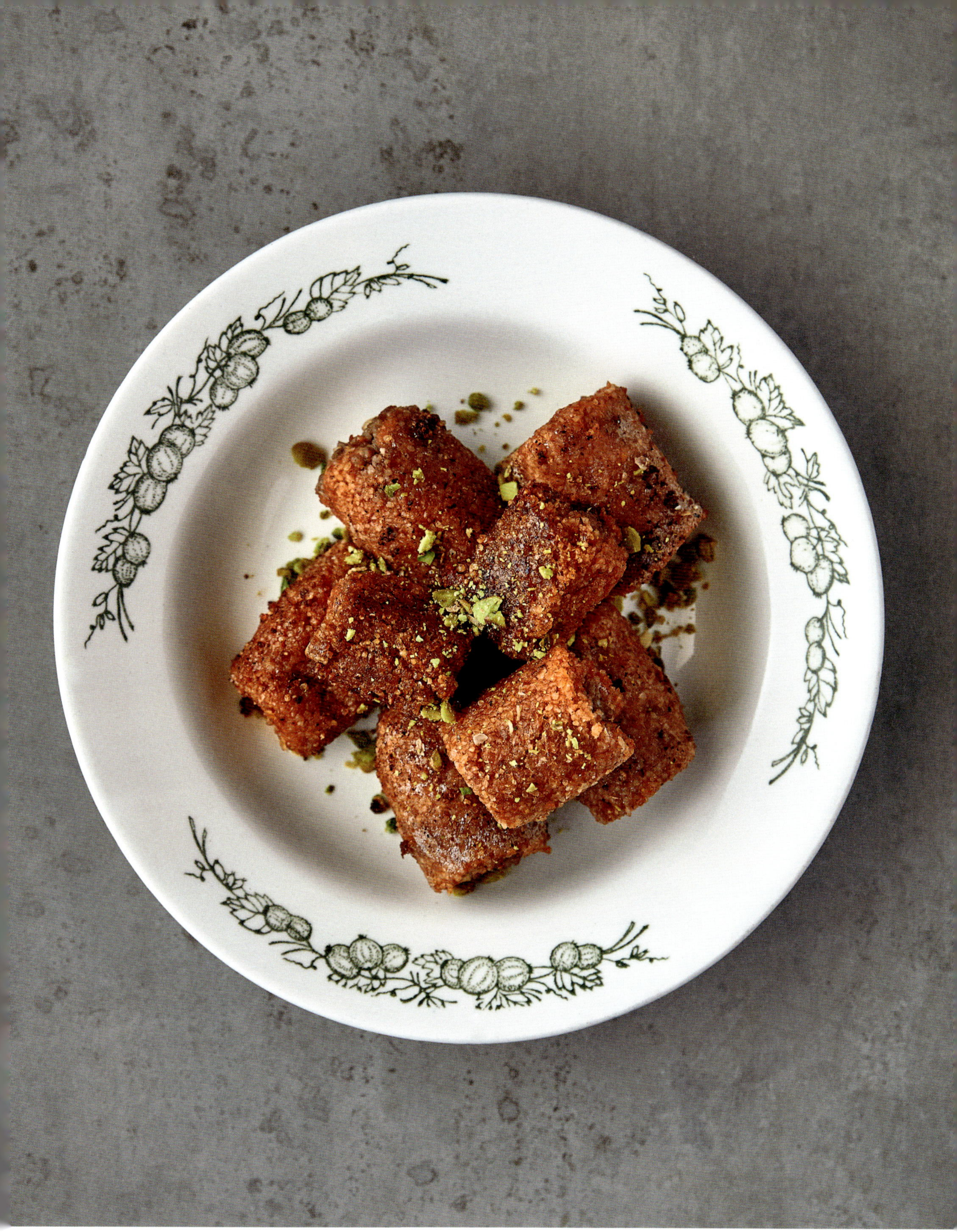

ESH EL BOLBOL

(NIGHTINGALE'S NEST)

- 20 to 25 servings (makes 40 to 50 pieces)
- Every season

This small lahmacun or pizza-like dish is a specialty from Aleppo and Hama. It is mostly prepared for special occasions. This name may remind you of another dish from Damascus, Syria, and Gaziantep, Turkey. But those versions are sweets, rather than the savory, meat-topped specialty seen below. The process is fairly intensive -- you're making a laminated dough -- so you may as well make a big batch while you're at it. Bake half to eat now and freeze the rest to enjoy later.

INGREDIENTS:

Topping:

1 kilogram ground lamb (30 percent fat)
100 to 250 grams pomegranate molasses (to taste)
1 teaspoon salt
1 tablespoon ground allspice
50 grams pine nuts

Dough:

1 1/2 kilograms flour
1 tablespoon (10 grams) salt
90 grams butter, at room temperature
3 eggs
660 grams water
Oil, for brushing
600 grams clarified butter

METHOD:

For the topping, mix the ground lamb, pomegranate molasses, salt, allspice, and pine nuts in a large bowl. Let rest while you prepare the dough. If the mixture becomes juicy after it rests, drain the excess liquid.

Combine the flour, salt, 90 grams of butter, eggs, and water in a large bowl, kneading to make a dough. Make mandarin-size balls that are about 9-cm (3 ½ inches) in diameter. Brush oil all over the balls, then place on a baking sheet, cover with plastic wrap, and let rest for 10 to 15 minutes.

Rub the clarified butter with your palms over your work surface (preferably marble) for 7 to 10 minutes, to both soften it and butter the work surface. Once soft and pliable, push the butter to one side. Roll out 1 piece of dough into a circle 16 to 18cm (6 to 7 inches) in diameter, then use your fingers to spread 2 tablespoons of the clarified butter over the dough. Fold over the circle to make a half moon. Repeat with the remaining dough pieces; cover with plastic wrap and let rest for 30 minutes.

Take each half moon-shaped dough and gently stretch with your fingers, until they are 3 cm (1 inch) wide and 60 to 70 cm (23 to 27 inches) long. Position 1 piece so that the short end is parallel to the edge of your work surface, then roll it up (like winding a thread over a spool). Repeat with the remaining pieces, then set aside for 10 minutes. Preheat the oven to 170ºC (325ºF).

Pinch walnut-sized pieces of dough from the dough rolls, then flatten them into discs. Arrange on a baking sheet, leaving a little space in between each disc (you'll need to do this in batches, or use multiple baking sheets). Evenly spread 1 tablespoon of the meat topping over each disc. Bake for 15 to 20 minutes, until golden brown.

Note: *Tahini and onion can be added to the topping. Served with salad and ayran, a diluted yogurt drink.*

MOHAMAD SHADY KHAYATA

KUNAFE NABULSIEH
(KUNAFE FROM NABLUS)

10 servings

Every season

This kunafe is a specialty dessert from Nablus, Palestine. It is served in restaurants or at sweet shops. The mild local cheese, similar to ricotta and mozzarella, should hold its shape when baked -- look for cheese labeled as meant for kunafe in Middle Eastern markets. Shady added a small amount of the sugar syrup to the kunafe during shredding, as he thinks this gives a nice color to the kunafe during baking -- you may do so if you like. Similar kunafe is prepared in Hatay, Şanlıurfa, and Gaziantep, Turkey, using local cheese prepared with goat or sheep's milk.

INGREDIENTS:

1 ½ kilograms sugar

600 milliliters (2 ½ cups) water

2 tablespoons lemon juice, or ½ teaspoon sour salt (citric acid)

400 grams clarified butter, melted

2 kilograms kunafe dough (also called kataifi shredded phyllo dough, available in Middle Eastern markets)

1 kilogram unsalted string cheese (see headnote)

Ground pistachios, to garnish

METHOD:

Combine the sugar and water in a medium saucepan and bring to a boil over medium heat. Boil, uncovered, for 20 to 25 minutes. Remove from heat and stir in the lemon juice. Let the syrup cool to room temperature while you prepare the rest.

Grease a rimmed baking sheet with 2 tablespoons of the melted butter, and then chill for a few minutes, to set. Preheat the oven to 170ºC (325ºF).

Add the remaining butter to the kunafe pastry, mixing well to combine, and then shred the pastry in a meat grinder (or pulse in a food processor), to create tiny pieces of pastry. Press ¾ of the shredded pastry into the tray, using your palms to flatten it evenly. Distribute the cheese over top. Sprinkle the remaining shredded pastry over the cheese layer. Bake (middle rack) for 30 to 35 minutes. Invert the baked kunafe onto a serving platter, and drizzle the syrup over the hot pastry. Garnish with ground pistachio nuts.

Note: *You can also add a bit of orange blossom water to the syrup, for a lovely floral boost.*

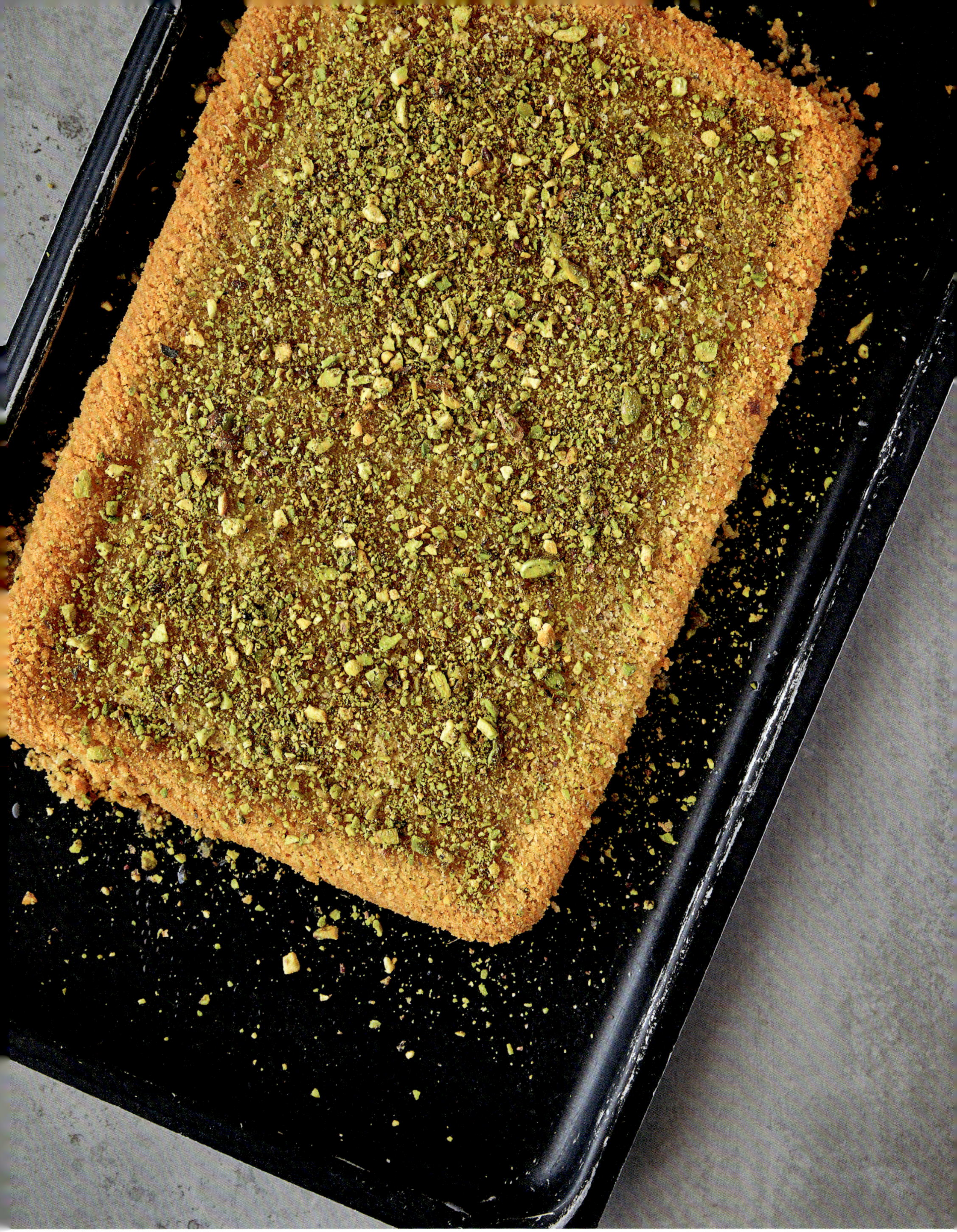

MUYASSAR HAMDAN

Muyassar's family is from Palestine, but she was born in and grew up in Jordan. Even from a young age, she loved to cook and seemed destined to start a food business of her own. She learned how to cook from her mother, while also testing and tweaking her own recipes until she was happy with the results. In 1990, Muyassar moved to Saudi Arabia and started a catering business that specialized in mansaf, a Jordanian specialty of lamb cooked in yogurt. But Saudi Arabia's infrastructure was not accommodating for Muyassar's husband, who uses a wheelchair, so about two years ago Muyassar and her husband left everything to relocate to Istanbul, where he is able to get around more easily. Muyassar restarted her catering company from scratch and now focuses on what are called eastern sweets (as opposed to Western-style cakes and pastries) -- she's known for her mamul, date-filled cookies that are commonly eaten during Eid al-Fitr and Eid al Adha.

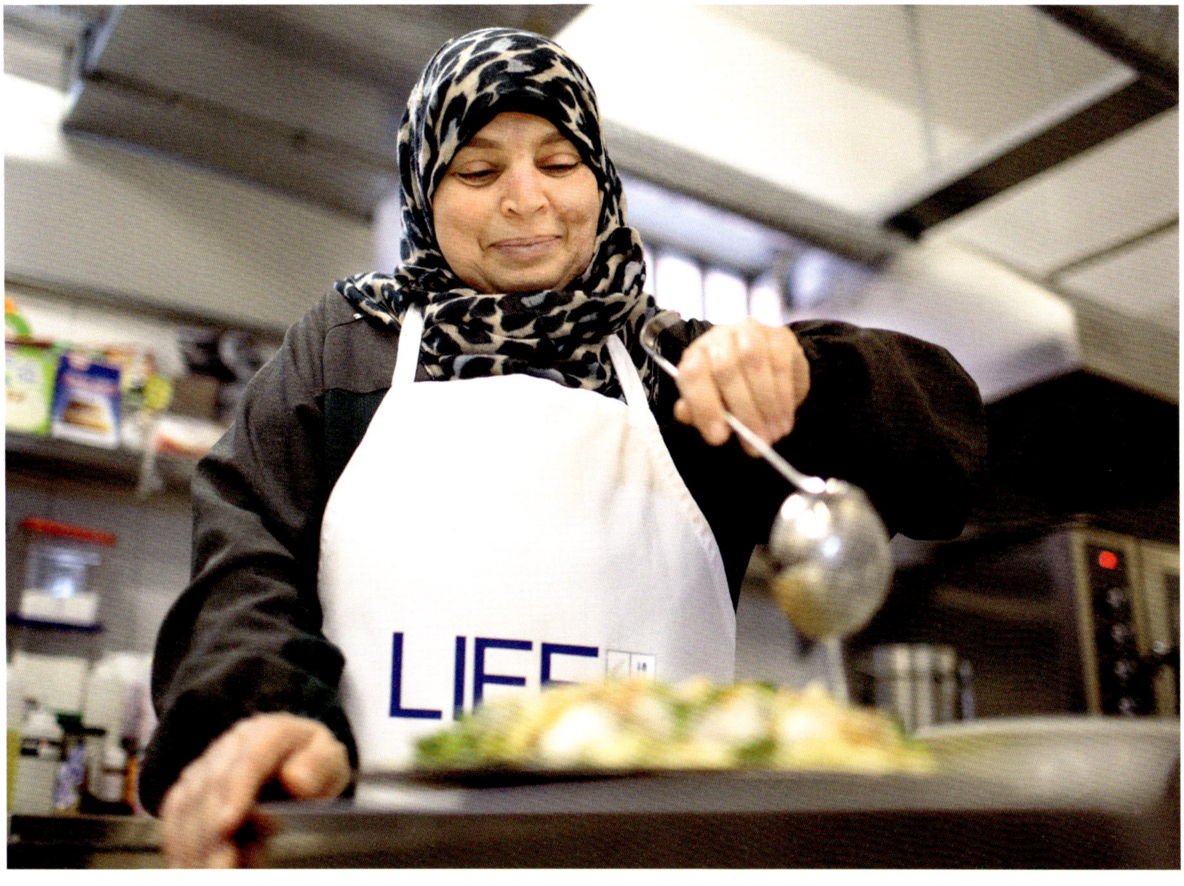
LIFE

MANSAF

(LAMB COOKED IN YOGURT)

5 servings

Every season

This is Muyassar's lighter take on mansaf, a dish traditionally prepared for big occasions like weddings, celebrations, funerals, and other life events. It was also cooked when there was a conflict between families -- they would come together, eat, and try to resolve the dispute -- and so it is associated with peace, happiness, sorrow, and respect. Mansaf has a way of bringing everyone around the table, no matter their relation.

Serve in a large round platter, if you've got one. It's also lovely garnished with toasted pine nuts and pistachios.

The original recipe uses jameed, a dried and salted sheep or goat milk yogurt that is not easy to find outside of Jordan. You may find it in stores or online, sold in liquid form (made by the brand Ziyad) -- follow package instructions to substitute for the dried jameed. If it's not available, leave it out and proceed as written with yogurt.

INGREDIENTS:

1 ½ kilograms bone-in lamb, cut into 200-gram portions

½ cup (120 milliliters) plus 5 tablespoons (70 milliliters) olive oil (may use ghee for a richer dish)

1 onion, peeled and quartered

5 cardamom pods

3 bay leaves

5 cups (1180 milliliters) hot water, plus more as needed

1 kilogram rice

2 kilograms (8 cups) yogurt

1 tablespoon cornstarch

250 grams jameed, chopped and soaked overnight in 2 cups (470 milliliters) of warm water (if available; see headnote)

2 teaspoons salt (or less if using jameed)

¾ teaspoon dried safflower petals

½ cup blanched almonds

2 pieces yufka (unleavened flatbread)

1/3 cup finely chopped parsley

METHOD:

Rinse the meat and pat dry. Warm 3 tablespoons of the oil in a large pot set over medium heat, then add the meat, cover, and cook for 10 minutes. Reduce the heat and add the onion, cardamom pods, and bay leaves; cook for 5 minutes more. Add 5 cups of water, then bring to a simmer and cook for 35 minutes.

Meanwhile, rinse the rice and set aside to drain. Place the yogurt, cornstarch, and soaked jameed and its liquid (if using) in a stand mixer with the whisk attachment, then beat until creamy.

Remove and discard the onion pieces, bay leaves, and cardamom pods from the pot. Ladle some of the meat stock out of the pot and into a large liquid measuring cup, leaving enough in the pot to just cover the meat. Strain the yogurt mix into the pot (to remove any lumps).

Increase the heat to high, bring to a boil, then reduce the heat so that it maintains a simmer. Cook, uncovered, for another 30 minutes, or until the meat is tender. Watch the level of yogurt and add some of the reserved stock if needed -- the liquid should be 15 to 20 cm (6 to 8 inches) high, and you'll want enough for serving.

FOOD, THE GREAT EQUALIZER

MUYASSAR HAMDAN

MANSAF
(LAMB COOKED IN YOGURT)

Warm the ½ cup of oil in a large pot set over medium heat, then add the rice and cook, stirring often, for 10 minutes. If you don't have 6 cups of reserved stock, add water to bring it up to 6 cups, then add it to the rice, along with the 2 teaspoons of salt (start with less salt if using jameed). Rub the safflower between your palms and add to the cooking rice. Cover and bring to a boil. Once the liquid reaches the level of the rice, turn the heat down to medium-low; cook, covered, until the liquid is absorbed, about 20 minutes. If the rice isn't tender, add a little more hot water and keep cooking, checking every few minutes.

Warm the remaining 2 tablespoons of oil in a small skillet and toast the almonds over medium heat for about 5 to 10 minutes, until golden.

Place 1 piece of yufka on your serving dish. Strain some of the yogurt-meat stock over the bread, then top with the rice, followed by the meat. Garnish with the toasted almonds almonds and parsley. Drizzle some liquid from the pot over top.

Cover with the second yufka. Ladle the yogurt sauce into a bowl and serve on the side.

FOOD, THE GREAT EQUALIZER

MUYASSAR HAMDAN

SHARING IS LOVING

SHARING IS LOVING

Artun Ünsal

During my childhood İstanbul was a different city. With a population of less than a million, neighborhoods felt especially close-knit. Practically everyone knew each other; if a new tenant moved to our apartment building, we kids watched our mothers bringing home-cooked meals to the newcomers, sharing because they had no opportunity to cook for themselves during the tiresome task of settling into a new home. During the week, people from our apartment building would stop by to welcome the new residents, bringing along some sort of treat to go with coffee. I remember those times as happy days, our mothers sharing parts of their own history with new arrivals.

Today the mahalle (neighborhood) life and its social relations have changed -- Istanbul is home to at least 15 million people, the buildings are taller, and childhood mainstreets are transformed into shopping centers and food courts. Such modernization and loss of close human connection isn't unique to Istanbul, of course. But do we not reach out to those in need because we have nothing to share, or because we forget that we should help our neighbors, no matter where they come from?
Often people move to a new country to escape the effects of climate change and war. If we exclude or isolate newcomers, we would no longer be human; sharing what we have and caring for our neighbors are simply matters of human ethics and character.

Food proves to be a powerful tool that brings us all together, as the LIFE Project exemplifies. People from many countries come together in the LIFE kitchens, learning from each other and mentors the skills needed to be successful in their own businesses and support themselves. In this way our community feels a little more tight-knit, as we see that sharing our culture is a welcoming act of love.

———

Born in Istanbul, Artun Ünsal studied law and politics in Paris, earned his PhD, and returned to Turkey to pursue a career in academics. He also worked as a journalist and food critic, and appeared on television programs and documentaries on food. He has written several books on Turkish food culture, with his latest, İktidarların Sofrası- Yemek, Siyaset ve Simgesellik (The Table of the Powerful- Food, Politics and Symbolism) coming out in 2019.

NAGLAA ASHOUR

When asked what she wanted to be when she grew up, in the sixth grade, Naglaa replied enthusiastically that she'd be a cook. Naglaa went on to study business administration and marketing in Egypt, but the kitchen and opportunity to gather family around her is what provides limitless joy. She enjoys learning about flavors from other cultures and incorporating them into her own cooking. To her, each taste has a story attached to it -- and remembering and telling these stories make the flavors stronger.

Naglaa moved to Turkey two years ago and wants to start a business that will fight food waste. One initiative would include taking unused or otherwise frequently discarded food from restaurants and repackaging them for those in need. Her organization would also raise awareness about food waste prevention techniques in home kitchens -- which might explain her desire to include a recipe for the bread pudding called Om Ali, made with baked puff pastry or stale croissants.

NAGLAA ASHOUR

OM ALI

(BREAD PUDDING)

8 servings

Prepared during feasts and events, weddings, and Ramadan

The story of this Egpytian dessert, as Naglaa describes, rivals its decadence: There once was a woman named Shajar al-Durr, who was bought as a slave by King Al-Saleh Najmuddin Ayoub. They had a son and eventually married. Shajar al-Durr was literate, educated, and beautiful -- so the king set her free. When King Najmuddin died, Shajar al-Durr kept the news secret to maintain control and rule Egypt. But the Abbasid caliphate in Baghdad did not like a woman sitting on the throne -- leading to many disputes between princes and leaders across the Levant -- so she married Prince Izzedine Aybak and made him responsible for the army, while also forcing him to divorce his wife (Om Ali, meaning Ali's mother) and abandon his son, Mansour Ali. Izzedine Aybak instead withdrew power from Shajar al-Durr and married someone else. Enraged, Shajar al-Durr took her revenge: One day she invited Izzedine Aybak into her home and had five strong men beat him to death in the bathroom. Once his son Ali found out, he, of course, enacted his own revenge, turning Shajar al-Durr over to his mother, who commanded her female slaves to beat her to death with clogs and slippers. To celebrate, Om Ali prepared the dessert that came to take her name.

This bread pudding is served after barbeques in some parts of Egypt, Syria, and Turkey. It's excellent with strawberries, chocolate, whipped cream, or ice cream.

INGREDIENTS:

- 4 sheets puff pastry (400 grams), each stretched/folded into rectangles that are 10-cm-by-20 cm (about 4-by-7 ¾ inches)
- 100 grams hazelnuts, chopped
- 4 ¼ cups (1 liter) milk
- ½ cup (100 grams) sugar, plus more for sprinkling
- 200 grams (205 milliliters) heavy cream
- ½ cup (100 grams) kaymak (see page 22)

Note: *You can use stale croissants instead of puff pastry pieces. Some cooks prefer to add the kaymak at the very end, just before serving.*

METHOD:

Preheat the oven to 180°C (350°F), then bake the puff pastry sheets on baking sheets for about 15 minutes, or until golden. Cut the baked pastry into 2-by-3-cm (¾-by-1 inch) rectangles, then put in a 23-by-33-cm (9-by-13-inch) baking dish. Top with the chopped hazelnuts.

Bring the milk and sugar to a boil in a medium saucepan set over medium-high heat, then add the heavy cream. Pour the mixture over the puff pastry pieces, making sure they are completely covered. Use your hands to tear and scatter the kaymak over top, then sprinkle with some sugar to help the top caramelize.

Bake (middle rack) until the puff pastry absorbs the milk and the top is golden brown, about 10 to 12 minutes. It will be a little jiggly. Serve hot.

SHARING IS LOVING

NAGLAA ASHOUR

BASBOUSA

(SEMOLINA CAKE)

6 servings

Every season, Ramadan

The Egyptian dessert is associated with happy occasions; it's made year-round, but especially during Ramadan. Most of its ingredients are available in every Egyptian house, and the recipe can be tweaked by using more nuts or high-quality butter. In Turkey, the cakes are sold in pastry shops and neighborhood simit carts.

Egyptians love this dessert -- so much so that they flirt with women by calling them basbousa.

INGREDIENTS:

For the cake:
- 1 cup (170 grams) butter, plus 1 tablespoon for greasing
- 1 tablespoon honey
- 2 cups (210 grams) semolina
- 200 grams yogurt
- 1 tablespoon baking powder

For the syrup:
- 1 cup (200 grams) sugar
- 1 cup (250 milliliters) water
- 1 ½ teaspoons freshly squeezed lemon juice
- 1 ½ teaspoons vanilla powder

To garnish:
- 100 grams almonds, blanched and peeled
- 100 grams shelled pistachios, chopped or ground

METHOD:

Preheat the oven to 180ºC (350ºF) and grease a 32-by-32-cm (12-by-12-inch) pan with the tablespoon of butter.

Melt the remaining cup of butter in a saucepan set over medium heat, then remove from heat and add the honey. Add the semolina and mix very well. Stir in the yogurt, just to combine, then stir in the baking powder. Bake for 25 to 35 minutes, until the edges are browned and firm, and the top has dots of golden brown.

During the last five minutes of baking, make the syrup. Boil the sugar and water in a small saucepan, stirring until the sugar dissolves. Add the lemon juice and vanilla. Boil for 4 to 5 minutes, to dissolve the sugar, then turn off the heat. Pour the hot syrup over the finished basbousa, cover with foil, and return to the oven for 10 minutes. Garnish with the nuts.

Note: *You can play around with the topping: use other nuts, grated or desiccated coconut, or even chocolate. Some cooks grease the baking dish with tahini to add a nutty flavor. Mamonia (Syrian semolina pudding) and İrmik Helva (Turkish semolina helva) may be interpreted as versions of basbousa.*

SHARING IS LOVING

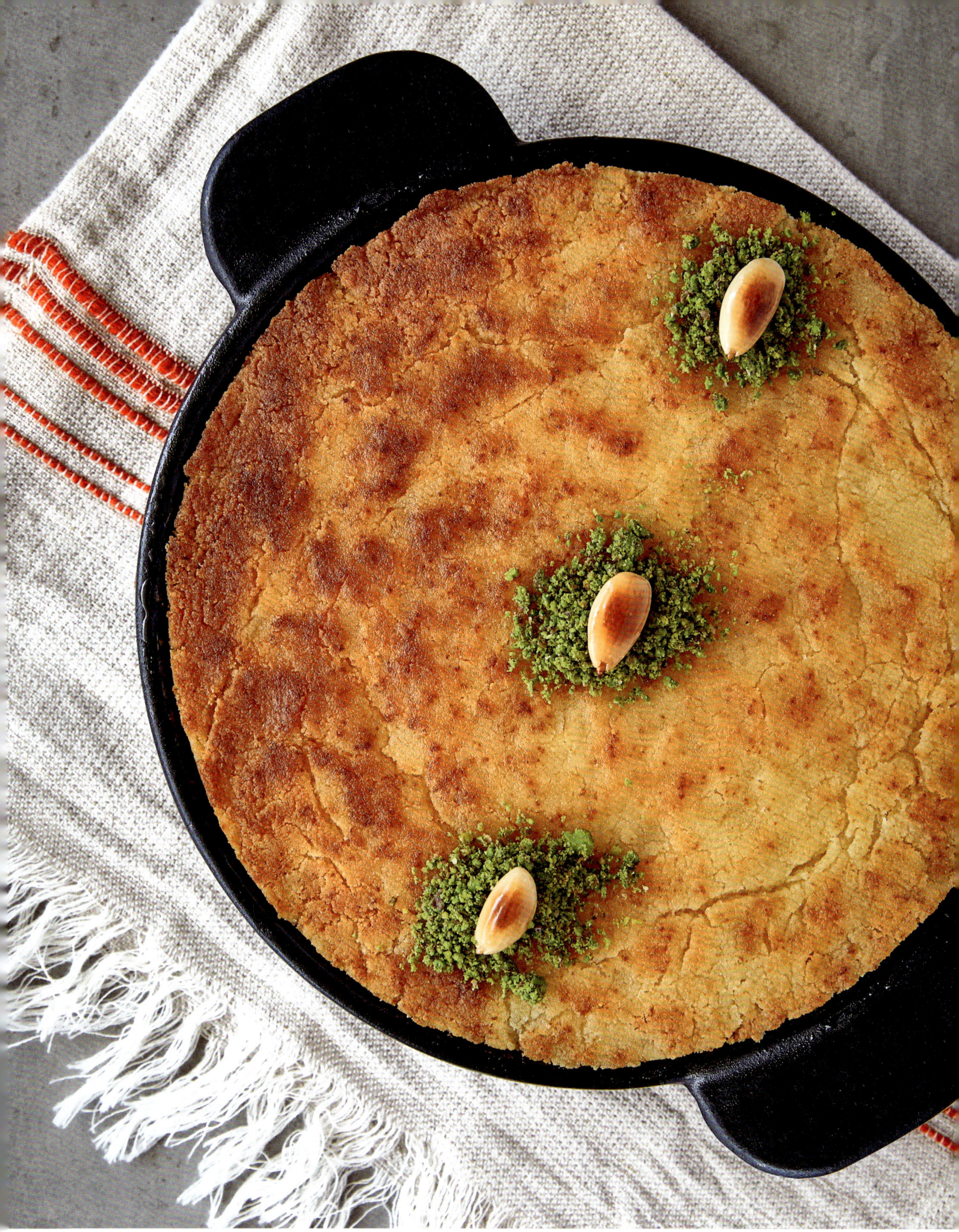

IDENTITY, CULTURE, AND CUISINE

IDENTITY, CULTURE, AND CUISINE

Musa Dağdeviren

Translated into English by Burçak Gürün Muraben

It is possible to overcomplicate culinary history with needlessly conflicting stories about the food's origins. Countries fight fiercely to claim baklava but this dessert existing in varying iterations is not a threat to anyone's national identity -- it is just a dish with different interpretations.

Cultural heritage is the product of geography and the hundreds of civilizations which flourished in it; local ingredients, techniques, and cooking utensils are evidence of a rich culinary history. Regional differences determine the food we eat. Each region has its own special dish, resulting in lore and myth around their creation, but also the people who live in these regions. It's said, for example, that the best cooks come from Antep. Some argue that you can talk about the cuisine of Tokat, but not Amasya. The locals in Iskilip (a town in central Anatolia, Çorum) might get animated when people say their cuisine is part of Çorum cuisine.

If we stepped back to examine our strong food convictions, we would realize that culinary culture is influenced by regional opportunities such as local crops, geographic features, and trade, as well as newcomers who settle and integrate their foodways into the existing ones. Turkish cuisine, for example, is influenced by the many and diverse culinary traditions which have thrived and interacted within its borders. We must remember this as more and more people seek refuge around the world, hoping for a new home but still holding on to parts of their old one. Culinary nationalism has its place, but it is important to remember that when it comes to cuisine we share, what counts is our ability to build a community around the table.

As a chef laboring to understand, learn, and teach the dishes of all the peoples of this country, I am Laz, Circassian, Albanian, Kurdish, Armenian, Bosnian, Assyrian, Turkish, Rum, Arabic, and Roma. I am Turkish, but a citizen of the world.

Musa Dağdeviren was born in Nizip, Turkey. He is an acclaimed chef and the author of The Turkish Cookbook, recently published by Phaidon, as well as the editor and publisher of Yemek, a Turkish food and culture magazine. Mr. Dağdeviren collaborates extensively with NGOs on many aspects of culinary culture, including food and identity, and currently carries out field-work all over Turkey to revive disappearing cooking techniques, vessels, and ingredients. He was featured on the fifth season of Netflix's "A Chef's Table."

NIZAR AKRAM ELKHARRAT

Nizar learned how to cook from his mother, whom he calls his first teacher in life. He's had a varied and multi-faceted career, working in hotels, restaurants, residential supply, humanitarian aid work, and even as an actor. Nizar was born in Damascus, Syria, but also lived in Cairo for a time. He moved to Turkey in 2014, where he heads the Syrian Community in Istanbul, a volunteer organization.

After moving to Turkey, Nizar excelled in cooking -- in part because he lived alone and had to cook for himself. He wants to open a catering business and is particularly passionate about helping Syrian women find their footing in their own food businesses. He also works as an export manager for a Syrian and Turkish company and continues to act in television shows.

NIZAR AKRAM ELKHARRAT

BATERSH

(SMOKY EGGPLANT PUREE)

4 servings

During summer

Batersh is the most famous dish from the west-central city of Hama, Syria. It is similar to the Turkish ali nazik (eggplant with yogurt) and hünkar beğendi (eggplant with a béchamel sauce). Make batersh during the summer, when eggplants are at their peak. Some cooks strain the yogurt a day in advance to make a more creamy and flavorful puree; you can also garnish it with minced parsley rather than green onion. Be sure to toast the pine nuts to bring out their intense sweet notes. Serve batersh as a main dish or an appetizer.

INGREDIENTS:

- 4 large globe eggplants (1 kilogram total)
- 1 ½ teaspoons salt
- 3 cloves garlic (20 grams)
- 1 tablespoon (15 milliliters) olive oil
- 2 cups (500 grams) yogurt
- 2 tablespoons (20 grams) tahini
- 2 tablespoons fresh lemon juice

For the topping:
- 3 tablespoons (30 grams) butter
- 2 shallots, chopped (40 grams total)
- 450 grams lamb loin, chopped into 1-cm (½-inch) cubes
- 2 tablespoons (10 grams) tomato paste
- 1 cup (250 milliliters) tomato juice
- ½ teaspoon freshly ground black pepper
- ½ teaspoon salt
- 1 teaspoon baharat, optional (see note)

To garnish:
- 3 tablespoons (30 grams) pine nuts, toasted
- ½ teaspoon Aleppo pepper flakes (may substitute ¼ teaspoon crushed red pepper flakes)
- 1 green onion, sliced (20 grams)
- 2 tablespoons (20 grams) clarified butter, melted

METHOD:

Preheat the oven to 200ºC (400ºF). Prick the eggplants with a fork and bake on a foil-lined baking sheet for 40 minutes, turning a few times, until the eggplants have collapsed and are well-charred on all sides. Wrap the eggplants with the foil and let rest for 15 to 20 minutes.

Carefully remove and discard the charred skin. Finely chop the eggplant flesh, then put in a bowl and mash with a fork or a wooden spoon. Mash the salt and garlic into a paste in a mortar and pestle, then add to the eggplant, along with the olive oil, yogurt, tahini, and lemon juice. Mix well, then spread onto a serving plate.

Make the topping: melt the butter in a large skillet over medium-high heat, then add the shallots and cook for a few minutes, to soften. Add the lamb and cook for 15 minutes on low heat (the lamb will not be cooked all the way through). Stir in the tomato paste, tomato juice, black pepper, salt, and baharat, if using. Continue cooking until all the juice is absorbed by meat, then spread over the eggplant puree. Garnish with the toasted pine nuts, red pepper flakes and finely chopped green onion, then drizzle the clarified butter over top.

Note: You can also char the eggplants over the flame of a gas stove, turning occasionally until collapsed. This will infuse them with an extra smoky flavor. To make baharat, combine 20 grams allspice, 5 grams black peppercorns, 5 grams cinnamon pieces, 3 grams cloves, 2 grams nutmeg, 2 grams cardamom, and 2 grams ground ginger. Grind in a spice grinder or mortar and pestle, then store in an airtight container.

NIZAR AKRAM ELKHARRAT

BASMASHKAT

(ROLLED STEAK WITH RICE FILLING)

5 servings

During winter and spring

Basmashkat is a traditional dish from Damascus, with many variations. Some cooks add peas, chopped onion, and grated carrot to the filling. Others use mushrooms and grated cheese instead of rice. The rolled steaks can be cooked in tomato puree (perhaps flavored with herbs) instead of boiled in plain water. To keep the filling snugly in the rolls, cooks will sew or tie the ends with string, or use toothpicks to keep them shut. In any case, the steak must be pounded so that it's no thicker than 1 cm. A skillful cook can fit a good amount of filling in the rolled steak, but don't be alarmed if you're not able to do so the first time.

INGREDIENTS:

600 grams thin sirloin steaks
100 grams ground beef
2 tablespoons (25 grams) butter
½ teaspoon salt
1 teaspoon (2 grams) ground cumin
½ teaspoon (1 gram) ground ginger
1 teaspoon (1 gram) freshly ground black pepper
½ teaspoon (1 gram) cardamom seeds, crushed
2 tablespoons (20 grams) pine nuts
1 teaspoon saffron threads, steeped in 2 tablespoons boiling water (may substitute safflower)
½ cup (100 grams) short-grain rice

For the sauce:
2 tablespoons (40 grams) unsalted butter
2 tablespoons (10 grams) flour
2 tablespoons (20 grams) tomato paste
½ teaspoon (1 gram) salt
½ teaspoon (1 gram) freshly ground black pepper
1 ½ cups plus 3 tablespoons (400 milliliters) warm water

METHOD:

Put a steak on a cutting board, cover it with a piece of wax paper, and use a mallet or rolling pin to pound the meat to an even thickness of 1-cm. Repeat with the remaining steaks.

Use your hands to mix the ground beef, butter, salt, cumin, ginger, black pepper, cardamom, pine nuts, saffron and its steeping liquid, and rice in a large bowl. Our filling is ready.

Bring a large pot of water to a boil. Put a steak on a piece of foil (the foil should be the size of a sheet of paper, or about four times the size of the steak). Place 1 tablespoon of rice filling along the bottom end of a steak. Roll the steak into a fat cigar shape, then position the roll along the bottom center of the foil. Wrap the roll with the foil and twist each end of foil to secure the steak rolls. Repeat with the remaining filling and steak. When all steaks are filled and wrapped, drop them into the boiling water and cook until the meat is tender, about 1 hour. Remove and let rest until they're cool enough to handle, then unwrap and arrange on a serving plate.

When the rolls are almost finished cooking, start the sauce. Melt the butter in a medium skillet over medium heat, then add the flour and cook, stirring, until the flour turns golden brown, about 10 minutes. Add the tomato paste, salt, and pepper, stirring until smooth. Add the warm water and mix well to prevent lumps. Simmer until the sauce thickens, about 10 minutes more. Pour the sauce over the finished steak rolls.

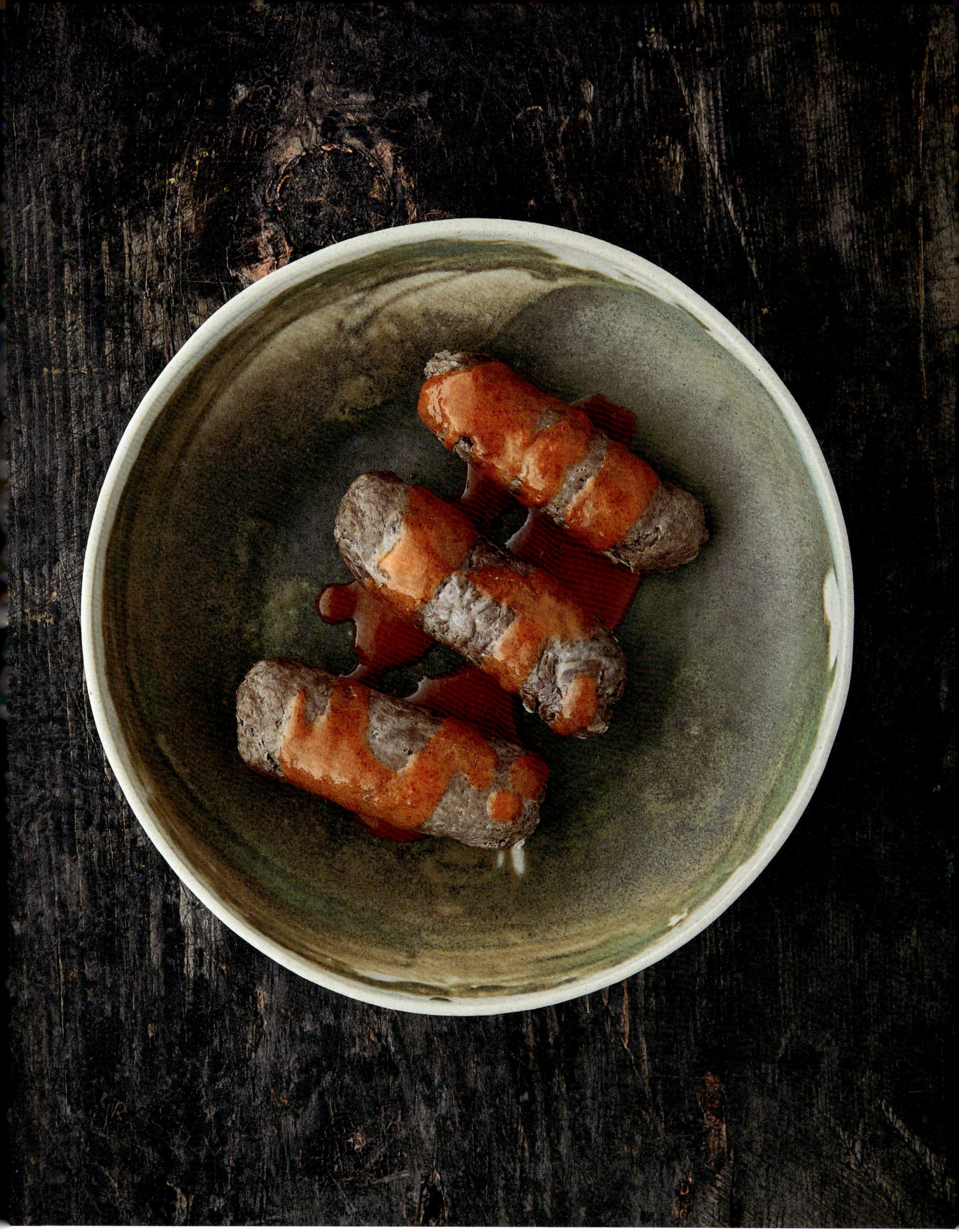

TATAR BARAK

(DUMPLINGS IN YOGURT-TAHINI SAUCE)

4 servings

During all seasons

These hat-like dumplings are popular in the Middle East and Central Asia. They require a good amount of time, as they're folded by hand. It's common for neighbors or family members to help, with some families even hosting a dumpling day filled with cooking and, of course, eating of dumplings.

INGREDIENTS:

For the dough:
- 1 ½ cups (160 grams) flour
- ½ cup plus 1 ½ teaspoons (125 milliliters) water
- ½ teaspoon salt
- 1 tablespoon (4 grams) milk powder
- 2 tablespoons (30 milliliters) olive oil, plus more for brushing
- 1 tablespoon (3 grams) wheat starch

For the filling:
- 3 tablespoons (40 milliliters) olive oil
- 2 tablespoons (20 grams) finely chopped onion
- 200 grams ground lamb
- ½ teaspoon salt
- ½ teaspoon freshly ground black pepper
- 2 tablespoons (12 grams) pine nuts

For the sauce and garnish:
- 2 cups (500 grams) yogurt
- ¼ cup (40 grams) tahini
- 1 teaspoon salt
- ¼ cup (60 milliliters) cream
- 3 tablespoons (15 grams) pine nuts, toasted in 3 tablespoons (30 grams) clarified butter

Note: *Variations include cooking the dumplings in a yogurt, starch and water sauce, and baking rather than boiling the dumplings. You can also garnish simply with chopped parsley.*

METHOD:

Make the dough: combine the flour, water, salt, milk powder, olive oil, and wheat starch in a large bowl, mixing to form a soft dough. Add more or less water as needed. Brush the dough with a little olive oil, then cover it with plastic wrap and let rest for 10 to 15 minutes.

While the dough is resting, make the filling: warm the oil in a large skillet set over medium-high heat. Add the onion and ground lamb and cook, stirring often, until the meat loses its pink color. Add the salt and pepper and keep cooking until the liquid evaporates. Stir in the pine nuts, then remove from heat.

Roll out the dough with a rolling pin to an even 2-mm (a little more than 1/16th-inch) thickness. (You should not need to flour or oil the work surface.) Cut 7-cm (2 ¾-inch) circles with a glass or other cutter. Add 1 tablespoon meat filling into the center of each circle, then fold each into a half moon shape, using your fingers to pinch and seal around the edges. Fold each half moon in half, so that the two pointed ends meet in the middle; pinch the ends together to form a hat-like shape.

Once you've shaped all the dumplings, bring a large pot of water to a boil. Slide the dumplings in and cook for 15 to 20 minutes, until tender. Use a slotted spoon to transfer the dumplings to a serving dish.

While the dumplings are cooking, prepare the sauce: strain the yogurt through a colander (to remove any lumps), then mix with the tahini, salt, and cream. Spoon over the cooked dumplings and top with the pine nuts in butter.

IDENTITY, CULTURE, AND CUISINE

NIZAR AKRAM ELKHARRAT

SILIQ BIL ZEYT

(CHARD WITH OIL)

4 servings

During Swiss chard season

The traditional way of preparing Swiss chard is to separate stalks from the leaves -- the leaves are used for this dish while the stalks are used for Chard Mutabal (recipe follows). Since the two have different textures and cooking times, it's best to prepare them separately. Sılıq Bil Zeyt is such a light and beautiful dish that it can accompany meat and chicken or be served plain as an appetizer.

INGREDIENTS:

½ cup (125 milliliters) olive oil
3 cloves garlic, minced
500 grams Swiss chard (leaves only), washed, dried, and cut into 2-cm (¾-inch) ribbons
2 tablespoons (10 grams) finely chopped cilantro
1 teaspoon (5 grams) salt
Juice of 1 lemon
2 tablespoons (30 grams) pomegranate seeds (optional)

METHOD:

Warm the oil in a large skillet set over medium heat, then add the garlic. Cook for 3 to 4 minutes, then add the chard leaves in batches, stirring with each addition. Cover and cook for 10 to 12 minutes. (Do not add any water -- the chard will release some liquid of its own.)

Stir in the cilantro, salt, and lemon juice. Cook on medium-high until the liquid evaporates, about 10 to 15 minutes. Garnish with pomegranate seeds, if using.

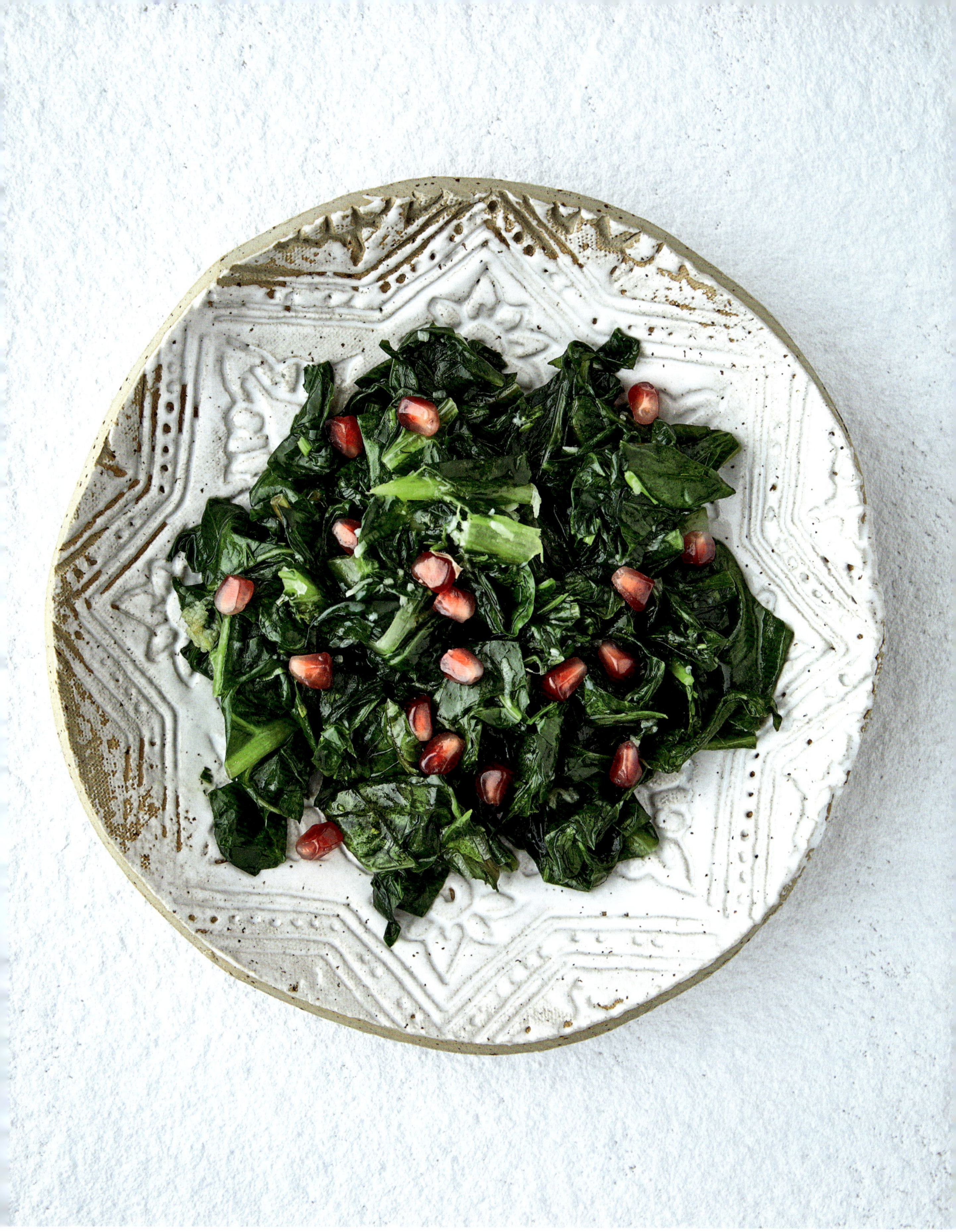

SILIQ MUTABAL

(CHARD STALKS IN YOGURT SAUCE)

4 servings

During Swiss chard season

When Sılıq Bil Zeyt (chard with oil) is prepared, the stalks of the chard are used for this dish -- yet another way to use every last bit of your ingredients.

INGREDIENTS:

3 tablespoons (40 ml) olive oil

1 clove garlic

2 cups (80 grams) chopped Swiss chard stalks, cut in ½-cm (¼-inch) chunks

1 cup (250 grams) yogurt

2 tablespoons (25 grams) tahini

Juice of ½ lemon

½ teaspoon (2 grams) salt

2 tablespoons (30 grams) pomegranate seeds

METHOD:

Warm the oil in a large skillet set over medium-high heat, then add the garlic and cook for a few minutes. Add the chard stalks, cover, and reduce the heat to low. Cook until the stalks are quite tender, about 30 minutes. Remove from heat and let cool slightly.

Add the yogurt, tahini, lemon juice, and salt. Mix well, transfer to a serving dish, and garnish with pomegranate seeds, if using.

Note: *In the original recipe, the chopped stalks are boiled, drained and combined with the remaining ingredients. To preserve the flavor and nutrients of the stalks, Nizar prefers to cook the stalks in their own juices. Partially steamed chard stalks also make excellent pickles.*

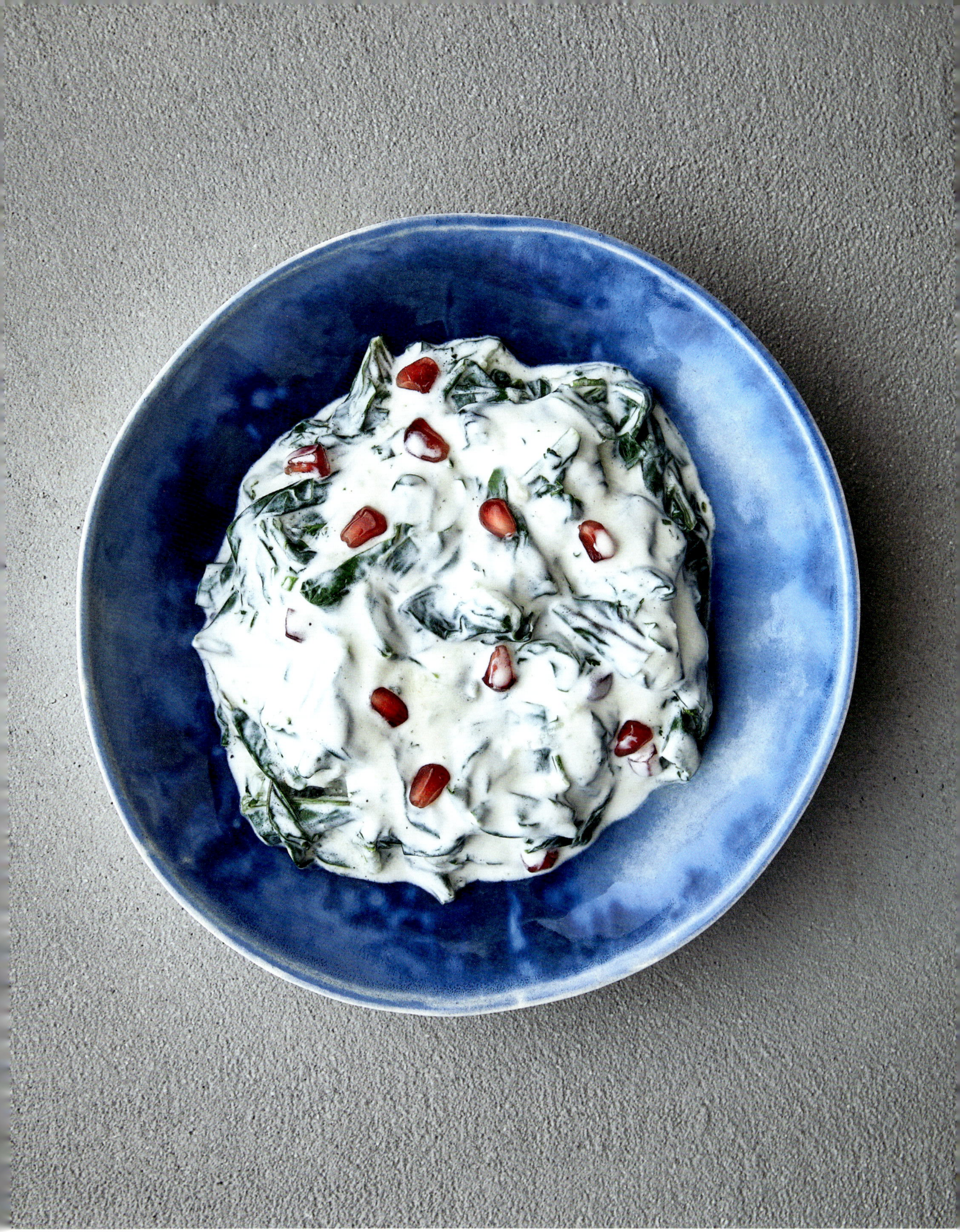

A TASTE FOR CHANGE?

A TASTE FOR CHANGE?

Paul Newnham

Food is extremely personal -- what we eat is tied to so many things. A compilation of religion, culture, place, family, and memories influence what we each see as tasting good. This element, taste, is critical; if we are to achieve any voluntary shifts in our food system, we need to strongly consider taste -- the chef's domain, passion, and livelihood.

Chefs have a growing influence on what we eat -- globally, people increasingly eat food prepared by someone outside of the home, which means chefs play an important role at the heart of our food system. Their voices impact trends as we look to them to help us address health concerns like allergies and special diets.

Being so central to the food system, chefs have great respect for the world's natural larder and work in tandem with these processes, accounting for seasonality and surplus. As a result, they can help introduce a colorful array of new ingredients onto our plates that are not only tasty but also improve health and reduce food waste. Through their menus, chefs can help us realize the value of food by illustrating its true cost and telling the stories of the people who grow it.

Educating chefs with a framework that connects their passion and knowledge with pressing global issues is critical. We must provide them with an action plan that is holistic and relevant.

The Chefs' Manifesto is one of many examples designed to help chefs have an impact on people, the planet, and farmers. Developed by chefs for chefs, it brings together more than 440 chefs from around the world to explore how they can help deliver a sustainable food system. As they bridge the gap between farm and fork, the Chefs' Manifesto empowers chefs with a framework tied to the United Nations Sustainable Development Goals. This framework consists of simple, practical actions chefs can take in the following eight areas:

Paul Newnham is the director of the SDG2 Advocacy Hub, a project coordinating global campaigns and advocacy groups to achieve the UN Sustainable Development Goal 2: to end hunger, achieve food security and improved nutrition, and promote sustainable agriculture by 2030. Mr. Newnham has over 20 years' experience in campaigning, youth mobilization, advocacy, marketing, and communication. He has worked in communities throughout Africa, Asia, the Middle East, Europe and the Americas. Mr. Newnham serves on the LIFE Project Advisory Council.

1. Ingredients grown with respect for the earth and its oceans
2. Protection of biodiversity and improved animal welfare
3. Investment in livelihoods
4. Value natural resources and reduce waste
5. Celebration of local and seasonal food
6. A focus on plant-based ingredients
7. Education on food safety, healthy diets, and nutritious cooking
8. Nutritious food that is accessible and affordable for all

Chefs have a critical role to help everyone explore tasty options that are good for farmers, people, and planet. This ensures that everyone's kitchens address global needs -- from refugee culinary training, to ending food waste, to using locally grown products.

NİSAN DOĞAN

Apricots have always played a role in Nisan's life. She was born and raised in Malatya, in Eastern Anatolia -- the region is the largest apricot producer in Turkey, and the production of fresh and dried apricots is one of the main sources of income for its residents, including Nisan's family. Nisan is the middle child, with two older and two younger siblings. She describes herself as the most quiet member of her family -- but when required, the most vocal. Her childhood memories often involve food, specifically apricots: her siblings and she would compete to see who could fit 30 apricot seeds into one dried apricot.

Nisan went to Istanbul to study law, eventually settling there and working as a lawyer. She has always cooked, though, and she and her family, noticing that healthy snacks were becoming more trendy, decided to start their own snack business called Grab The Sun -- they specialize in sun-dried and chocolate-covered apricots. With the business and market training received through the LIFE Project, Nisan will be able to help her family's business grow, even as she continues to practice law.

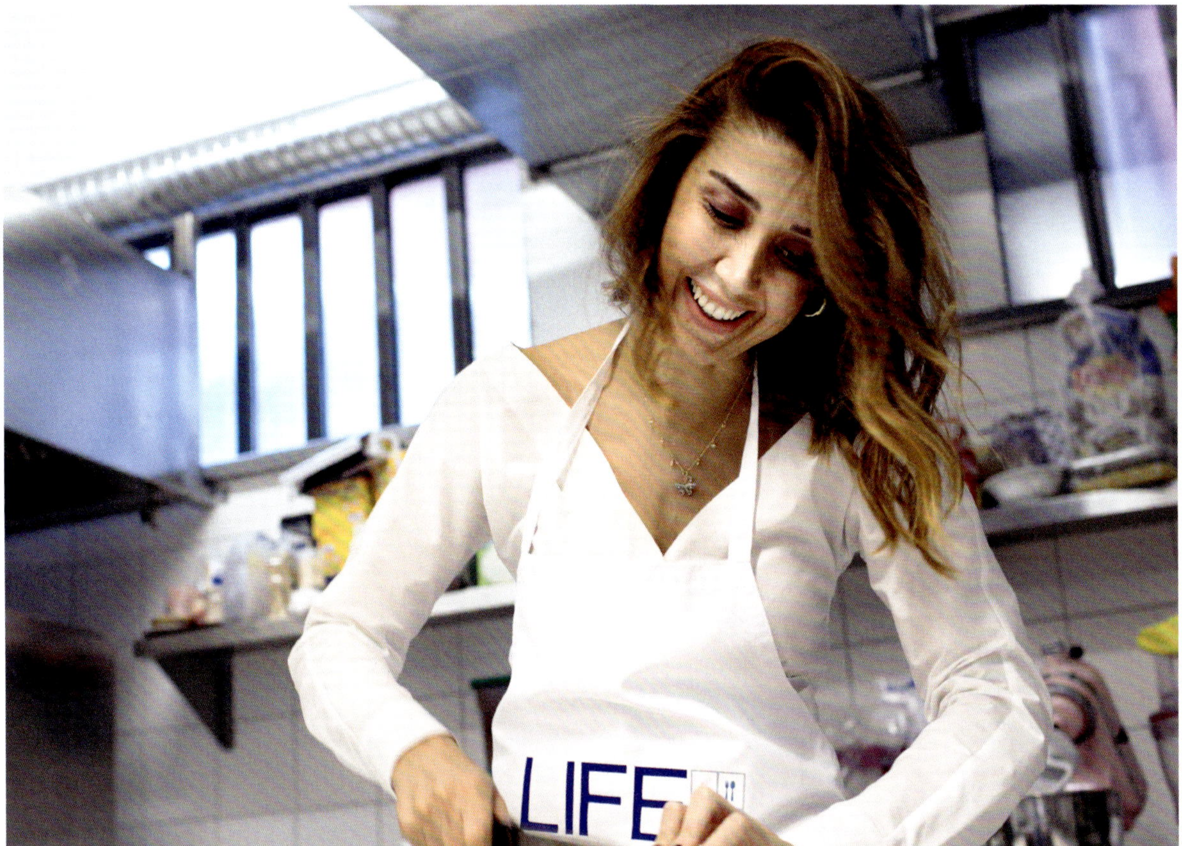
LIFE

CEVİZLİ KAYISI KAVURMASI

(DRIED APRICOTS WITH WALNUTS)

10 servings

Fall, winter, and spring

Since Malatya is famous for its wide variety of pungent, sweet, and colorful apricots, the fruit is used in many dishes. This dried apricot dessert is quite popular -- it's easy and just the thing for when a guest arrives after dinner, or an unexpected guest comes for afternoon tea.

INGREDIENTS:

For the apricots:

250 grams dried apricots
Water, for soaking
50 grams butter
2 cups (250 grams) walnuts, coarsely ground or chopped
1 cup (200 grams) kaymak (see page 22; may substitute clotted cream)

For the syrup:

4 cups (945 milliliters) water
2 cups (400 grams) sugar
2 to 3 cloves (to taste)
1 tablespoon fresh lemon juice

METHOD:

Soak the dried apricots in water for one hour, until softened. Drain and put them on paper towels, then pat dry.

Make the syrup: stir the water, sugar, and cloves in a medium saucepan over medium heat. Bring to a boil, stirring to dissolve the sugar, then add the lemon juice and continue boiling for 5 minutes. Remove from heat.

Warm the butter in a large skillet set over medium heat, then add the apricots. Cook for 7 to 8 minutes, turning over to make sure both sides are glazed by butter.
The color of the apricots should be light brown. Pour the syrup over the apricots, then top with the ground walnuts. Boil gently over medium heat for a few minutes, then remove from heat and let cool.

When the syrup and apricots are at room temperature, drain the excess syrup, keeping the walnuts with the apricots. (Reserve the syrup to serve on the side or use in cakes and cookies.)
Arrange in a serving dish and serve with the kaymak.

Note: *You can halve or quarter the dried apricot before soaking in water, so that they'll absorb even more sugar and butter (and have a richer taste). Some may prefer sprinkling the ground walnuts on the cooked apricots before serving with the clotted cream, rather than cooking the walnuts. This sweet can be served with tea or coffee and take the place of cookies for those who don't consume gluten.*

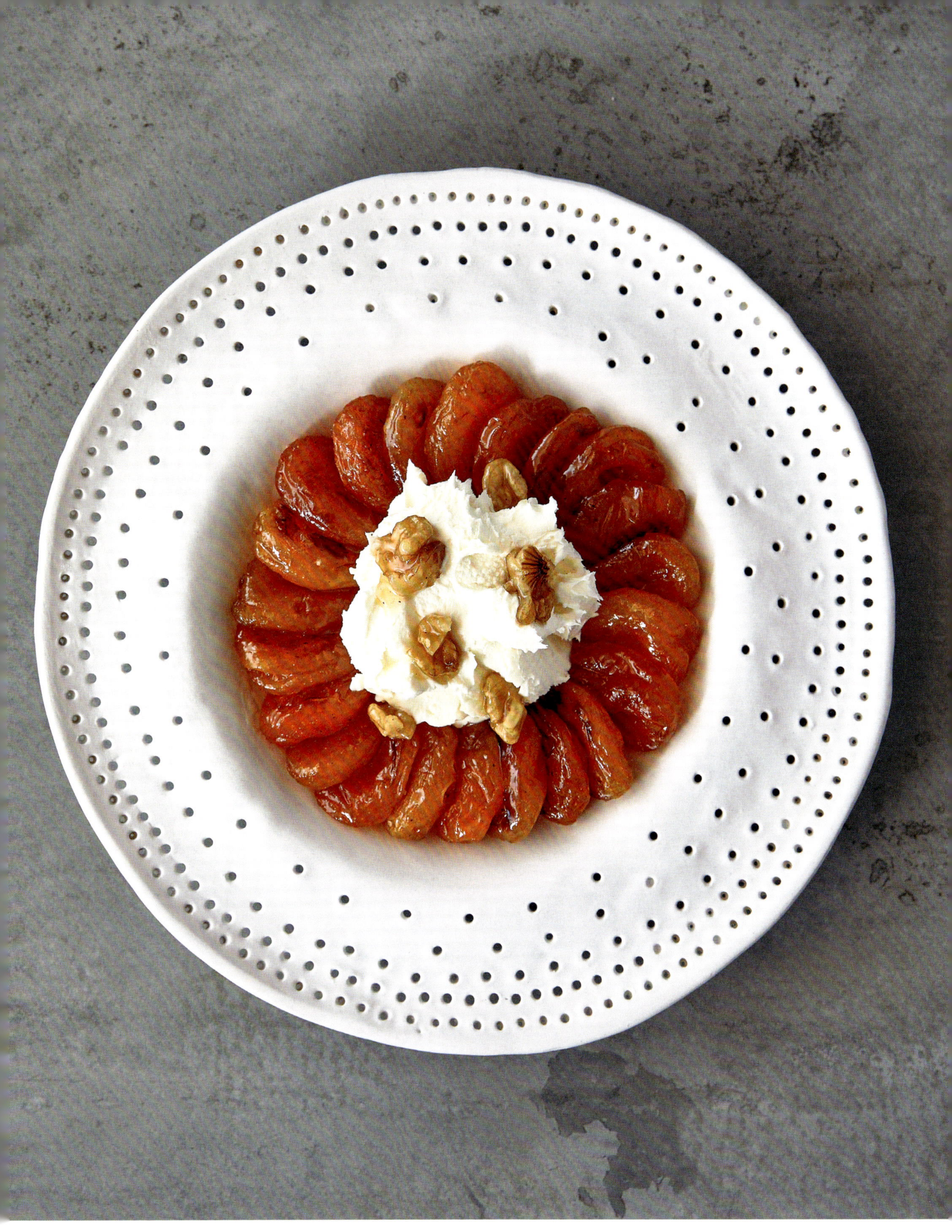

ÖZGÜL İNALİ

Özgül began her career as a retailer in Istanbul's bustling Grand Bazaar, one of the oldest (and largest) covered markets in the world, before working in accounting for several years. When pregnant with her first child, she quit her office job, embraced her entrepreneurial spirit, and, after having her baby, opened a retail store to sell children's items. A crisis in the textile sector forced her to close her business, but Özgül still wanted to work and help support her family. She turned to food, something that's been in her life ever since her childhood in Kars, Turkey. Özgül first opened a butcher shop, and, in order to use up leftover meat and avoid waste, she opened a doner kebap shop right next door. An investor then approached her with an offer to partner in another kebap restaurant. She's since moved on to run a Çiğ Köfte (popular chain restaurant) for five years, all the while honing and developing her business skills -- and of course, cooking the delicious food from her hometown.

ÖZGÜL İNALİ

HANGEL

(MANTI WITHOUT FILLING)

8 servings

Every season

This is an indispensable dish from Kars. Although it's in the same family as manti (dumplings), these fresh noodles are not stuffed -- rather, you'll make a dough and top them with a garlicky yogurt sauce and golden fried onions. Özgül's mother used to prepare this for neighbors and friends -- after a while, friends started dropping by just to eat hangel, as she made the most delicious version.

INGREDIENTS:

For the garnish and sauce:
- 1 cup (250 milliliters) olive oil
- 3 medium onions, coarsely chopped (750 grams total)
- 2 cloves garlic
- Pinch of salt
- 2 cups (500 grams) yogurt

For the dough:
- 4 cups (450 grams) flour, plus more for sprinkling
- 1 cup (250 milliliters) water
- 1 egg
- 2 tablespoons (12 grams) salt

METHOD:

To make the garnish, warm the oil in a deep skillet over medium-low heat, add the onion, and cook until the onion is soft and caramelized, about 25 minutes.

Meanwhile, make the sauce: crush the garlic with a pinch of salt, then stir into the yogurt. Spread about 5 tablespoons of the yogurt over a serving dish.

Make the dough by kneading the flour, water, egg and salt in a large bowl until firm. Divide into four pieces. Let rest while you tend to the onions.

Lightly flour a work surface, then roll each piece to a thickness of ¼ cm (a little less than ⅛ inch). Cut into 2- to 3-cm (¾- to 1-inch) squares. Sprinkle some flour over the squares to keep them from sticking.

Bring a large pot of water to a boil, then drop in the dough squares and cook for 5 to 7 minutes, until they float to the top. Strain in a colander and rinse with cold water, then transfer to the serving dish. Top with the remaining yogurt and drizzle with the oil and onions.

Note: *You can prepare the dough in advance and lay over a piece of cloth to dry, so that it's even easier to prepare for unexpected guests or family members. In Kars, hangel is also served with butter and çeçil cheese (local string cheese), if the yogurt and onion sauce is not preferred.*

A TASTE FOR CHANGE?

ÖZGÜL İNALİ

PATLICAN GÜVEÇ

(EGGPLANT AND LAMB STEW IN AN EARTHENWARE POT)

8 servings

Summer, when eggplants are best

This dish is full of happy memories for Özgül -- she learned how to make it from her manager, who would prepare it three times per week for his colleagues. After preparing the vegetables in the earthenware pot, it is traditionally baked at the local bakery, then brought back to be served family-style, right from the pot.

INGREDIENTS:

500 grams boneless leg of lamb, cut into 2- to 3-cm (¾- to 1-inch) cubes

2 tablespoons plus ½ cup (125 milliliters) olive oil

300 grams pearl onions, peeled

6 cloves garlic, coarsely chopped

4 Japanese eggplants (1300 grams), chopped into 2-cm (¾-inch) cubes

4 medium tomatoes (600 grams), peeled and coarsely chopped

4 long green peppers (225 grams), cut into pieces 2 to 3 cm (¾ to 1 inch) long

2 hot green peppers (120 grams), optional

1 teaspoon pepper paste

1 cup (250 milliliters) water

½ teaspoon freshly ground black pepper

1 teaspoon salt

1 teaspoon crushed red pepper flakes

1 teaspoon fresh thyme

METHOD:

Preheat the oven to 160ºC (320ºF).

Rub meat with 2 tablespoons of the olive oil, then put at the bottom of a large earthenware pot (or an enameled cast iron pot). Top with the onions, garlic, eggplants, tomatoes, and peppers.

Mix the remaining oil with the pepper paste, water, black pepper, salt, red pepper flakes and thyme. Drizzle over the vegetables. Cover with parchment paper, and put the lid on. Bake for 2 hours, until the meat is tender. Serve with lavash.

Note: *Zucchini, green beans, potatoes and peas can be added for a richer flavor and a colorful look. The pepper paste can be omitted. If there are a lot of visitors around the table, serve with rice or bulgur pilaf, as well as salad, plain yogurt, and pickles.*

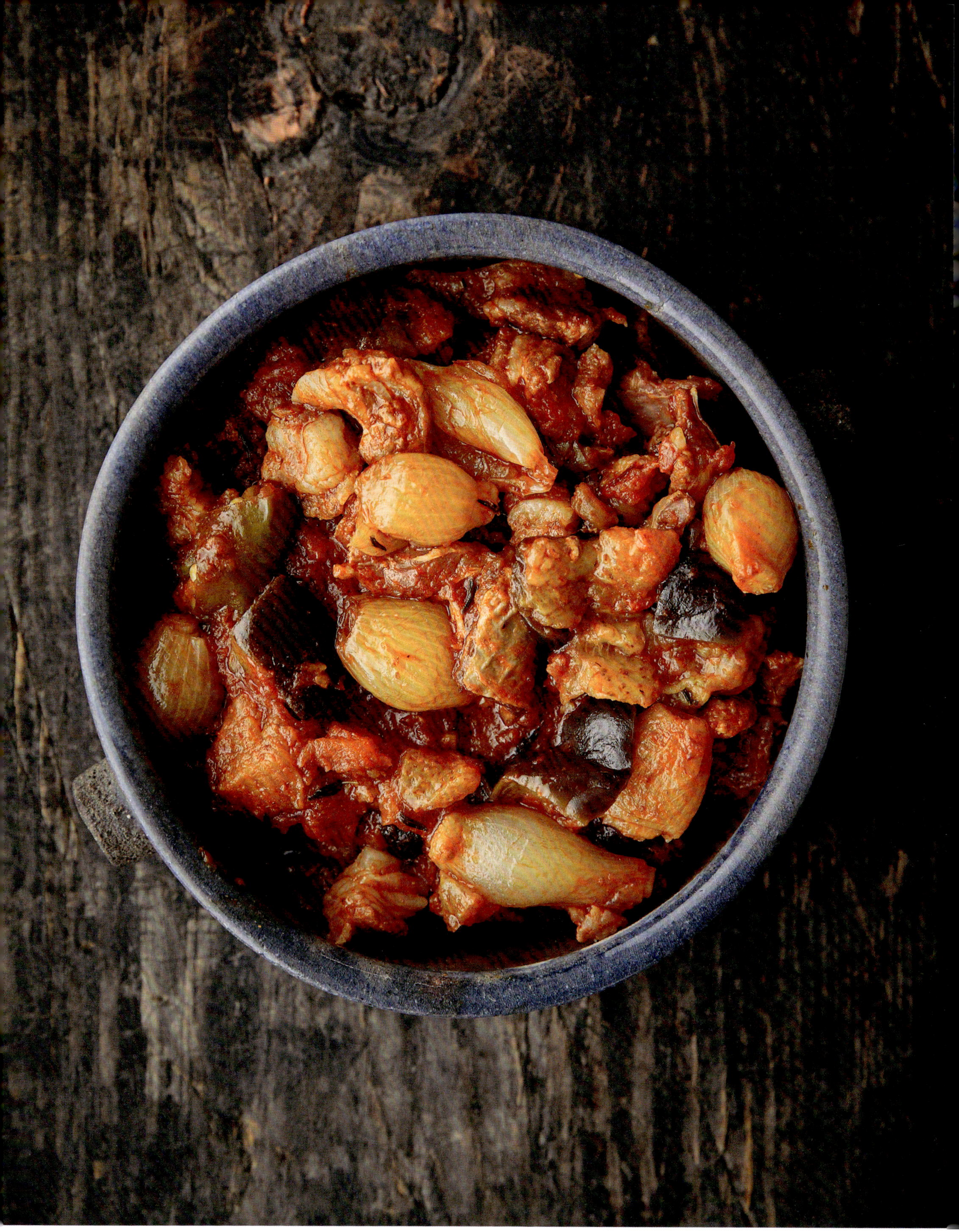

FOOD TO CREATE NEW BEGINNINGS

FOOD TO CREATE NEW BEGINNINGS

David Hertz

Cooking is more than just reproducing a recipe with techniques and precision -- it's a way of relating to the world through understanding traditions, culture, and history. Gastronomy can play a role in overcoming adversity.

In 2004, during my first visit to a favela -- an unregulated hillside town in Brazil -- I was inspired by the perseverance of young people who were constantly searching for opportunities to further their development. A few years later I founded Gastromotiva, with the belief that gastronomy has the power to connect people and begin change in communities. Our project was first implemented in a vulnerable community in São Paulo. We taught students the potential, power, and responsibility that comes with learning about culinary culture.

Since then our organization has trained and employed more than five thousand cooks, helping them get high-paying jobs in the hospitality industry. Our students learn to believe in themselves and their abilities and through the program they learn the importance of working together, listening to each other, and sharing knowledge. Once they've finished the program, the students go on to share their new skills with friends and family, thus expanding our reach. We have supported more than 300 local businesses and provided food education for more than 100,000 families that live in the favelas.

We want to share our core beliefs that education can elevate people out of poverty, and that restoring dignity can change a person's outlook on life and prove the world can be inclusive and fair. From our projects in Brazil, we've expanded to work in Mexico and South Africa, and formed a new partnership with the World Food Program in El Salvador. We hope to further increase our reach and expand all over Latin America.

And we want more. We want to spread the Social Gastronomy Movement, an organization we founded in collaboration with Cargill, that uses the power of food, cooking, and gastronomy to address global societal issues. We actively connect and convene key actors to stimulate learning, share ideas, co-create, and form partnerships.

At the heart of this community is the importance of food as the connective tissue that brings people together. The knowledge obtained through groups that participate in social gastronomy -- including the LIFE Project -- can translate the principles of using food for good to support the needs of the local community. Because only together can we free the world from hunger, malnutrition, and poverty.

David Hertz is a Brazilian-born chef who co-founded Gastromotiva, a socio-gastronomic organization that helped launch the Social Gastronomy Movement, a global initiative to advance social inclusion and eliminate food waste and hunger. During the 2016 Olympics in Rio de Janeiro, Mr. Hertz opened Refettorio Gastromotiva, a no-food-waste cooking school and restaurant, in collaboration with chef Massimo Botura and journalist Alexandra Forbes. He was recently named the 2019 recipient of The Charles Bronfman Prize, given to a humanitarian under fifty whose innovative work, informed by Jewish values, has significantly improved the world.

SAWSAN BAWADEKJI

Aleppo's cuisine is known for its complex flavors, created by a mix of spices, aromatic oils, and various fruits used in cooking. Sawsan was born and raised in this Syrian city, where she learned to cook from her mother, making traditional Aleppine dishes such as kibbeh and stuffed vegetables.

Sawsan studied Education Sciences at the university and went on to become an elementary school teacher and school supervisor. Once she married and moved to Idlib, where her husband is from, and settled into a comfortable life -- she enjoyed cooking for her growing family and was very active in her community. This changed once Sawsan moved to Turkey with her son and daughter in 2011. It was a difficult transition: she no longer had the close connections and community that she did in Syria, she didn't speak Turkish, and she felt like an outsider for being a refugee. During her time in the LIFE Project -- learning next to people from many backgrounds, sitting at the same table, and sharing a meal -- she was able to rebuild a network for herself. Today she feels more confident in her ability to communicate and integrate into the Turkish community.

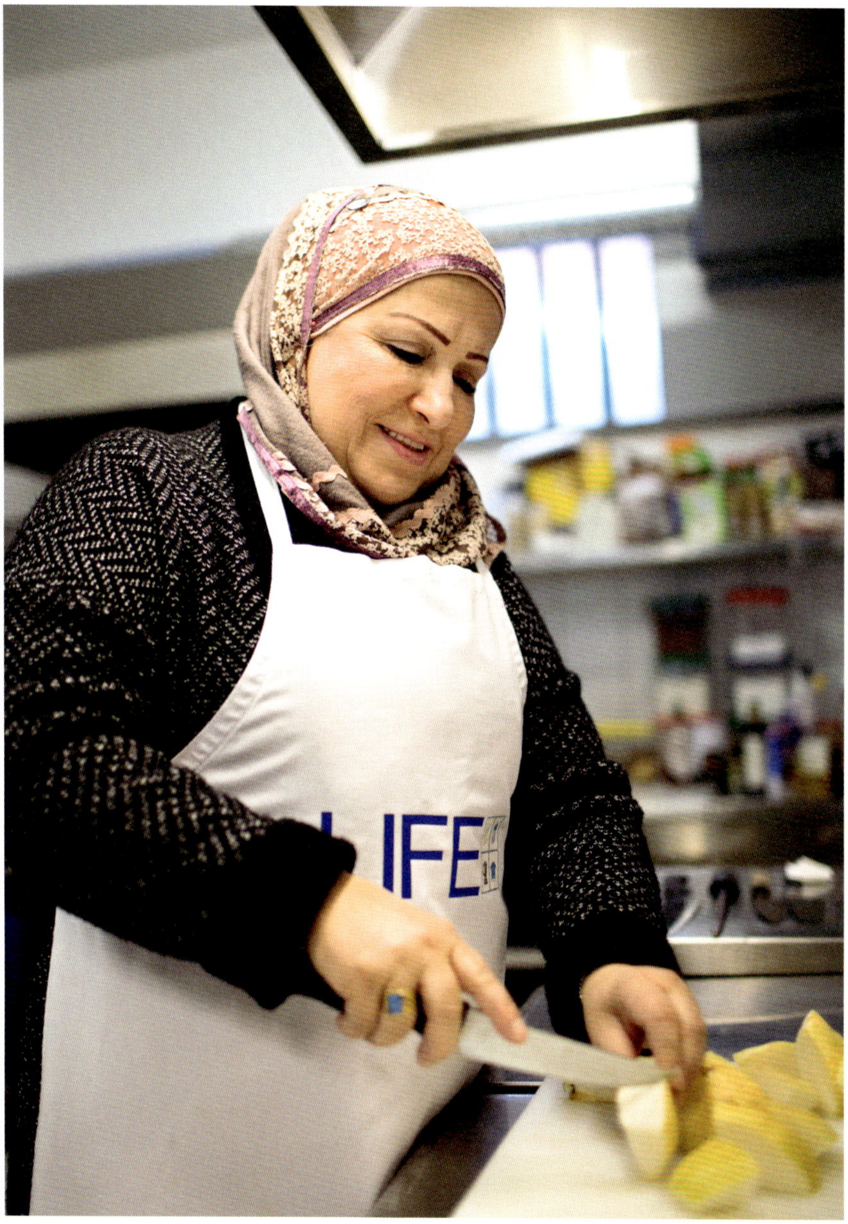
LIFE

SAFARJALIYEH
(QUINCE AND LAMB STEW)

🍴 8 servings

❀ Winter, family celebrations, and holidays

A sprinkle of dried mint ties together the aroma and flavor of the sweet quince combined with the sour notes of pomegranate molasses and tomato paste. For Sawsan, all these ingredients create a magnificent symphony of tastes. You can serve safarjaliyeh with kibbeh or add kibbeh directly to the pot. (Safarjaliyeh with chickpea-size bulgur balls and kibbeh is called Analı, Kızlı, which means "Mothers and Daughters" in southeastern Turkey.) Some cooks use chicken rather than lamb.

INGREDIENTS:

Water, for the quinces

2 tablespoons lemon juice

1 kilogram quinces

150 grams ground lamb fat (optional)

1 cinnamon stick (6 to 7 cm/2 ¼ to 2 ¾ inches)

2 to 3 cloves (to taste)

½ teaspoon (2 grams) Aleppo spice mix (Al-Bhar Al-Halabi), plus more for serving (see note)

3 bay leaves

1 teaspoon (5 grams) freshly ground black pepper

6 to 8 cardamom pods (to taste)

2 kilograms lamb shanks or 1.2 kilograms boneless leg of lamb, cut into 4- to 5-cm (1 ½- to 2-inch) chunks

1 onion (250 grams), peeled but left whole

4 cups (945 milliliters) hot water

2 tablespoons crushed garlic (20 grams)

1 tablespoon dried mint

1 teaspoon (4 grams) salt

7 cups (1650 milliliters/1 kilogram) fresh pomegranate juice (or 1 tablespoon pomegranate molasses mixed with 7 cups of water)

7 cups (1650 milliliters/1 kilogram) tomato juice (or 1 tablespoon tomato paste mixed with 7 cups of water)

½ teaspoon sour salt (or 2 tablespoons/5 grams lemon juice)

METHOD:

Fill a large bowl about halfway with water, then add the lemon juice. Peel, quarter, and core the quinces, then cut each quarter in half widthwise, so that you have 8 quince pieces. Drop the chunks into the bowl as you work (to prevent discoloration).

Cook the ground lamb fat in a large pot set over medium heat for 15 minutes. (If you're not using the lamb fat, warm 3 tablespoons of oil for a few minutes and proceed.) Add the cinnamon stick, cloves, Aleppo spice mix, bay leaves, black pepper, and cardamom pods, stir, and cook until very aromatic, about 30 seconds. Add the lamb chunks and onion. Cook, turning the meat over periodically, until browned on all sides and any liquid has evaporated.

Add the 4 cups of hot water, garlic, dried mint, and salt. Cook, covered, for 45 minutes, or until the meat is tender. Stir in the tomato and pomegranate juices, cover, and cook for another 10 minutes, then add the chopped quinces and the lemon juice (or sour salt) and cook (uncovered) for 10 to 15 minutes, until the quince pieces are easily pierced with the tip of a sharp knife.

Remove the whole onion, then sprinkle with a little more of the spice mix before serving.

Note: To make the Aleppo Spice Mix (Al-Bhar Al-Halabi), toast 500 grams white peppercorns, 200 grams black peppercorns, 100 grams cloves, 50 grams dry ginger, and 50 grams cardamom. Grind with 50 grams nutmeg and 50 grams cinnamon, then store in an airtight container. (You can scale this down if you'd like.)

SAWSAN BAWADEKJI

RIS EL FREEKEH

(FREEKEH WITH RICE AND LAMB)

8 servings

Every season

Rice, bulgur, and freekeh are key ingredients in Middle Eastern cuisine. They can accompany stews or be the star of the meal, especially when aromatic samna (clarified butter) is added. This beautiful dish is more complex than its simple name implies, with velvety rice and crunchy nuts complementing the toasty freekeh and heady spiced lamb shanks. It is presented at the table three ways: One dish holds a mixture of freekeh and rice, topped with ground lamb, nuts, and braised lamb pieces; another holds only the freekeh with the same toppings, and the third just the rice with its toppings. Use glass serving dishes if you have them, to show off the many lovely layers.

INGREDIENTS:

For the lamb stock and lamb:
- 1 teaspoon unsalted butter
- ½ kilogram boneless lamb shank pieces
- 1 onion (220 grams), peeled
- 1 cinnamon stick (4 to 5 cm/1 ½ to 2 inches)
- 2 bay leaves
- 6 to 8 cardamom pods (to taste)
- 1 teaspoon Aleppo spice mix (see recipe, page 214)
- 7 cups (1650 milliliters) hot water

For the nut and ground lamb topping and garnish:
- 2 tablespoons clarified butter
- 50 grams peeled almonds
- 50 grams raw pistachio nuts
- 50 grams raw cashews or pine nuts
- ½ kilogram ground lamb
- ½ teaspoon salt
- ½ teaspoon freshly ground black pepper
- ½ teaspoon ground allspice, optional (for the final garnish)

For the grains:
- 2 cups (350 grams) rice
- Water, for soaking the rice
- ½ kilogram freekeh
- 2 teaspoons (20 grams) clarified butter
- 6-10 cardamom pods (to taste)
- 2 teaspoons salt

METHOD:

Start the stock: melt the butter in a large pot set over medium heat, then add the lamb shanks, onion, cinnamon stick, bay leaves, cardamom kernels, and the Aleppo spice mix. Cook for 10 minutes, stirring occasionally. Add the water, cover, and cook until the meat is tender, about 40 to 50 minutes. Let cool slightly, then strain and reserve the stock, setting the shanks aside for garnishing later. You should have 9 cups (2250 milliliters) of stock; add water if needed.

While the stock is cooking, make the topping: warm 1 tablespoon of the clarified butter in a large skillet set over medium heat, then add the nuts and cook, stirring, for 10 to 12 minutes, until lightly toasted. Set the nuts aside in a bowl, then add the remaining tablespoon of clarified butter to the skillet and stir in the lamb, salt, and pepper. Cook, stirring often, for about 30 minutes, until the liquid has evaporated and the lamb is browned. Combine the nuts and ground lamb -- this is your garnish.

Next, prepare the grains: start the rice soaking in a bowl of water; let sit for 30 minutes, then strain.

Rub the freekeh in between two damp kitchen towels to get rid of any dust. Warm 1 teaspoon of the clarified butter in a large pot set over medium heat, then stir in the freekeh and toast for 15 minutes. Add 3 to 5 cardamom pods (to taste), 1 teaspoon of salt, and 6 cups (1500 milliliters) of the reserved lamb stock. Cover and cook for 30 to 35 minutes, until all the liquid is absorbed by the freekeh. For the last 10 minutes, put the meat chunks over top, to help meld the flavors.

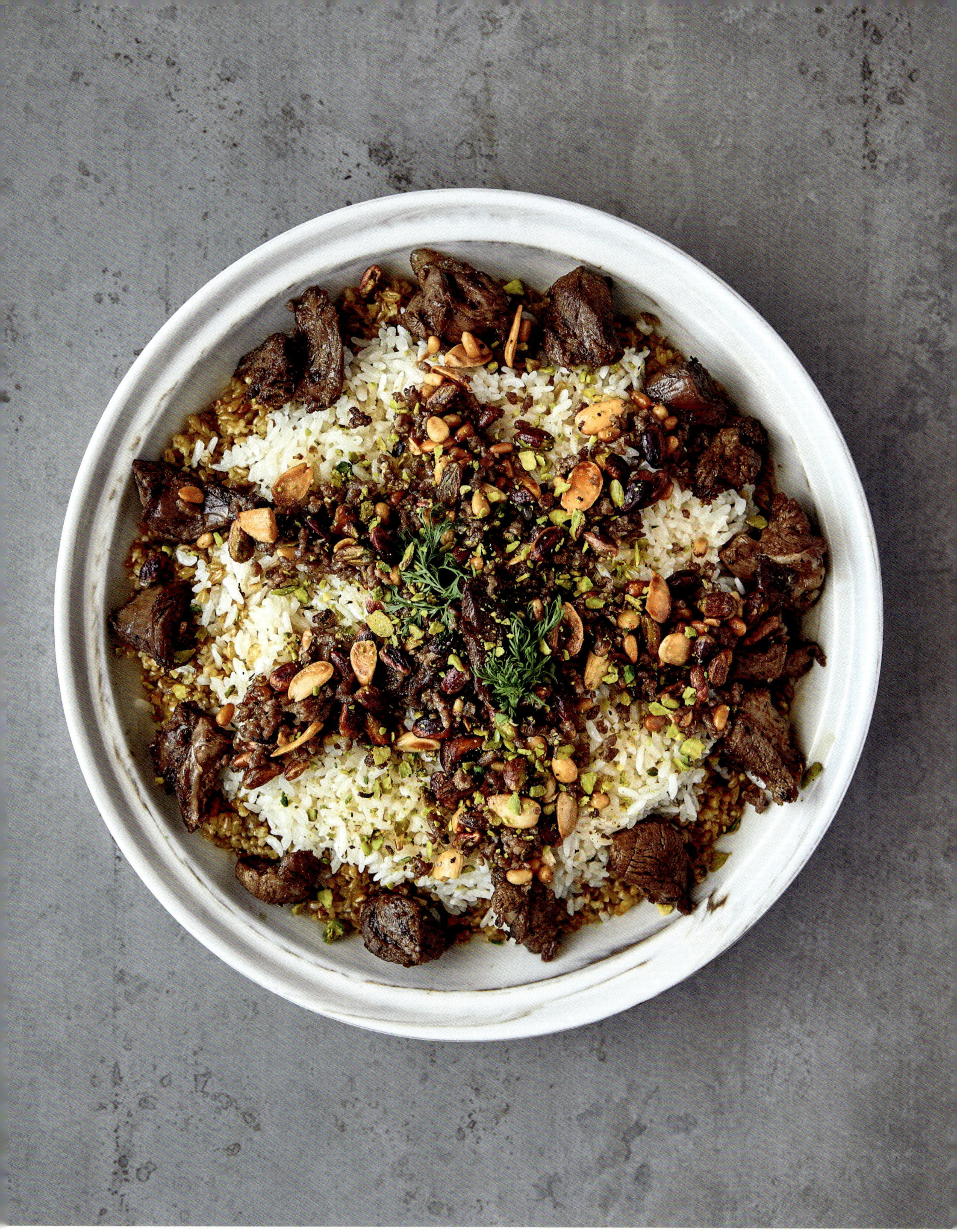

RIS EL FREEKEH
(FREEKEH WITH RICE AND LAMB)

Warm the remaining teaspoon of clarified butter in a medium pot set over medium heat, then add the soaked and strained rice. Cook, stirring frequently, for 10 minutes. Add the remaining 3 to 5 cardamom pods (to taste), the remaining teaspoon of salt, and the remaining 3 cups (750 milliliters) of meat stock. Cook, covered, for 20 to 25 minutes, until the liquid is absorbed.

When ready to serve, divide the freekeh and the rice into two batches, and the nut mixture and lamb chunks into three batches. Spread one half of the freekeh into a serving dish and top with one half of the rice, followed by ⅓ of the nut mixture and ⅓ of the lamb chunks.

For the second dish, spread the remaining half of the freekeh, then top with ⅓ of the nut mixture and ⅓ of the lamb chunks.

For the third dish, spread the remaining rice, then top with the remaining nuts and lamb chunks. Sprinkle with allspice, if you like.

Note: *For freekeh there is an optional step to infuse even more smoky flavor. Heat a piece of coal over your stove's burner. Make a small bowl out of aluminum foil, then pour in 3 tablespoons (60 milliliters) of olive oil and nestle the oil-filled foil bowl into the cooked freekeh.*

Add the hot coal to the oil, then let the smoke infuse the freekeh for 3 to 4 minutes. Remove the coal and drizzle the oil over the dish. (This is similar to the technique used by Fatima Fouad on page 61.)

FOOD TO CREATE NEW BEGINNINGS

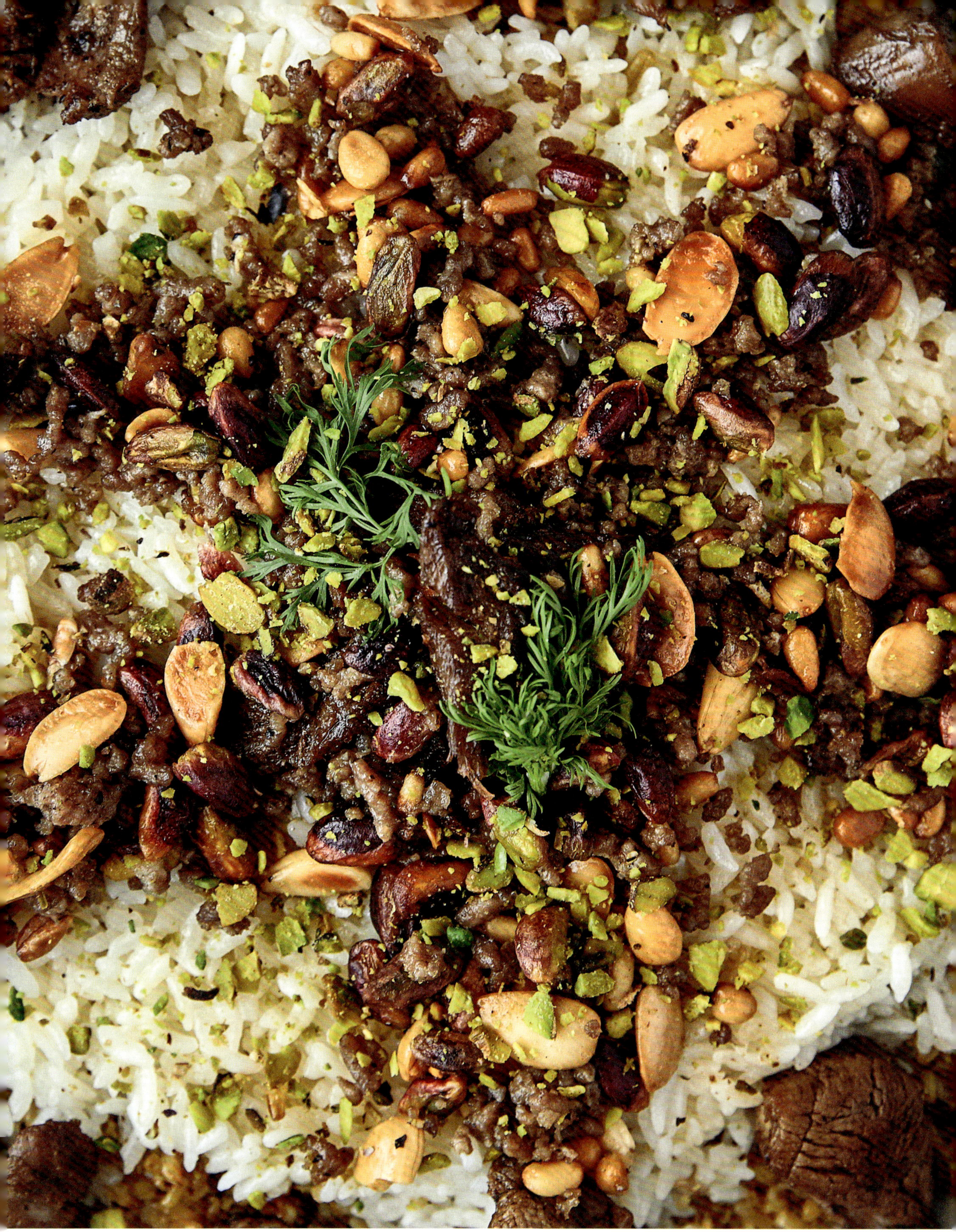

SAWSAN LUTFI

Sawsan was born and raised in Damascus, learning from a young age to cook with its colorful and diverse cuisine. She studied French literature at university, but in her free time she focused on cooking, developing her skills by recreating Damascene dishes with her own touch. After Sawsan married and had children, her passion for cooking grew; she combined recipes she learned from her mother, mother-in-law, and television to create her signature recipes.

Once Sawsan moved to Istanbul, she decided to pursue a career in food. Language was a barrier at first, but Sawsan is resilient and enrolled in Turkish language courses as well cooking classes focused on Turkish cuisine. To bolster her skills even more, she took baking classes -- she loves to bake cakes, as they combine her love for art and food. Unfortunately Sawsan also developed diabetes during this time. Rather than count that as a setback, she researched healthful food products and gluten-free and vegan cooking techniques so that she can still pursue her passion for baking, but with a slightly more healthful angle. Sawsan would like to open a restaurant or pastry shop that makes alternative products for those on vegan and/or gluten-free diets. Bringing joy to those who taste her food is Sawsan's ultimate goal.

SAWSAN LUTFI

BATATA BEL-FIRIN MA DAJAJ
(POTATO BAKED WITH CHICKEN)

10 servings

Every season

This filling and delicious combination of chicken, potatoes, garlic, and onions is widely prepared in the Middle East. Sawsan's traditional Damascene version makes enough for a crowd -- or for a few eaters who would like leftovers. Instead of deep-frying the potatoes, you can brush them generously with oil and bake in a 200ºC (400ºF) oven until golden.

INGREDIENTS:

2 kilograms small potatoes

1 teaspoon salt

1 liter oil, for frying (see headnote)

4 onions (440 grams)

¼ cup olive oil

10 skin-on, bone-in chicken legs

5 to 6 cups (1180 to 1400 milliliters) water, plus more for the initial chicken boiling

5 to 6 cloves garlic (to taste), crushed

1 mild, medium green pepper, finely chopped

½ teaspoon ground cinnamon

½ teaspoon curry powder

½ teaspoon ground turmeric

½ teaspoon Aleppo spice mix (optional; see page 214)

½ teaspoon freshly ground black pepper

5 cardamom pods

For the sauce (to be added after the chicken legs are placed in the baking dish):

Juice of 2 lemons

1 pinch curry powder

1 pinch freshly ground black pepper

2 tablespoons olive oil

6 to 7 cloves garlic, crushed

½ teaspoon salt

Note: *You can make the chicken and its broth up to one day ahead. Use the leftover chicken broth to make a soup with one chopped/grated carrot, one chopped/grated potato, and a handful of vermicelli or rice.*

METHOD:

Peel and cut the potatoes into discs, sprinkle with the salt, and let sit on the cutting board for 5 minutes. Blot any moisture with a towel. If you have a deep fryer, that's ideal; if not, fill a deep pot with the oil and heat to about 180ºC (350ºF). Fry the potatoes until slightly golden brown, about 15 to 20 minutes. (You may need to do this in batches.) Put the fried potatoes in a 23-by-33-cm (9-by-13-inch) baking dish.

Cut 2 of the onions in half from top to bottom, then slice thinly in half moons. Chop the remaining 2 onions and reserve for later. Warm the olive oil in a large skillet set over medium heat, then add the sliced onions. Once they start sizzling, reduce the heat to low and cook, stirring from time to time, until they are slightly golden, about 20 to 25 minutes. Arrange the cooked onions over the fried potatoes.

Meanwhile, bring a large pot of water to a boil. Slide in the chicken legs and cook for 8 to 10 minutes, or until a layer of fat appears on top. Strain and add 5 to 6 cups of fresh water (to cover the chicken by 5 cm/2 inches), the reserved chopped onion, green pepper, garlic, black pepper, cinnamon, curry powder, cardamom pods, turmeric, and Aleppo spice, if using. Simmer, covered, for 45 minutes over medium heat, or until the chicken is tender. Near the end of cooking, preheat the oven to 180ºC (350ºF).

Place the chicken legs over the potatoes and onions. Ladle in enough of the broth to just cover the potatoes. (Reserve the rest of the broth for another use; see note.) Stir together the sauce ingredients in a small bowl, then pour over the chicken. Bake uncovered for 35 to 40 minutes, until golden and crisped on top.

SAWSAN LUTFI

NATURAL TALENTS FOR A LIVING

NATURAL TALENTS FOR A LIVING

Anissa Helou

Syria sits in the Fertile Crescent, where wheat was first domesticated, and the country's cuisine is rich with history. You will find distinct regional variations in Syrian cooking, each delicious. Food occupies an important part in the life of all Syrians, and practically all women -- young or old, rich or poor -- know how to cook, whether they are town dwellers or rural folk. Even for those working outside of their home -- without much time to spend in the kitchen -- there is a whole network of women who prepare vegetables so that those with little time can prepare traditional family meals quicker.

Shortly after the uprising in 2011, when a peaceful rebellion turned into an armed conflict due to the government's brutal repression, Syrians began to flee their country in large numbers. One way for them to earn a living in the countries they fled to was to use their natural talents -- and one of the great and most natural talents of Syrians is cooking.

This culinary aptitude has been a boon to many Syrian people, especially women, who have found themselves fallen on hard circumstances. Many started to cook to earn a living -- some on their own initiative and others within the framework of a community, such as the LIFE Project -- with the unexpected and comforting result of making Syrian cuisine better known in the countries where refugees have resettled.

Within these pages, several Syrian cooks share recipes that may be both familiar and new to you -- baba ganoush (eggplant salad) from Inam Alshayeb, basmashkat (steak stuffed with rice) from Nizar Akram Elkharrat, and safarjaliyeh (quince and lamb stew) from Sawsan Bawadekji, for example. Their recipes offer yet another perspective to their stories, allowing us all to share part of their culture at our own tables.

Anissa Helou is a chef, food writer, journalist, broadcaster, consultant, and blogger focusing on the cuisines and culinary heritage of the Middle East, Mediterranean, and North Africa, and more recently the Islamic world. She also serves on the LIFE Project Advisory Council. Ms. Helou was born in Beirut and raised between Beirut, Lebanon, and Mashta el-Helou, Syria. In 2013 she helped a group of Egyptian entrepreneurs open Koshari Street in London's Covent Garden, where they serve her gourmet version of Koshari, the ultimate Egyptian street food. Ms. Helou is the author of nine award-winning cookbooks; her latest, "Feast: The Food of the Islamic World" (Ecco, 2018), won the James Beard Foundation International Cookbook Award.

SHATHAA ALRAMADHANI

Shathaa is a practical, open-minded cook, always eager for feedback and keen to adjust and adapt her recipes with feedback from others. These qualities will serve her well as she works to start a catering business that specializes in cuisine from Iraq, her home country.
Shathaa is from Mosul and studied linguistics at the University of Baghdad; she moved to Turkey in 2016 with her husband and three children. They first settled in Mersin, in the south, and then moved to Istanbul when their daughter started attending a university there.
In addition to her catering plans, Shathaa dreams of writing a cookbook of her own.

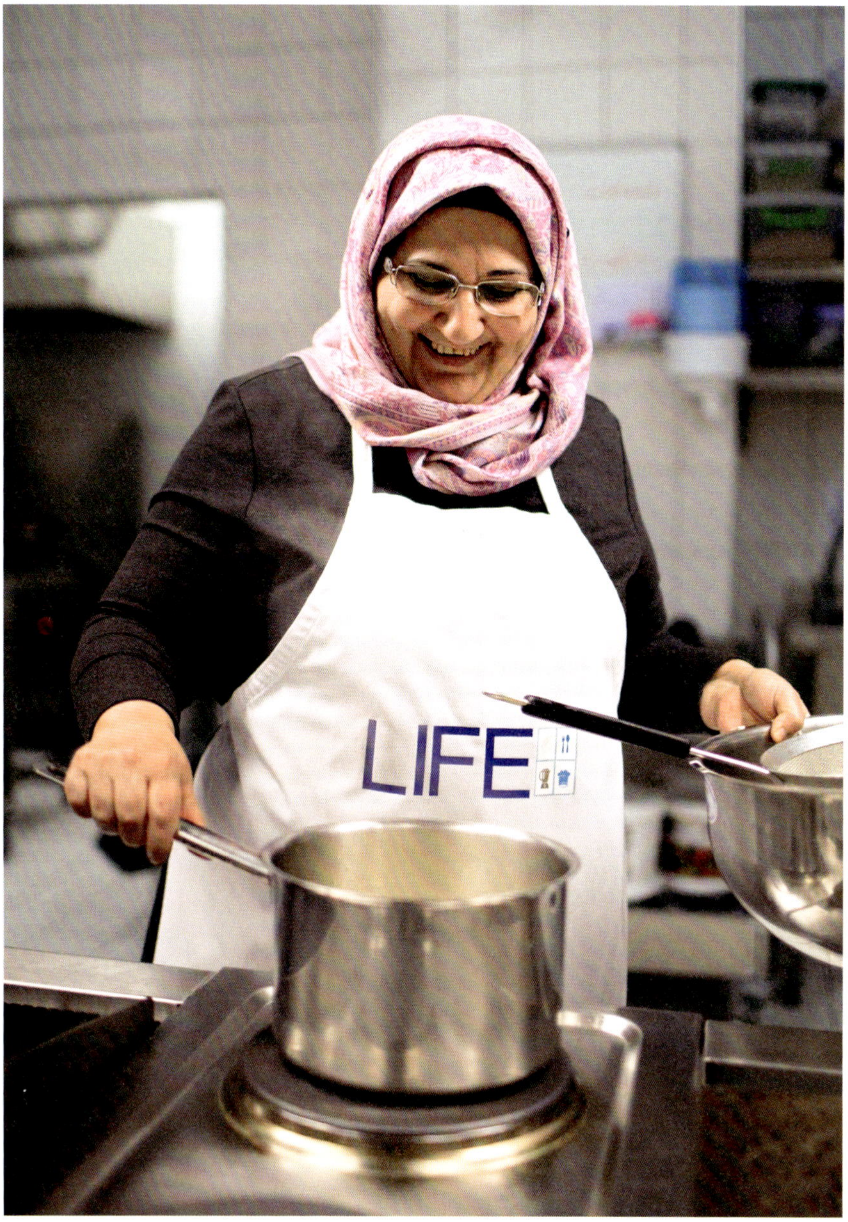
LIFE

KIBBEH EL RIZ

(RICE KIBBEH)

8 servings (makes 14 to 16 kibbeh)

All seasons

This is an old Baghdadi recipe, where the kibbeh crust can be prepared with rice or bulgur. In the original recipe, Iraqi amber rice -- highly prized but rarely exported -- is used, making for a highly aromatic kibbeh. But this recipe can be made with nearly any rice available. The finished product may remind you of Japanese onigiri or Sicillian arancini. Serve with lentil soup and salad.

INGREDIENTS:

For the dough:

2 cups (300 grams) rice

1 potato (300 grams), peeled and finely chopped

4 cups (945 milliliters) water

1 teaspoon (2 grams) salt

½ teaspoon ground turmeric (may substitute saffron threads or safflower petals), optional

1 egg

Filling:

2 tablespoons olive oil

½ kilogram lean ground lamb

1 teaspoon (1 gram) freshly ground black pepper

1 teaspoon (1 gram) ground allspice

½ teaspoon (1 gram) salt

2 tablespoons (30 grams) raisins (optional)

2 tablespoons chopped parsley (optional)

4 cups (945 milliliters) olive or vegetable oil, for frying (see note)

Note: *If you'd rather not deep fry, you can shallow fry the kibbeh in a thin layer of oil in a nonstick skillet. You can also prepare two fillings, as Shathaa did: one with raisins and one without. Shape the raisin-filled kibbeh into patties and the others into torpedo-shaped croquettes (so that you can tell the difference when serving). Finely chopped onion and cilantro can also be added to the filling.*

METHOD:

Bring the rice, potato, water, salt, and turmeric to a boil in a medium pot set over medium heat. Cook until the potatoes are soft and the rice mushy, about 20 to 25 minutes. Remove from heat, cover, and set aside to cool.

Meanwhile, make the filling: warm the olive oil in a large skillet over medium-high heat, then add the lamb and cook, stirring frequently, for 40 to 45 minutes, until the liquid has evaporated. Add the pepper, allspice, salt, raisins, and parsley. Cook for 5 minutes more, making sure everything is mixed well. Remove from heat.

When the rice mixture is at room temperature, add the egg and knead well, mixing with your hands until you have a malleable dough. (You can also use a stand mixer with a paddle attachment.) Have a bowl of cold water nearby to moisten your hands and fingers.

Take a lump of dough about the size of a large egg. Make an indentation in the center, add 1 tablespoon of the filling, and close the kibbeh by rolling it between your hands to form a torpedo-like shape. (Keep your fingers wet to help seal the kibbeh.)
The thickness of the shell is expected to be 6 to 8 mm (about ¼ inch), but it can be thicker while you're learning. Deep fry in olive or vegetable oil till they are slightly golden, about 10 to 12 minutes.

SHATHAA ALRAMADHANI

YELDA KUMBASAR

For many years, Yelda worked for a textile company in Istanbul, handling subcontracting, accounts, and other such administrative tasks. But this was neither her passion nor what made her happy -- for that, she cooked and baked. Her friends and family enjoyed her culinary creations so much that she decided to improve her skills and take a baking course (and eventually, quit her textile job). At the end of her course, she learned that she could enroll in an entrepreneurship program through the Small and Medium Industry Development Organization (KOSGEB); by the end, she was awarded as one of the best amongst 450 trainees.

In 2006, Yelda found the ideal location to open a business of her own -- an abandoned and overgrown garden in the Çengelköy district of Istanbul. Although close to the city center, in this valley surrounded by pine, cypress, and nettle trees -- with a view of the Bosphorus strait -- nature surrounds. After extensive renovations, Yelda now has a cafe, herb garden, and beautiful event space, where she hosts private dinners, workshops, weddings, and more, offering tailor-made menus for her customers.

Yelda was born in Artvin, a city in Turkey not far from the Black Sea. She moved to Istanbul with her family as a child.

Find Yelda on Instagram at @yeldaninbahcesi.

YELDA KUMBASAR

AŞURE

(NOAH'S PUDDING)

20 servings

Prepared during the 10th of Muharram, the first month of the Hijri calendar

As the story goes, aşure was invented when the cook in Noah's ark gathered all of the dwindling ingredients left after floating along for several months, combining a little of this and that to create a delicious dish that was shared with everyone. Even though it was the last food left, it was shared and enjoyed by all -- for that reason, aşure symbolizes sharing and is made in large batches for just that purpose. For Yelda, aşure also contains hope, as all broken things do; by sharing aşure, you are also spreading hope.

INGREDIENTS:

For the aşure:

1 cup (220 grams) dry chickpeas, soaked for 8 hours and then boiled until tender

1 cup (200 grams) navy beans, soaked for 8 hours and then boiled until tender

2 cups (220 grams) pearled wheat, boiled for 15 to 20 minutes

2 cups (500 milliliters) water

3 ½ cups (700 grams) sugar

20 dried apricots, cut into small cubes

1 tablespoon (15 grams) wheat starch

½ cup (125 milliliters) milk

Zest of 3 oranges

To garnish:

1 tablespoon (8 grams) cinnamon powder, or to taste

2 cups (250 grams) hazelnuts, coarsely chopped

1 cup (100 grams) walnuts, coarsely chopped

1 cup (100 grams) pistachios (preferably Turkish Antep), chopped

Seeds of 2 medium pomegranates

10 dried figs, sliced into strips

METHOD:

Put the chickpeas, navy beans, and pearled wheat in a large pot with the water. Bring to a boil over medium-high heat, then reduce to maintain a gentle boil and cook for 20 to 25 minutes. Add the sugar and boil 7 to 9 minutes more, until dissolved. Add the dried apricots and cook for 5 minutes.

Stir the starch into the milk, then add to the pot along with the orange zest; boil for 5 to 10 more minutes, until creamy. Remove from heat and let sit for 10 to 15 minutes. Divide among serving bowls, sprinkle each with a pinch of cinnamon, then top with the hazelnuts, walnuts, pistachios, pomegranate seeds, and figs.

You can also use currants, raisins, and lemon zest, plus grape molasses in addition to the sugar. Aşure has various recipes depending on the family, income, and region. A pinch of rice is added to give a creamy texture, if starch is not used. The finished dish can be garnished with sesame seeds as well.

YELDA KUMBASAR

KURU BAKLAVA

(DRY BAKLAVA)

16 servings (makes 48 pieces)

Every season

Yelda describes these one-bite, not-too-sweet treats as an ideal pairing with coffee. They are rich in tahini and hazelnuts, both heart-healthy ingredients, and thus recall a Turkish saying that drinking a cup of coffee with a friend corresponds to forty years of heart-felt memories.

INGREDIENTS:

1 cup tahini
1 cup extra-virgin olive oil
½ cup (100 grams) sugar
8 phyllo sheets (38-by-33 cm/15-by-15 inches; may be labeled as baklava phyllo)
400 grams hazelnuts, finely ground

METHOD:

Preheat the oven to 180°C (350°F) and line a baking sheet with parchment paper. Blend the tahini, oil, and sugar until smooth. Set aside about 2 tablespoons of the tahini mixture. Brush a little less than ¼ of the remaining mixture over 1 phyllo sheet, then top with another phyllo sheet. Brush again with some of the tahini mixture, then sprinkle with some of the ground hazelnuts. Roll lengthwise and place on the parchment-lined baking sheet. Repeat with the remaining tahini mixture and phyllo sheets, for a total of 4 rolls.

Brush the reserved tahini mixture over the top of the rolls, then bake for 20 to 25 minutes, or until golden. Cool slightly before slicing.

Note: *You can play around with the filling, flavoring it with pistachios, walnuts, and/or currants in addition to or instead of the hazelnuts. (You can even skip brushing the tahini on top of the rolls!) Your creativity has no limits.*

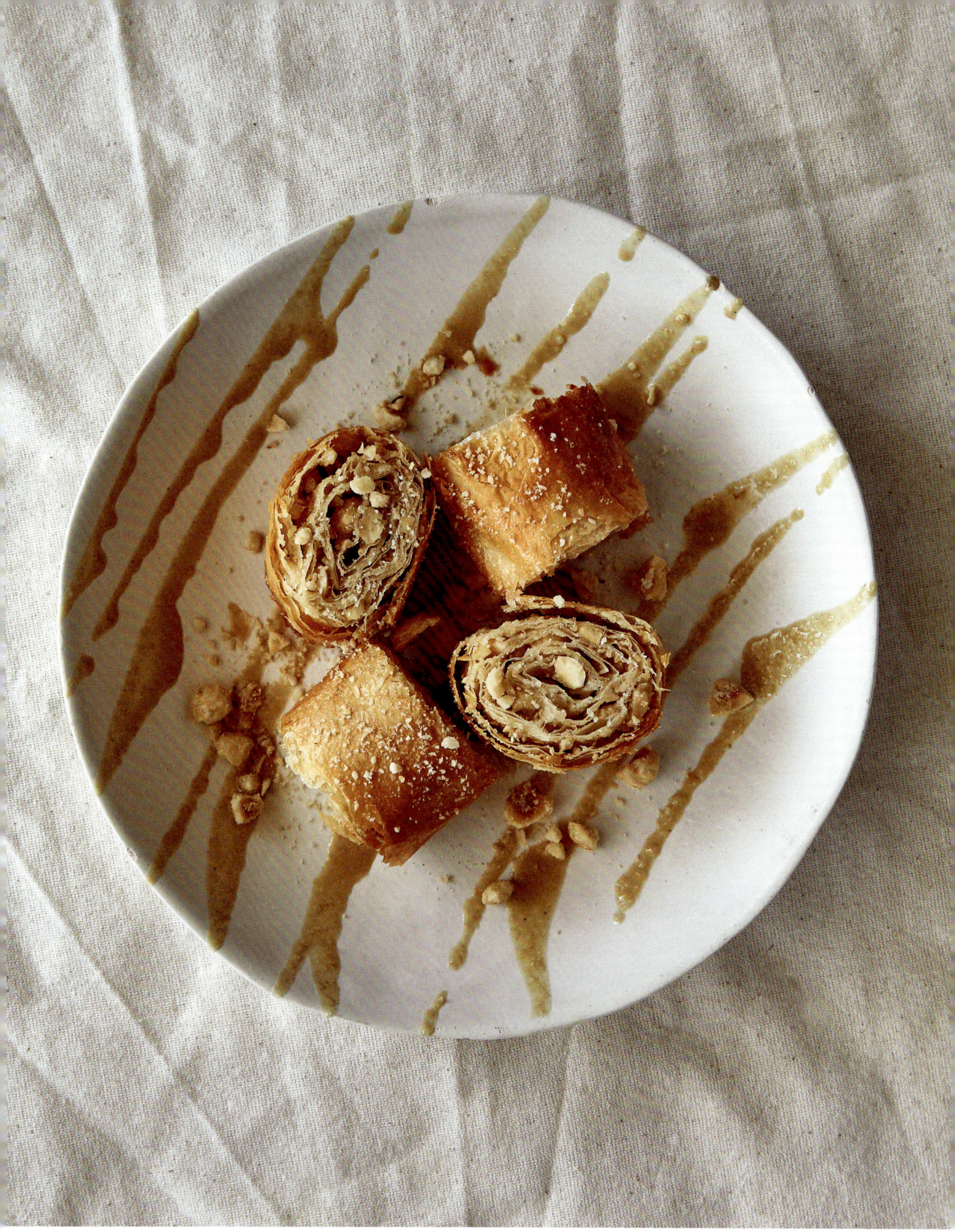

FOOD POWER

FOOD POWER

Mitchell Davis

It is often said that food brings people together -- but the reality is more complicated than that. Food is just as likely to keep people apart. Whether it pushes or pulls, the power of food comes less from its nutritive value than its cultural richness—a concoction of memory and emotion, taste and tradition, intention and identity, opportunity and hope.

The power of food, beyond its capacity to nourish, is something most people don't often think about.. But just as food, or good food, rather, can heal our bodies, food can also heal our society. Climate change, social inequality, economic development, public health—when food is made central to our solutions to these problems, the results are better, more broadly engaging, and more palatable than many of the alternatives.

As individuals and organizations around the world are realizing the role food can play in solving what ails us, chefs, food entrepreneurs, home cooks, and others are playing their part by making good food available to more people. Increasingly, thanks to programs like those run by the James Beard Foundation, Gastromotiva, and Chefs Manifesto, they are also advocating for policies that support positive food system change.

Change is necessary because for some time we thought we could treat food like other material, transactional objects, manipulating and exploiting it without consequence. As we see our health deteriorate, the environment degrade, and our communities splinter, we realize the externalities of mass-produced, commodity food can't be ignored. That's not to say good food must be precious or rare. Quite the contrary. If we think of food as a public good rather than an economic commodity, as an expression of cultural identity rather than fuel, as a source of empowerment rather than a handout, as joy rather than medicine, we can begin to reorganize our food systems to reflect not only the true value of what we eat but also of the people who produce, distribute, prepare, and serve it.

Mitchell Davis, a LIFE Project Advisory Council member, is the James Beard Foundation's Chief Strategy Officer, as well as a cookbook author and food journalist. In 2013, he assembled and led the team that was selected by the U.S. Department of State to create the USA Pavilion at the World Expo Milano 2015. He has written three cookbooks and co-authored two, including the ground-breaking electronic book My Provence (Alta Editions) with famed French chef Laurent Gras. Mr. Davis has made multiple television appearances, and his writing appears regularly in books, magazines, and academic journals.

There is perhaps no object or artifact besides food that is a nexus of so many global systems. They flow through history and time, bend around science and technology, entwine in political economies, weave through every religion and culture, pass through your mouth, and end up in your cells. You are all that you eat. Good food is paradoxical, both local and global, individual and universal, natural and manmade.

De gustibus non est disputandum -- In matters of taste, there can be no disputes. Everyone seems to love so many of the same delicious things: warm bread, savory soups, a ripe tomato, fresh-baked cookies, the sorts of time-tested recipes you find in this book. The power of food to bring people together also lies in the joy of eating -- a pleasure that's even better when shared.

INDEX

A
Algerian
- Kuskus (Couscous with Lamb) 134
- Mhajeb/Mahjouba (Vegetable and Cheese Turnovers) 132

almonds:
- Basbousa (Semolina Cake) 182
- Gonca Gül Tatlısı (Rosebud Cookies) 78
- Harissa/Harisa (Peanut Dessert) 64
- Kibbeh bil Sanieh (Kibbeh in a Tray) 70
- Makloubeh (Upside-down Rice with Eggplant and Lamb) 90
- Mansaf (Lamb Cooked in Yogurt) 172
- Ouzi (Lamb and Rice Pilaf Wrapped in Phyllo Pastry) 140
- Ris El Freekeh (Freekeh with Rice and Lamb) 216
- Zurbian (Rice with Lamb) 58

apricots, dried: Cevizli Kayısı Kavurması (Dried Apricots with Walnuts) 202
arugula: Salatet Jarjeer (Arugula Salad) 158
Ashour, Naglaa 178
Asida (Corn Porridge) 104
Astarlı Sütlaç (Rice Pudding) 50
Aşure (Noah's Pudding) 232

B
Baba Ganoush (Smoky Eggplant Salad/Dip) 120
baharat 188
bananas: Muz Fattah (Banana Bread) 66
Basbousa (Semolina Cake) 182
Basmashkat (Rolled Steak with Rice Filling) 190
Batata Bel-Firin ma Dajaj (Potato Baked with Chicken) 222
Batersh (Smoky Eggplant Puree) 188
Batikh, Iman 108
Bawadekji, Sawsan 212

beef:
- Basmashkat (Rolled Steak with Rice Filling) 190
- Fahsa (Beef Stew) 96
- Kibbeh bil Sanieh (Kibbeh in a Tray) 70
- Saçta Kıyma Böreği (Lamb-Filled Skillet Borek) 36
- Zurbian (Rice with Lamb) 58

Bint Al-Sahn (The Daughter of the Plate) 100
black-eyed peas: Pirpirim Aşı (Purslane Dish) 48

bread:
- Fattoush (Bread Salad) 124
- Mansaf (Lamb Cooked in Yogurt) 172
- Muz Fattah (Banana Bread) 66
- Shafoot/Shafut (Bread in Yogurt Sauce) 94

bread crumbs: Muhammara (Walnut and Pepper Dip) 126

bulgur 21
- Harput Köftesi (Bulgur Koftes in Tomato and Pepper Paste Sauce) 82
- Kibbeh bil Sanieh (Kibbeh in a Tray) 70
- Kibbeh Mabrumeh (Rolled Kibbeh) 164
- Mujaddara (Lentil Pilaf) 144
- Pirpirim Aşı (Purslane Dish) 48
- Tabbouleh (Fine Grain Bulgur Salad) 146

C
cake: Basbousa (Semolina Cake) 182

carrots:
- Kuskus (Couscous with Lamb) 134
- Portakal Suyu İle Zeytinyağlı Kereviz (Celery Root with Olive Oil and Orange Juice) 42
- Shurbet Khudar w Dajaj (Vegetable Soup with Chicken) 56
- Tavuklu Pazı Sarma (Swiss Chard Stuffed with Chicken) 76

cashews:
- Gonca Gül Tatlısı (Rosebud Cookies) 78
- Makloubeh (Upside-down Rice with Eggplant and Lamb) 90
- Ouzi (Lamb and Rice Pilaf Wrapped in Phyllo Pastry) 140
- Ris El Freekeh (Freekeh with Rice and Lamb) 216
- Zurbian (Rice with Lamb) 58

celery root: Portakal Suyu İle Zeytinyağlı Kereviz (Celery Root with Olive Oil and Orange Juice) 42
Cevizli Kayısı Kavurması (Dried Apricots with Walnuts) 202

cheese:
- Hünkar Beğendi (Sultan's Delight) 40
- Kunafe Nabulsieh (Kunafe from Nablus) 168
- Mhajeb/Mahjouba (Vegetable and Cheese Turnovers) 132
- Peynirli Sıkma (Cheese-Filled Wraps) 34

chicken:
- Batata Bel-Firin ma Dajaj (Potato Baked with Chicken) 222
- Shurbet Khudar w Dajaj (Vegetable Soup with Chicken) 56
- Tavuklu Pazı Sarma (Swiss Chard Stuffed with Chicken) 76

chickpeas:
- Aşure (Noah's Pudding) 232
- Hedik/Diş Buğdayı (Wheat Boiled with Chickpeas) 84
- Kuskus (Couscous with Lamb) 134
- Pirpirim Aşı (Purslane Dish) 48

clarified butter 22
- Batersh (Smoky Eggplant Puree) 188
- Esh El Bolbol (Nightingale's Nest) 166
- Kibbeh Mabrumeh (Rolled Kibbeh) 164
- Kunafe Nabulsieh (Kunafe from Nablus) 168
- Kuskus (Couscous with Lamb) 134

Ouzi (Lamb and Rice Pilaf Wrapped in Phyllo Pastry) 140
  Ris El Freekeh (Freekeh with Rice and Lamb) 216
  Tatar Barak (Dumplings in Yogurt-Tahini Sauce) 192
  Zurbian (Rice with Lamb) 58
cookies: Gonca Gül Tatlısı (Rosebud Cookies) 78
corn flour 21
  Asida (Corn Porridge) 104
couscous: Kuskus (Couscous with Lamb) 134
cucumbers:
  Fattoush (Bread Salad) 124
  Laban Bi Khiar (Cucumber with Yogurt) 142

D

Dağdeviren, Musa 185
Dalae Mahshi Bil-Ruzz (Stuffed Rack Of Lamb) 112
Davis, Mitchell 237
Doğan, Nisan 200
dumplings
  Shish Barak (Dumplings Cooked in Yogurt Sauce) 152
  Tatar Barak (Dumplings in Yogurt-Tahini Sauce) 192

E

eggplant:
  Baba Ganoush (Smoky Eggplant Salad/Dip) 120
  Batersh (Smoky Eggplant Puree) 188
  Hünkar Beğendi (Sultan's Delight) 40
  Makloubeh (Upside-down Rice with Eggplant and Lamb) 90
  Patlıcan Güveç (Eggplant and Lamb Stew in an Earthenware Pot) 208
eggplant, dried: Mahshi Betincan Ma Fitir (Mushrooms Cooked with Stuffed Eggplants) 110
Egyptian
  Basbousa (Semolina Cake) 182
  Om Ali (Bread Pudding) 180
Erol, Cem 53
Es, Ayşe 32
Esh El Bolbol (Nightingale's Nest) 166

F

Fahsa (Beef Stew) 96
Fakhdet Lahmeh (Leg of Lamb) 156
Fattoush (Bread Salad) 124
fenugreek 22
  Fahsa (Beef Stew) 96
Fırat, Mert 107
freekeh 22
  Ris El Freekeh (Freekeh with Rice and Lamb) 216
food waste, 19
Fouad, Fatima 54

G

Georgian, Tavuklu Pazı Sarma (Swiss Chard Stuffed with Chicken) 76
ghee: see clarified butter
Algherawi, Maysaa 150
gluten-free/gluten-free option
  Astarlı Sütlaç (Rice Pudding) 50
  Baba Ganoush (Smoky Eggplant Salad/Dip) 120
  Batata Bel-Firin ma Dajaj (Potato Baked with Chicken) 222
  Batersh (Smoky Eggplant Puree) 188
  Cevizli Kayısı Kavurması (Dried Apricots with Walnuts) 202
  Dalae Mahshi Bil-Ruzz (Stuffed Rack Of Lamb) 112
  Fahsa (Beef Stew) 96
  Fakhdet Lahmeh (Leg of Lamb) 156
  Harissa/Harisa (Peanut Dessert) 64
  Hünkar Beğendi (Sultan's Delight) 40
  Kibbeh El Riz (Rice Kibbeh) 228
  Laban Bi Khiar (Cucumber with Yogurt) 142
  Mahshi Betincan Ma Fitir (Mushrooms Cooked with Stuffed Eggplants) 110
  Makloubeh (Upside-down Rice with Eggplant and Lamb) 90
  Patlıcan Güveç (Eggplant and Lamb Stew in an Earthenware Pot) 208
  Portakal Suyu İle Zeytinyağlı Kereviz (Celery Root with Olive Oil and Orange Juice) 42
  Safarjaliyeh (Quince and Lamb Stew) 214
  Salatet Jarjeer (Arugula Salad) 158
  Shakriyeh (Lamb Stew with Yogurt) 128
  Shurbet Khudar w Dajaj (Vegetable Soup with Chicken) 56
  Siliq Bil Zeyt (Chard with Oil) 194
  Siliq Mutabal (Chard Stalks in Yogurt Sauce) 196
  Zahawiq (Green Chile Sauce) 62
  Zurbian (Rice with Lamb) 58
Gonca Gül Tatlısı (Rosebud Cookies) 78

H

Halıcı, Nevin 149
Hamdan, Muyassar 170
Hammo, Fatima 68
Hangel (Mantı Without Filling) 206
Harissa/Harisa (Peanut Dessert) 64
Harput Köftesi (Bulgur Koftes in Tomato and Pepper Paste Sauce) 82
hazelnuts:
  Aşure (Noah's Pudding) 232
  Gonca Gül Tatlısı (Rosebud Cookies) 78
  Kuru Baklava (Dry Baklava) 234
  Om Ali (Bread Pudding) 180
Hedik/Diş Buğdayı (Wheat Boiled with Chickpeas) 84
Helou, Anissa 225

Hertz, David 211
Hösükoğlu, Filiz 45, 46
hulba, with Fahsa (Beef Stew) 96
Hünkar Beğendi (Sultan's Delight) 40

I

İnali, Özgül 204
Iraqi, Kibbeh El Riz (Rice Kibbeh) 228

J

Jordanian, Mansaf (Lamb Cooked in Yogurt) 172

K

Kakınç, Zeynep 137
Kawakibi, Mohamad Yahya 108
kaymak 22
    Om Ali (Bread Pudding) 180
    Cevizli Kayısı Kavurması (Dried Apricots with Walnuts) 202
Elkharrat, Nizar Akram 186
Khayata, Mohamad Shady 162
Kheawe, Hanaddy 88
Kibbeh bil Sanieh (Kibbeh in a Tray) 70
Kibbeh El Riz (Rice Kibbeh) 228
Kibbeh Mabrumeh (Rolled Kibbeh) 164
Kumbasar, Yelda 230
Kunafe Nabulsieh (Kunafe from Nablus) 168
Kuru Baklava (Dry Baklava) 234
Kuskus (Couscous with Lamb) 134

L

Laban Bi Khiar (Cucumber with Yogurt) 142
Al-Laith, Hayat Ali Naji
lamb:
    Batersh (Smoky Eggplant Puree) 188
    Dalae Mahshi Bil-Ruzz (Stuffed Rack Of Lamb) 112
    Esh El Bolbol (Nightingale's Nest) 166
    Fakhdet Lahmeh (Leg of Lamb) 156
    Harput Köftesi (Bulgur Koftes in Tomato and Pepper Paste Sauce) 82
    Hünkar Beğendi (Sultan's Delight) 40
    Kibbeh bil Sanieh (Kibbeh in a Tray) 70
    Kibbeh El Riz (Rice Kibbeh) 228
    Kibbeh Mabrumeh (Rolled Kibbeh) 164
    Kuskus (Couscous with Lamb) 134
    Ouzi (Lamb and Rice Pilaf Wrapped in Phyllo Pastry) 140
    Mahshi Betincan Ma Fitir (Mushrooms Cooked with Stuffed Eggplants) 110
    Makloubeh (Upside-down Rice with Eggplant and Lamb) 90
    Mansaf (Lamb Cooked in Yogurt) 172
    Patlıcan Güveç (Eggplant and Lamb Stew in an Earthenware Pot) 208
    Ris El Freekeh (Freekeh with Rice and Lamb) 216
    Saçta Kıyma Böreği (Lamb-Filled Skillet Borek) 36
    Safarjaliyeh (Quince and Lamb Stew) 214
    Shakriyeh (Lamb Stew with Yogurt) 128
    Shish Barak (Dumplings Cooked in Yogurt Sauce) 152
    Shorbet Lahme (Wheat and Lamb Soup) 98
    Tatar Barak (Dumplings in Yogurt-Tahini Sauce) 192
    Zurbian (Rice with Lamb) 58
lentils:
    Mujaddara (Lentil Pilaf) 144
    Pirpirim Aşı (Purslane Dish) 48
Lutfi, Sawsan 220

M

Mahshi Betincan Ma Fitir (Mushrooms Cooked with Stuffed Eggplants) 110
Makloubeh (Upside-down Rice with Eggplant and Lamb) 90
Mamuniyeh (Semolina Helva) 114
Mansaf (Lamb Cooked in Yogurt) 172
Mhajeb/Mahjouba (Vegetable and Cheese Turnovers) 132
Mendelson Forman, Johanna 31
Mortada, Dalia 117
Muhammara (Walnut and Pepper Dip) 126
Mujaddara (Lentil Pilaf) 144
mushrooms: Mahshi Betincan Ma Fitir (Mushrooms Cooked with Stuffed Eggplants) 110
Muz Fattah (Banana Bread) 66

N

Nathan, Joan 161
Newland, Kathleen 73
Newnham, Paul 199
nigella seeds 22
    Bint Al-Sahn (The Daughter of the Plate) 100
    Muz Fattah (Banana Bread) 66

O

Om Ali (Bread Pudding) 180
Ouzi (Lamb and Rice Pilaf Wrapped in Phyllo Pastry) 140

P

Palestinian, Kunafe Nabulsieh (Kunafe from Nablus) 168
Patlıcan Güveç (Eggplant and Lamb Stew in an Earthenware Pot) 208
peanuts: Harissa/Harisa (Peanut Dessert) 64
pepper paste: see red pepper paste
Peynirli Sıkma (Cheese-Filled Wraps) 34

phyllo:
- Kuru Baklava (Dry Baklava) 234
- Ouzi (Lamb and Rice Pilaf Wrapped in Phyllo Pastry) 140

pine nuts:
- Basmashkat (Rolled Steak with Rice Filling) 190
- Batersh (Smoky Eggplant Puree) 188
- Dalae Mahshi Bil-Ruzz (Stuffed Rack Of Lamb) 112
- Esh El Bolbol (Nightingale's Nest) 166
- Kibbeh Mabrumeh (Rolled Kibbeh) 164
- Makloubeh (Upside-down Rice with Eggplant and Lamb) 90
- Ouzi (Lamb and Rice Pilaf Wrapped in Phyllo Pastry) 140
- Ris El Freekeh (Freekeh with Rice and Lamb) 216
- Tatar Barak (Dumplings in Yogurt-Tahini Sauce) 192

pistachio nuts:
- Astarlı Sütlaç (Rice Pudding) 50
- Basbousa (Semolina Cake) 182
- Gonca Gül Tatlısı (Rosebud Cookies) 78
- Kibbeh Mabrumeh (Rolled Kibbeh) 164
- Kunafe Nabulsieh (Kunafe from Nablus) 168
- Mamuniyeh (Semolina Helva) 114
- Ris El Freekeh (Freekeh with Rice and Lamb) 216

Pirpirim Aşı (Purslane Dish) 48
Portakal Suyu İle Zeytinyağli Kereviz (Celery Root with Olive Oil and Orange Juice) 42

pomegranate molasses:
- Baba Ganoush (Smoky Eggplant Salad/Dip) 120
- Esh El Bolbol (Nightingale's Nest) 166
- Fattoush (Bread Salad) 124
- Muhammara (Walnut and Pepper Dip) 126
- Pirpirim Aşı (Purslane Dish) 48
- Safarjaliyeh (Quince and Lamb Stew) 214
- Salatet Jarjeer (Arugula Salad) 158

pomegranate seeds:
- Astarlı Sütlaç (Rice Pudding) 50
- Aşure (Noah's Pudding) 232
- Baba Ganoush (Smoky Eggplant Salad/Dip) 120
- Fattoush (Bread Salad) 124
- Shafoot/Shafut (Bread in Yogurt Sauce) 94
- Siliq Bil Zeyt (Chard with Oil) 194
- Siliq Mutabal (Chard Stalks in Yogurt Sauce) 196

potatoes:
- Batata Bel-Firin ma Dajaj (Potato Baked with Chicken) 222
- Kibbeh El Riz (Rice Kibbeh) 228
- Kuskus (Couscous with Lamb) 134
- Fakhdet Lahmeh (Leg of Lamb) 156
- Portakal Suyu İle Zeytinyağli Kereviz (Celery Root with Olive Oil and Orange Juice) 42
- Tavuklu Pazı Sarma (Swiss Chard Stuffed with Chicken) 76
- Zurbian (Rice with Lamb) 58

puff pastry: Om Ali (Bread Pudding) 180
purslane: Pirpirim Aşı (Purslane Dish) 48

Q

quince: Safarjaliyeh (Quince and Lamb Stew) 214

R

Alramadhani, Shathaa 226
red pepper paste 22
- Harput Köftesi (Bulgur Koftes in Tomato and Pepper Paste Sauce) 82
  - Kibbeh Mabrumeh (Rolled Kibbeh) 164
  - Muhammara (Walnut and Pepper Dip) 126
  - Patlican Güveç (Eggplant and Lamb Stew in an Earthenware Pot) 208
  - Saçta Kıyma Böreği (Lamb-Filled Skillet Borek) 36

rice, 21
- Astarlı Sütlaç (Rice Pudding) 50
- Basmashkat (Rolled Steak with Rice Filling) 190
- cooked with vermicelli, 156
- Dalae Mahshi Bil-Ruzz (Stuffed Rack Of Lamb) 112
- Kibbeh El Riz (Rice Kibbeh) 228
- Mahshi Betincan Ma Fitir (Mushrooms Cooked with Stuffed Eggplants) 110
- Makloubeh (Upside-down Rice with Eggplant and Lamb) 90
- Mansaf (Lamb Cooked in Yogurt) 172
- Ouzi (Lamb and Rice Pilaf Wrapped in Phyllo Pastry) 140
- Ris El Freekeh (Freekeh with Rice and Lamb) 216
- Zurbian (Rice with Lamb) 58

Ris El Freekeh (Freekeh with Rice and Lamb) 216
rose water: Harissa/Harisa (Peanut Dessert) 64

S

Saçta Kıyma Böreği (Lamb-Filled Skillet Borek) 36
Safarjaliyeh (Quince and Lamb Stew) 214
safflower 22
- Astarlı Sütlaç (Rice Pudding) 50
- Basmashkat (Rolled Steak with Rice Filling) 190
- Kibbeh El Riz (Rice Kibbeh) 228
- Mansaf (Lamb Cooked in Yogurt) 172

Salatet Jarjeer (Arugula Salad) 158
Salcan, Gülhan 80
Schleifer, Yigal 87
semolina 22
- Basbousa (Semolina Cake) 182
- Gonca Gül Tatlısı (Rosebud Cookies) 78
- Harput Köftesi (Bulgur Koftes in Tomato and Pepper Paste Sauce) 82
- Mamuniyeh (Semolina Helva) 114

Mhajeb/Mahjouba (Vegetable and Cheese Turnovers) 132
Shafoot/Shafut (Bread in Yogurt Sauce) 94
Shakriyeh (Lamb Stew with Yogurt) 128
Alshayeb, Inam 118
Shish Barak (Dumplings Cooked in Yogurt Sauce) 152
Shorbet Lahme (Wheat and Lamb Soup) 98
Shurbet Khudar w Dajaj (Vegetable Soup with Chicken) 56
Siliq Bil Zeyt (Chard with Oil) 194
Siliq Mutabal (Chard Stalks in Yogurt Sauce) 196
Smaili, Latifa 130
spice blends:
    Aleppo Spice Mix (Al-Bhar Al-Halabi) 214
    baharat 188
    rice spice mix for zurbian 61
    seven spices for shish barak 155
    spice mix for Shurbet Khudar w Dajaj 56
    Yemeni spice for fahsa 96
sustainability in the kitchen, 19
Swiss chard:
    Siliq Bil Zeyt (Chard with Oil) 194
    Siliq Mutabal (Chard Stalks in Yogurt Sauce) 196
    Tavuklu Pazı Sarma (Swiss Chard Stuffed with Chicken) 76
Syrian
    Baba Ganoush (Smoky Eggplant Salad/Dip) 120
    Basmashkat (Rolled Steak with Rice Filling) 190
    Batata Bel-Firin ma Dajaj (Potato Baked with Chicken) 222
    Batersh (Smoky Eggplant Puree) 188
    Dalae Mahshi Bil-Ruzz (Stuffed Rack Of Lamb) 112
    Esh El Bolbol (Nightingale's Nest) 166
    Fakhdet Lahmeh (Leg of Lamb) 156
    Fattoush (Bread Salad) 124
    Kibbeh El Riz (Rice Kibbeh) 228
    Kibbeh Mabrumeh (Rolled Kibbeh) 164
    Laban Bi Khiar (Cucumber with Yogurt) 142
    Mahshi Betincan Ma Fitir (Mushrooms Cooked with Stuffed Eggplants) 110
    Makloubeh (Upside-down Rice with Eggplant and Lamb) 90
    Mamuniyeh (Semolina Helva) 114
    Muhammara (Walnut and Pepper Dip) 126
    Mujaddara (Lentil Pilaf) 144
    Ouzi (Lamb and Rice Pilaf Wrapped in Phyllo Pastry) 140
    Ris El Freekeh (Freekeh with Rice and Lamb) 216
    Safarjaliyeh (Quince and Lamb Stew) 214
    Salatet Jarjeer (Arugula Salad) 158
    Shakriyeh (Lamb Stew with Yogurt) 128
    Shish Barak (Dumplings Cooked in Yogurt Sauce) 152
    Siliq Bil Zeyt (Chard with Oil) 194
    Siliq Mutabal (Chard Stalks in Yogurt Sauce) 196
    Tabbouleh (Fine Grain Bulgur Salad) 146

Tatar Barak (Dumplings in Yogurt-Tahini Sauce) 192

T

Tabbouleh (Fine Grain Bulgur Salad) 146
tahini 23
    Batersh (Smoky Eggplant Puree) 188
    Kuru Baklava (Dry Baklava) 234
    Muhammara (Walnut and Pepper Dip) 126
    Siliq Mutabal (Chard Stalks in Yogurt Sauce) 196
    Tatar Barak (Dumplings in Yogurt-Tahini Sauce) 192
Tatar Barak (Dumplings in Yogurt-Tahini Sauce) 192
Tavuklu Pazı Sarma (Swiss Chard Stuffed with Chicken) 76
Tek, Fatma Hülya 74
Al-Tinawi, Maha 138
tomatoes:
    Baba Ganoush (Smoky Eggplant Salad/Dip) 120
    Fahsa (Beef Stew) 96
    Fattoush (Bread Salad) 124
    Hünkar Beğendi (Sultan's Delight) 40
    Kuskus (Couscous with Lamb) 134
    Mhajeb/Mahjouba (Vegetable and Cheese Turnovers) 132
    Patlıcan Güveç (Eggplant and Lamb Stew in an Earthenware Pot) 208
    Pirpirim Aşı (Purslane Dish) 48
    Salatet Jarjeer (Arugula Salad) 158
    Shorbet Lahme (Wheat and Lamb Soup) 98
    Shurbet Khudar w Dajaj (Vegetable Soup with Chicken) 56
    Tabbouleh (Fine Grain Bulgur Salad) 146
    Zahawiq (Green Chile Sauce) 62
Turkish
    Astarlı Sütlaç (Rice Pudding) 50
    Aşure (Noah's Pudding) 232
    Cevizli Kayısı Kavurması (Dried Apricots with Walnuts) 202
    Gonca Gül Tatlısı (Rosebud Cookies) 78
    Hangel (Mantı Without Filling) 206
    Harput Köftesi (Bulgur Koftes in Tomato and Pepper Paste Sauce) 82
    Hedik/Diş Buğdayı (Wheat Boiled with Chickpeas) 84
    Hünkar Beğendi (Sultan's Delight) 40
    Kuru Baklava (Dry Baklava) 234
    Patlıcan Güveç (Eggplant and Lamb Stew in an Earthenware Pot) 208
    Peynirli Sıkma (Cheese-Filled Wraps) 34
    Pirpirim Aşı (Purslane Dish) 48
    Portakal Suyu İle Zeytinyağlı Kereviz (Celery Root with Olive Oil and Orange Juice) 42
    Saçta Kıyma Böreği (Lamb-Filled Skillet Borek) 36

INDEX

U

Ünsal, Artun 177

V

vanilla powder 23
- Basbousa (Semolina Cake) 182
- Gonca Gül Tatlısı (Rosebud Cookies) 78
- Harissa/Harisa (Peanut Dessert) 64

vegetarian mains
- Hangel (Mantı Without Filling) 206
- Hedik/Diş Buğdayı (Wheat Boiled with Chickpeas) 84
- Mhajeb/Mahjouba (Vegetable and Cheese Turnovers) 132
- Peynirli Sıkma (Cheese-Filled Wraps) 34

vermicelli, rice with 156

W

walnuts:
- Aşure (Noah's Pudding) 232
- Baba Ganoush (Smoky Eggplant Salad/Dip) 120
- Cevizli Kayısı Kavurması (Dried Apricots with Walnuts) 202
- Gonca Gül Tatlısı (Rosebud Cookies) 78
- Hedik/Diş Buğdayı (Wheat Boiled with Chickpeas) 84
- Kibbeh bil Sanieh (Kibbeh in a Tray) 70
- Kibbeh Mabrumeh (Rolled Kibbeh) 164
- Muhammara (Walnut and Pepper Dip) 126
- Salatet Jarjeer (Arugula Salad) 158

wheat berries:
- Hedik/Diş Buğdayı (Wheat Boiled with Chickpeas) 84
- Shorbet Lahme (Wheat and Lamb Soup) 98

wheat, pearled: Aşure (Noah's Pudding) 232

wheat starch 23
- Aşure (Noah's Pudding) 232
- Harissa/Harisa (Peanut Dessert) 64
- Shish Barak (Dumplings Cooked in Yogurt Sauce) 152
- Tatar Barak (Dumplings in Yogurt-Tahini Sauce) 192

Y

Yemeni
- Asida (Corn Porridge) 104
- Bint Al-Sahn (The Daughter of the Plate) 100
- Fahsa (Beef Stew) 96
- Harissa/Harisa (Peanut Dessert) 64
- Muz Fattah (Banana Bread) 66
- Shafoot/Shafut (Bread in Yogurt Sauce) 94
- Shorbet Lahme (Wheat and Lamb Soup) 98
- Shurbet Khudar w Dajaj (Vegetable Soup with Chicken) 56
- Zahawiq (Green Chile Sauce) 62
- Zurbian (Rice with Lamb) 58

Yıldız, Esin 38

yogurt:
- Asida (Corn Porridge) 104
- Basbousa (Semolina Cake) 182
- Gonca Gül Tatlısı (Rosebud Cookies) 78
- Hangel (Mantı Without Filling) 206
- Laban Bi Khiar (Cucumber with Yogurt) 142
- Mansaf (Lamb Cooked in Yogurt) 172
- Shafoot/Shafut (Bread in Yogurt Sauce) 94
- Shakriyeh (Lamb Stew with Yogurt) 128
- Shish Barak (Dumplings Cooked in Yogurt Sauce) 152
- Siliq Mutabal (Chard Stalks in Yogurt Sauce) 196
- Tatar Barak (Dumplings in Yogurt-Tahini Sauce) 192
- Zurbian (Rice with Lamb) 58

yogurt, strained: 142 (see note)

yufka: Mansaf (Lamb Cooked in Yogurt) 172

Z

Zahawiq (Green Chile Sauce) 62
- Fahsa (Beef Stew) 96

zahawiq, red 62 (see note)

zucchini:
- Kuskus (Couscous with Lamb) 134
- Shurbet Khudar w Dajaj (Vegetable Soup with Chicken) 56
- Zurbian (Rice with Lamb) 58

NOTES

NOTES

NOTES

NOTES

LIFE Project
Livelihoods Innovation through
Food Entrepreneurship (LIFE) Project

Print and Binding
Ofset Filmcilik ve Matbaacılık Sanayi ve Ticaret A.Ş.
   Çağlayan Mah. Şair Sok. No:4,
   34410 Kağıthane, Istanbul.
   T. +90 (212) 295 86 01
   F. +90 (212) 295 64 55
   www.ofset.com.tr
   Certificate No: 45354

All rights reserved. No part of this publication may be reproduced, distributed or transmitted in any form or by any means including information storage and retrieval systems, without written permission of the copyright owner, except by a reviewer who may quote less than one-page passages in a review with full acknowledgment of author, publisher, and source.

ISBN 978-0-578-61307-9
Istanbul, 2019

Follow the journey of these and other members
of the LIFE Project in Turkey at lifeforentrepreneurs.com,
or on Instagram and Twitter at @life_proj and @lifeprojecttr.